Books in the Great Lives from God's Word series

DAVID
A Man of Passion and Destiny

ESTHER
A Woman of Strength and Dignity

JOSEPH
A Man of Integrity and Forgiveness

MOSES
A Man of Selfless Dedication

ELIJAH
A Man of Heroism and Humility

PAUL
A Man of Grace and Grit

JOB
A Man of Heroic Endurance

FASCINATING STORIES OF FORGOTTEN LIVES
Rediscovering Some Old Testament Characters

GREAT DAYS WITH THE GREAT LIVES
Daily Insight from Great Lives of the Bible

It is with profound feelings of gratitude
for the exemplary life of my maternal grandfather
that I dedicate this book to

The Honorable Justice Louis Orville Lundy
1877–1960

The man my brother, sister, and I called "granddaddy"
was a gentle, humble, and pure-hearted man
who faithfully served as Justice of the Peace
in our hometown of El Campo, Texas.

When I was a little boy growing up under his godly influence,
spending time with him was as close as I could have imagined
what it must have been like spending time with Jesus.

I loved and admired him more deeply than words can express.

GREAT LIVES FROM GOD'S WORD

Profiles in Character from

CHARLES R.
SWINDOLL

THOMAS NELSON
Since 1798

NASHVILLE DALLAS MEXICO CITY RIO DE JANEIRO

Published in Nashville, Tennessee, by Thomas Nelson. Thomas Nelson is a registered trademark of Thomas Nelson, Inc.

Published in association with Yates & Yates, www.yates.com.

Thomas Nelson, Inc., titles may be purchased in bulk for educational, business, fund-raising, or sales promotional use. For information, please e-mail SpecialMarkets@ThomasNelson.com.

ISBN: 978-1-4002-0258-4 (trade paper)

Library of Congress Cataloging-in-Publication Data

Swindoll, Charles R.
    Jesus : the greatest life of all / Charles R. Swindoll.
        p. cm.— (Great lives from god's word)
    ISBN 978-0-8499-0190-4
    1. Jesus Christ—Biography. I. Title.
BT301.3.S93 2008
232.9'01—dc22
[B]   2007042207

Printed in the United States of America

09 10 11 12 13 RRD 5 4 3 2 1

Contents

Jesus: The Greatest Life of All

CONTENTS

Part 3: The Substitute

Part 4: The King

Introduction

Jesus: The Greatest Life of All

F rankly, I sat there silent and stunned. It was difficult for me to believe what I was hearing. But I could neither deny it nor ignore it.

I'm referring to the answers that were given to this simple three-word question: "Who is Jesus?" The adults who were asked that question were mainly in their twenties and thirties, well educated, and intelligent. Understand, this was not in some distant, far-removed region of our world. It occurred at a large shopping mall not even five miles from our church in the busy, rapidly growing community of Frisco, Texas, only a few miles north of the Dallas metroplex. Nevertheless, these people didn't have a clue.

To help our congregation become aware of the spiritual vacuum in which we find ourselves, one of our staff members came up with the idea of on-the-street video interviews with a random sampling of individuals in the local mall. The questions he asked were not complicated or designed to manipulate or embarrass anyone; they were clear, courteous, simple, and to the point. The results of his informal survey helped convince all of us that our plans to expand made good sense. Truth be told, most of us had no idea what we would discover.

As the video flickered across a small projection screen in one of our church conference rooms, my mouth dropped open and my eyes grew wide. Subconsciously, I began to lean forward in my chair. The crowning moment came when the interviewer asked several people, "Who is Jesus?" Here are a few of the answers he received:

> MAN 1. That's a trick question. (Laughs) I don't know how to answer that.

> WOMAN. I mean, I believe that he was a real person and that he died on the cross, but I don't believe that he was God's Son.

> MAN 2. He was, you know . . . He was just another person that found religion and all that, so it's . . . I mean . . . He's nothing like . . . He's, of course, a good person and all that, and he's a really big part of religion, so . . . You know . . . All people that find religion are, you know, important. So people have different views.

> Man 3. He is . . . uh . . . (Turns to younger man) Help me out here. (Young man shrugs) Jesus Christ is, uh . . . the Son of God? (Looks again to the younger man)

I stared in amazement as my heart sank. Bright, attractive, with-it people stood within a few miles of several churches that teach the Bible, some of them (like ours) many times every week, yet none of them could answer the question "Who is Jesus?" with even a hint of confidence. I came to two conclusions that day. First, without question, we need to build a larger facility where folks like that can gather and interact with the truth as it is recorded in the Scriptures. Second, I need to begin writing my next biblical biography in the Great Lives series, and this time I knew I had to write about Jesus Christ.

All historians accept the fact that Jesus existed and that He was a Galilean Jew who lived and taught during the first century. Many would also agree that He was martyred because His teachings were so radical and controversial. Most would not agree on what He taught because, from their point of view, successive generations of His followers reshaped, amplified, and systematized His original teachings into what we know today as Christianity. For most historical scholars, the Jesus of history and the Christ of faith have little relation to each other. Many opinions surround the person and work of Jesus Christ.

Robert Bowman and J. Ed Komoszewski illustrate this in their book, *Putting Jesus in His Place*:

> Interpretations of Jesus are fraught with bias. He's a powerful figure whom people want on their sides—and they're willing to re-create him in their image to enlist his support. Animal-rights activists imagine a vegetarian Jesus. New Agers make him an example of finding god within. And radical feminists strip him of divinity so that Christianity doesn't appear sexist. Frankly, it's hard to escape the feeling that our culture has taken Jesus' question, "Who do you say that I am?" and changed it to "Who do you want me to be?"[1]

Candidly, I would argue that most scholarly historians, for all their knowledge, are less equipped to answer the question "Who is Jesus?" than most anyone else today.

What you hold in your hands is more than a mere chronicle of a historical figure's exploits. That is because Jesus was no mere man. I don't pretend to offer a cool, rational, unbiased analysis of a man's life. However, I have paid attention to historical details, and to the best of my knowledge, I have not been irrational.

Jesus' story has deep roots in Israel's soil, and His ministry was—and is—the culmination of Hebrew culture and theology; therefore, I have given great attention to His place in history. Nevertheless, because His influential life transcends history, I have not shied away from the complex and provocative theological issues Jesus addressed during His years of ministry on our planet.

Biographies tend to give us insight into how the life of someone in our past continues to impact us today . . . but as you read about the life of Jesus Christ, I hope you will do more. I hope that your thinking about *everything* will be challenged. I certainly hope you will view the life of Jesus with greater clarity. But in the process, I hope you will begin to see the world differently—your own world as well as the world outside yourself.

Most of all, I hope that before you reach the final chapter, you will not only have gained a clearer understanding of Jesus' place in history, but you will have come to know Him personally and deeply, as you determine your own answer to the question "Who is Jesus?"

Finally, I wish to express my appreciation to my many friends at Thomas Nelson Publishers for their continued encouragement since 1997, when I released my first volume in the Great Lives series. Since this is my ninth and final biblical biographical study in the series, it is appropriate that I pause to thank all of you in the Thomas Nelson family who have remained excited about each volume.

And a special word of thanks is due Mark Gaither, for his splendid work as my keen-eyed and disciplined editor and who remained enthusiastic about this project from start to finish. Well done, Mark! You are "a good and faithful servant" who deserves much applause for your hard work on this book. I am confident you will receive many rewards for your faithful assistance as you stand in eternity before the One we both love and worship: Jesus, the greatest life of all.

Chuck Swindoll

Chuck Swindoll
Frisco, Texas

Part One

The Child

Chapter One

The Identity of Deity

He was an immensely popular teacher despite His unassuming nature and ordinary looks. The places He taught could scarcely hold the tightly packed multitudes that mobbed Him everywhere He went. On this particular day, the building bulged with virtually every Jewish teacher and cleric in Israel. Even the foremost religious authorities of Jerusalem, Israel's political and religious elite, came to hear the teaching of an untrained carpenter from the insignificant town of Nazareth. Every person present had the same question on his or her mind.

WHO *IS* THIS MAN?

As He taught from the beloved books of the Jewish Bible—the law of Moses, the oracles of the prophets, and the wisdom writings—a small band of men strategized on behalf of their paralyzed comrade. They had heard that Jesus (*Yeshua* in the Hebrew tongue) had the ability to heal the sick, so they traveled to where He would be teaching. But upon arrival, they were disappointed to find Him seated near the center of a large house and surrounded by a crowd of Pharisees and religious teachers, none of whom would yield for a disabled person, someone bearing a disease they considered divine judgment for sin.

The band of men would have to do some creative thinking. They had carried their disabled friend a long way, and they were not about to give up. So they climbed the outside staircase, located the ceiling directly above Jesus' head, and started pulling tiles. As the rabbi taught, sand and dust trickled down onto His tunic, and within a few moments, a stretcher descended.

Ever since the paralytic had heard of the miraculous man from Nazareth, he dreamed of hearing the words, "Arise, take up your pallet and walk." But Jesus said something different. Surprising words. Outrageous words. "Friend, your sins are forgiven" (Luke 5:20).

The teachers and religious officials immediately understood the immense implications of Jesus' declaration.

> "Who is this man who speaks blasphemies? Who can forgive sins, but God alone?"
>
> Luke 5:21

C. S. Lewis explains why the religious leaders had good reason to be upset:

> Now unless the speaker is God, [forgiving sins] is really so preposterous as to be comic. We can all understand how a man forgives offences against himself. You tread on my toe and I forgive you, you steal my money and I forgive you. But what should we make of a man, himself unrobbed and untrodden on, who announced that he forgave you for treading on another man's toes and stealing other men's money? Asinine fatuity is the kindest description we should give of his conduct. Yet this is what Jesus did. He told people that their sins were forgiven, and never waited to consult all the other people whom their sins had undoubtedly injured. He unhesitatingly behaved as if He was the party chiefly concerned, the person chiefly offended in all offences. This makes sense only if He really was God whose laws are broken and whose love is wounded in every sin. In the mouth of any speaker who is not God, these words

would imply what I can only regard as a silliness and conceit unrivalled by any other character in history.[1]

Note the unanimous response of the religious leaders: "Who is this man?"

Fast-forward a few weeks, perhaps months. Another house packed with religious leaders; another opportunity to teach. Jesus, like the other dinner guests, reclined at a low table, propped on one elbow with His feet angled away from the food. As was the custom, uninvited guests were permitted to sit against the walls and listen to the dinner conversation. However, they were never to intrude . . . and, in that culture, certainly not a woman!

But as Jesus taught, a woman crept toward the table, fell at His feet, and drenched them with her tears. Then, in an extravagant gesture of worship, she anointed His feet with expensive perfume, pouring out the entire container. In response, the Teacher turned, lifted her face to meet His gaze, and said to her, "Your sins have been forgiven" (Luke 7:48).

Again, take note of how the religious authorities responded:

> Those who were reclining at the table with Him began to say to themselves, "Who is this man who even forgives sins?"
>
> Luke 7:49

As Jesus continued His ministry of teaching, healing, and forgiving sins, He attracted a multitude of disciples, whom He empowered to spread the good news of God's grace and to heal in His name. Before long, Herod Antipas, Rome's puppet ruler over the region of Galilee, heard that a great teacher had captured the imagination of his subjects.

> Now Herod [Antipas] the tetrarch heard of all that was happening; and he was greatly perplexed, because it was said by some that John had risen from the dead, and·by some that Elijah had appeared, and by others that one of the prophets of old had risen again. Herod said, "I myself had John beheaded; but who is this man about whom I hear such things?" And he kept trying to see Him.
>
> Luke 9:7–9

Earlier, John the Baptizer had publicly confronted Herod for having an extramarital affair with the wife of Philip, the ruler's blood brother. To silence John and to appease John's enemies in the royal court, Herod had ordered his execution. When reports of Jesus reached the most powerful ears in the land, Herod repeated the question that had been sweeping the country: "Who is this man?"

Even Jesus' disciples remained perplexed for much of His ministry. They had witnessed a number of miraculous healings and heard scores of lessons. They knew Him to be special. They had even come to recognize Him as the long-awaited Jewish Messiah, but they failed to comprehend who He really was.

After one long day of teaching, they saw something they would never forget.

> On that day, when evening came, He said to them, "Let us go over to the other side." Leaving the crowd, they took Him along with them in the boat, just as He was; and other boats were with Him. And there arose a fierce gale of wind, and the waves were breaking over the boat so much that the boat was already filling up. Jesus Himself was in the stern, asleep on the cushion; and they woke Him and said to Him, "Teacher, do You not care that we are perishing?" And He got up and rebuked the wind and said to the sea, "Hush, be still." And the wind died down and it became perfectly calm. And He said to them, "Why are you afraid? How is it that you have no faith?" They became very much afraid and said to one another, "Who then is this, that even the wind and the sea obey Him?"
>
> Mark 4:35–41

I grew up in Houston, Texas, and have been fishing in and around the Gulf of Mexico numerous times. I've seen all sorts of conditions on the water, including waves so choppy that we could barely make it back to shore with an outboard motor. I can only imagine the terror of having only sails and oars to work with. I've also seen what fishermen call a "slick" on the water. That's when the surface is so calm, it's like glass . . . not even a ripple.

Imagine straining against the oars in an effort to reach the safety of shore as turbulent waves toss around your ship like a toy. Then someone stands up and scolds the elements like He would a child—"Stop it! Calm down, right now!"—and the chop immediately turns slick. I don't know about you, but I suspect my reaction might be like those twelve bewildered men in the boat with Jesus. They trembled with fear and asked, "Who is this man?"

Mark 6:1–3 records yet another surprising reaction, this time among the people of Jesus' own hometown. While Jesus was born in Bethlehem, He grew up in a northern village in Galilee called Nazareth.

> Jesus . . . came into His hometown; and His disciples followed Him. When the Sabbath came, He began to teach in the synagogue; and the many listeners were astonished, saying, "Where did this man get these things, and what is this wisdom given to Him, and such miracles as these performed by His hands? Is not this the carpenter, the son of Mary, and brother of James and Joses and Judas and Simon? Are not His sisters here with us?" And they took offense at Him.
>
> Mark 6:1–3

Nazareth, being a small town, was filled with people who knew Jesus well. He was known as Yeshua, the son of Mary and Joseph, the carpenter from whom the boy had learned His trade. Jesus had at least four brothers and an undetermined number of sisters. The people of Nazareth saw Him learn in the synagogue and participate in the customary rites of passage. We are told in another part of the Gospel narrative that Yeshua grew to gain the respect of the community (Luke 2:52) and had extraordinary ability handling Scripture and understanding theology (Luke 2:47). Many of the Nazarenes had played with little Yeshua as a child and made the difficult transition to adulthood as His peers.

Then, one day, Jesus returned to Nazareth after a long absence. While His reputation had become larger than life, the townspeople probably snickered at the absurd rumors. After all, they knew Him "back when." But when they discovered the rumors to be true and His power to be genuine, they couldn't believe their eyes. Even the people who knew Jesus best were heard to ask, "Who is this man?"

It's a sad but undeniable truth that no one expects to find greatness among the people he or she knows well. Jesus pointed to this fact when He commented, "A prophet is not without honor except in his hometown and among his own relatives and in his own household" (Mark 6:4).

NO ORDINARY MAN

As I read the accounts of Jesus in the Bible, I find that time has done little to change how people respond to an encounter with Jesus. Like today, many wrote off reports of His miracles as myth. Like today, others who accepted His miracles as genuine attributed them to the work of evil or something else. Like today, some saw His works and accepted them as blessings from God but rejected the One who brought them.

I also find that a relative few—perhaps numbering in the hundreds—saw the miraculous deeds of Jesus as proof that they had met someone very, very special. And their response was to stop what they were doing and consider the possibility that something remarkable was happening, something that deserved closer examination.

One such man was Nicodemus, a member of what might be considered the Jewish Supreme Court in ancient days. He was a Pharisee, which means he belonged to a philosophical and political party that advocated strict adherence to the Old Testament Law. Consequently, he knew his Bible and lived by every command and every prohibition in it—plus many more. Nicodemus was a conservative scholar, a civic leader, a religious expert, and according to the understanding of his culture, he was as good as a man could get. And in their thinking, his great wealth and power indicated that God thought so too. Yet something about Jesus intrigued the old teacher, perhaps because, deep down, something was missing, despite his impressive religious involvement.

One of Jesus' disciples, John, wrote an account of Jesus' life and ministry, and in the second chapter of this work, he recorded that Jesus took authority over the Jewish temple by shutting down the crooked business dealings taking place within its walls. The temple authorities challenged

Him, asking, "What sign do you show us as your authority for doing these things?" (John 2:18). He answered them directly and then went on to conduct a very public ministry involving miraculous healings. As a result, "many believed in His name, observing His signs which He was doing" (John 2:23).

Nicodemus was, undoubtedly, one of the many observers. As a temple leader and a prominent Jewish citizen, he watched this young, thirty-something miracle worker take the Hebrew religious capital by storm. He heard the blind say, "I can see!" He had seen the disabled leap for joy, and lepers peel off their bandages to reveal fresh, babylike skin. Yet these were no mere faith-healer tricks. These were undisputed, publicly verified, dramatic physical transformations. Had there been any fraud, Jesus' enemies in the religious establishment would have made a fool of Him immediately. But the signs were genuine, so scores of people began to call Jesus "Messiah," the long-promised king who would lead Israel to greatness. The longer Nicodemus watched, the more he became convinced that Jesus was no charlatan. This young Teacher had a connection with God that the old leader didn't. That piqued his curiosity.

John also called Nicodemus "a member of the Jewish ruling council" (John 3:1 NIV). In those days, the Jews were ruled by a religious assembly of seventy men called the Sanhedrin. This body governed much like a congress or parliament and a supreme court combined. They made laws, held trials, upheld justice, and governed the country.

Bill Counts, in his book *Once a Carpenter*, writes, "So far as we know, Jesus never encountered a more prestigious, knowledgeable, refined representative of Judaism than Nicodemus."[2] Nicodemus was very well known, so we shouldn't be surprised that he came to see Jesus under the cover of night. Wherever famous people go, a band of gossipers will surely follow. He obviously didn't want the general public—and especially the other sixty-nine members of the Sanhedrin—to know that he'd been visiting Jesus, the miracle worker.

Later in the chapter, in verse 10, Jesus called Nicodemus "*the* teacher of Israel," not "*a* teacher of Israel." This suggests that Nicodemus was not only one of the seventy rulers, but he was probably the best known or perhaps the most respected. In other words, this was not a narrow-minded, religious bully. He was very astute, very articulate, and very committed to what he believed to be truth, yet he had lost touch with the truth about God and what He desires.

I admire Nicodemus. While he displayed all the signs of a man who knew what he believed to be true and would not easily change his view, he nevertheless allowed for the possibility that Jesus represented something worth investigating. He was understandably skeptical. Let's face it, most intelligent people are. But the young Teacher had been displaying signs that no reasonable person could ignore.

Perhaps "skeptical" describes you. Maybe you aren't quite sure what to do with Jesus. Maybe you, like the people in Jesus' day, have heard His name and the rumors but had little time or interest in knowing more until now. Maybe you recently encountered one of Jesus' followers and the experience has piqued your interest. Or, just as likely, you've been turned off by a number of overzealous Christians and so you've decided to learn more about Him on your own. Whatever your motivation, I invite you to read on. You may be reluctant to accept His miracles as genuine or admit that He was anything more than a man. If so, you are not that different from the people who encountered Him in the houses, synagogues, dinner parties, and byways of Palestine. Nevertheless, those who wanted to be intellectually honest had to admit that Jesus was no ordinary man—and someone that remarkable deserved a closer look.

Whether viewed face-to-face or through the lens of history, the question remains the same: *who is this man?* Historians who doubt the existence of the supernatural might object to a biography that accepts the miracles of Jesus at face value. Regardless, I intend to present Him in this book the same as He presented himself to eyewitnesses more than two millennia ago: as a perplexing, confrontational, natural, *and* supernatural man. I will then leave the question of what to do with Jesus up to you. But let me warn you before you begin: your encounter with Jesus will not allow you any middle ground, any more than it did the people who met Him in person. He not only did extraordinary things, but He also made an extraordinary claim.

WHO DO YOU SAY THAT I AM?

As Jesus neared the end of His earthly ministry, questions about His identity reached a climax.

> Now when Jesus came into the district of Caesarea Philippi, He was asking His disciples, "Who do people say that the Son of Man is?" And they said, "Some say John the Baptist; and others, Elijah; but still others, Jeremiah, or one of the prophets."
>
> Matthew 16:13–14

Everyone agreed that Jesus was someone special, and everyone had his own theory as to how or why. John the Baptizer back from the dead? An ancient prophet returning to announce the revival of Israel? As theories abounded, only a very few thought of Jesus as the Hebrew Messiah. Eventually, when Jesus thought the time was right and that His disciples had enough evidence, He put them on the spot. His companions would have to make a decision. He asked them, "But who do you say that I am?" (Matthew 16:15).

The "you" in that question is plural. *Who do all of you say that I am?* The group probably stammered and squirmed before one brave disciple blurted out, "You are the Christ" (Matthew 16:16).

The word "Christ" in this verse comes from the Greek term *christos*. The Hebrew used the term *mashiach*, from which we get "Messiah." Both words mean "anointed one." In ancient Near Eastern cultures, a person would participate in a ceremony in which a small amount of oil was poured over his head as a symbol of special recognition. It could be a reward for valor on the battlefield or victory over a national enemy. Most often, it was the way a leader was commissioned. And in Israel, to be "the Lord's anointed" was to be the king.

For centuries, hopeful Jews looked for a very special king—an ultimate Messiah, promised by prophets of old, who would supersede all of Israel's past "anointed ones." He would usher in a new way of relating to God, He would establish an unprecedented time of peace and prosperity, and He

11

would rule the world from Israel (Jeremiah 31:31–34). This person would not be merely a christ, but *the* Christ.

Peter declared that Jesus was indeed this long-awaited, ultimate king of Israel. But he didn't stop there. He went on to affirm another truth about Jesus.

> Simon Peter answered, "You are the Christ, the Son of the living God."
>
> Matthew 16:16

In the Hebrew vernacular, to be a "son" was to share all of the father's qualities in common and to inherit the father's privileges and power. No one dared call himself a son of God, or he would be guilty of blasphemy. Only someone having God's divine qualities and powers, and possessing God's ruling authority, could call himself "the Son of God." And for Peter to give Jesus this title meant that Jesus was a worthy object of worship, just like the God faithful Jews had worshiped in the temple for centuries.

Jesus didn't object. Instead, He praised Peter, saying,

> "Blessed are you, Simon Barjona, because flesh and blood did not reveal this to you, but My Father who is in heaven."
>
> Matthew 16:17

In other words, *Yes! You've got it! This is a supernatural insight you have received from heaven. I am in fact deity.*

Who is this man? If we are to believe the man himself, He is God.

NO MIDDLE GROUND

Many try to take what they consider to be an intellectually balanced position. They readily accept that Jesus existed, that He was a Galilean Jew who lived and taught during the first century, that He was martyred for His teachings, and that those teachings were both radical and influential. But they deny Jesus' miracles and reject even the suggestion that He is deity.

Unfortunately, this view of Jesus fails to explain why so many were willing to follow Him, even to a martyr's death, and why He continues to impact the world so profoundly. Think of men like Alexander the Great, Caesar Augustus, and Constantine, men who conquered vast stretches of the known world. Think of Plato, Newton, and Einstein, men who revolutionized the thinking of humankind. Think of all the musicians, composers, philosophers, builders, and leaders who impacted the world so positively. Other men have conquered more, written more, and built more. But none has impacted the world more profoundly, permanently, or—for millions of people—more personally than the carpenter from Nazareth.

Divorce Him from the supernatural, and we are left with a history that makes less sense, not more. Apart from the supernatural aspect of His life, Jesus was quite ordinary. And when you combine His deeds with His claims, you cannot avoid intellectual extremes and call yourself logical. C. S. Lewis explained the dilemma this way:

> I am trying here to prevent anyone saying the really foolish thing that people often say about Him: "I'm ready to accept Jesus as a great moral teacher, but I don't accept His claim to be God." That is the one thing we must not say. A man who was merely a man and said the sort of things Jesus said would not be a great moral teacher. He would either be a lunatic—on the level with the man who says he's a poached egg—or else he would be the Devil of Hell. You must make your choice. Either this man was, and is, the Son of God: or else a madman or something worse. You can shut Him up for a fool, you can spit at Him and kill Him as a demon; or you can fall at His feet and call Him Lord and God. But let us not come with any patronising nonsense about His being a great human teacher. He has not left that open to us. He did not intend to.[3]

THE WHOLE TRUTH ABOUT JESUS WAS . . . AND IS

Near the end of the first century, very few firsthand witnesses to the life of Jesus remained alive, and false teachers—ironically, many of whom denied that Jesus was entirely human—had begun to twist the story of His life to suit their religious and philosophical views. So the aging apostle John set out to write the story of Jesus in response. In his own words, his purpose in writing was "so that you may believe that Jesus is the Christ, the Son of God; and that believing you may have life in His name" (John 20:31).

Whereas the other Gospel writers took a more classically historical approach, John wrote boldly from a philosophical perspective. The opening words of his account reach back to a time before Genesis 1:1. He tells us that "In the beginning," before God created the heavens and the earth, the Word existed. The Greek states, literally, "In beginning, was existing the Word" (John 1:1).

In this verse, "Word" comes from the Greek term *logos*, which held incredibly profound significance for the philosophers of Jesus' day. *Logos* was first coined by Heraclitus roughly five hundred years before Christ, and it grew to become a universal, cosmic, religious principle.

In Stoicism *logos* expresses the ordered and teleologically oriented nature of the cosmos. It can thus be equated with God and with the cosmic power of reason of which the material world is a vast unfolding.[4]

Influenced both by the Old Testament and by Hellenic thought, Philo [a Jewish philosopher living at the time of Christ] made frequent use of the term *logos*, to which he gave a highly-developed significance and a central place to his theological scheme. He derived the term from Stoic sources and, in accordance with his discovery of Greek thought in the Hebrew Scriptures, made use of it on the basis of such passages as Ps. 33:6 to express the means whereby the transcendent God may be the Creator of the universe and the Revealer of himself to Moses and the Patriarchs. On the Greek side he equates the Logos with the Platonic concept of the World of Ideas so that it becomes both God's plan and God's power of creation.[5]

The apostle John borrowed this *logos* concept to give it new significance as a nickname, of sorts, for the Son of God. And in applying it, he crafted his sentences very carefully, literally writing, "In beginning was being the *logos*." (Not, "In *the* beginning . . .")

By leaving out the definite article "the," John suggests that we cannot identify a past moment to call "beginning." He's pointing to something that existed before eternity past, farther back than our finite minds can conceive. Before the earth, before the planets and stars, before light or darkness, matter or time—in a beginning that never really had a beginning, the *logos* was already existing. He had no "starting point." Eternally existing, the *logos* was with God and the *logos* was God. And then John wrote something truly remarkable:

> And the Word became flesh, and dwelt among us, and we saw His glory, glory as of the only begotten from the Father, full of grace and truth.
>
> John 1:14

In other words, God became a man!

Is it any wonder the people in Jesus' day—even His own disciples—struggled to comprehend who He was? What an incredible thought! God becoming a man.

Ray Stedman described the problem well:

> But if we find it difficult, how much more did His own disciples! They, of all people, would be least likely to believe that He was God, for they lived with Him and saw His humanity as none of us ever has or ever will. They must have been confronted again and again with a question that puzzled and troubled them, "Who is this man?" . . .
>
> I have often pictured them sleeping out under the stars with our Lord on a summer night by the Sea of Galilee. I can imagine Peter or John or one of the others waking in the night, rising up on an elbow, and as he looked at the Lord Jesus sleeping beside him, saying to himself, "Is it true? Can this man be the eternal God?"[6]

The apostle Paul, who became a disciple after Jesus was crucified, wrote,

[Jesus] is the image of the invisible God, the firstborn of all creation. For by Him all things were created, both in the heavens and on earth, visible and invisible, whether thrones or dominions or rulers or authorities—all things have been created through Him and for Him. He is before all things, and in Him all things hold together.

Colossians 1:15–17

"In Him," Paul went on to write, "all the fullness of Deity dwells in bodily form" (Colossians 2:9). Before Jesus became a man, He was the Word by which the utterance, "Let there be light," resulted in the existence of light. He created the world long centuries before entering it as a baby in a stable just outside a little hamlet called Bethlehem.

Who is this man? He is Jesus of Nazareth. He is God in human flesh. This is how He presented Himself to the world and, in the end, how we must either accept or reject Him.

Chapter Two

A Relationship, a Courtship, a Miracle

If you know a little about the birth of Jesus, it might be best for you to forget it and start from scratch. The story has been so sanitized and romanticized over the centuries that even Hollywood—as jaded a culture as can be found anywhere—failed to capture the gritty pathos that surrounded His arrival. The 2006 movie *The Nativity Story* helped to recapture the humanity and the Jewishness of the events surrounding Jesus' birth, but it still painted a somewhat idealistic picture. And if there is any one word we cannot use to describe Jesus' birth, it's *ideal.*

Without question, 6 BC was a lousy time to live in Judea. Herod the Great had seized the throne of Israel through bloody intrigue and with political support from Rome. Then, once in power, he guarded his stolen title, "King of the Jews," so ruthlessly he even put his own sons to death when any of them posed a significant political threat. Macrobius, a fifth-century writer, recorded, "When [Caesar Augustus] heard that Herod king of the Jews had ordered boys in Syria under the age of two years to be put to death and that the king's son was among those killed, he said, 'I'd rather be Herod's pig than Herod's son!'"[1]

Caesar's comment illustrated the sad irony of Israel's condition. Herod, though not really Jewish, pretended to be a good Jew by eliminating pork from his diet, but he indulged an insatiable appetite for murder. He built a magnificent temple for the God of Israel—an architectural wonder in its day—and gave its administration to one corrupt high priest after another. He taxed Jews through the temple in keeping with the Old Testament Law and then used the proceeds to break the first commandment, building cities and temples in honor of the emperor and his pantheon of Roman deities. It was a time of unprecedented economic and political advancement for the rich and horrific oppression for everyone else. By the first century BC, a dark cloud had settled over Israel, blocking any ray of hope.

Then, somewhere in the hill country of Judea, a woman named Elizabeth became pregnant with her first child. This would not have been remarkable except that she was well past childbearing years, perhaps having experienced menopause some years earlier. She and her husband, Zacharias, had prayed all their married years to have a child, but Elizabeth had been unable to conceive. Her neighbors would have called her "barren," a condition often attributed to God's judgment for sin.

Neither Elizabeth nor Zacharias was guilty of any greater sin than their neighbors; however, her barrenness did symbolize God's judgment on Israel's unfaithfulness. According to the *Dictionary of Biblical Imagery:*

> The image of the barren wife is one of the Bible's strongest images
> of desolation and rejection. . . . In Isaiah's prophecy the promise that
> God will restore the blessedness of life is expressed through trans-
> forming the imagery of the barren land and the barren woman. In
> the day of restoration the desolate land will burst into bloom (Is
> 35:1–7) and the barren woman will sing and rejoice because of an
> unexpected and abundant fertility.[2]
>
> Isaiah 54:1

Just when it became clear that the couple had no hope of bearing children, an angel appeared to Zacharias and told him that Elizabeth would bear a son and that he was to name the boy John. He would be a very unique child with a very special purpose: he would be the forerunner of the Messiah. Elizabeth's barrenness and advanced age—a double symbol of hopelessness—became the means by which God would announce to the world that nothing is impossible for Him. The infant son of a small-town priest and his aged wife would grow to become John the Baptizer. And even before the boy could walk and talk, he bore God's message to the world: *What I did through Elizabeth is what I will do for all of humanity. The barren womb of Israel will bear a son.*

COMPLICATIONS

Several days' journey to the north of Jerusalem, in a tiny peasant village, a young woman named Mary—*Mariam* in Hebrew—helped her family scratch a living out of the Galilean soil. Roughly two hundred people farmed land and tended animals in the obscure town of Nazareth, which sat in a slight depression high in the mountains overlooking the vast Jezreel Valley. This made it a perfect place for a garrison of Roman soldiers to keep watch over the region.

I can tell you from my days in the military that a group of soldiers in a tiny town with nothing to do can only lead to trouble. Consequently, the Jews of Nazareth gained a reputation for immorality that became legendary, perhaps because of their regular contact with these Gentiles and the depraved habits of military men in that day. The reputation of the Nazarenes may or may not have been deserved, but to the religious mind in Israel, it didn't matter. Appearances meant everything. Later, when the disciple Nathaniel heard that Jesus grew up in Nazareth, he curled his lip and muttered, "Can anything good come out of Nazareth?" (John 1:46).

With such a high premium given to keeping up religious appearances, it's little wonder that the manner in which Jesus was born would raise a few eyebrows. Matthew's Gospel explains why:

> This is how the birth of Jesus Christ came about: His mother Mary was pledged to be married to Joseph, but before they came together, she was found to be with child through the Holy Spirit.
> Matthew 1:18 NIV

The Jews of first-century Palestine saw marriage as a joining of two families. And because the stakes were so high, they never would have entrusted such an important decision to the whims of teenage emotions. As in many cultures, both past and present, first-century Hebrew parents arranged the marriages of their sons and daughters. According to rabbinical law, this could take place sometime after the age of consent: twelve for girls, thirteen for boys. While the children weren't given the final word in the matter, their personal desires were usually taken into account.

Once the decision was made to pursue the match, the fathers discussed every detail of the arrangement and prepared a legal contract, which would be read during the marriage ceremony. Vows were made, tokens were exchanged, and the families celebrated. At the conclusion of the ceremony, the boy and girl would enter the betrothal period, which could be no less than one month, but typically lasted one year.

During the betrothal period, the newly married couple was husband and wife in every respect except that they were to live with their respective families and refrain from sex. This interval between the vows and the home-taking served several purposes. First, it gave the groom time to prepare the couple's new home, usually a one-room addition to his parents' house. Second, it gave the bride time to complete several purification rituals and to demonstrate that she was sexually pure. Proof of paternity was of supreme importance in Jewish law, so a divorced woman or widow had to wait no fewer than ninety days in order to prove she did not carry her former husband's child. Third, unlike many other cultures, Jews didn't expect a young girl to leave her family one morning and lie in the bed of a stranger that night. The betrothal period gave the husband and wife plenty of time to bond under the strict supervision of their families before coming together as a couple. Though they lived apart, the community viewed the couple as married. To end the marriage during the betrothal period required an official divorce decree. And if either of them engaged in sex with someone else, it was considered adultery, which could carry the penalty of death by stoning.

When the bride had completed her purification and the groom was ready to receive her, the groom and his wedding party would arrive at her house, where he called for his bride to join him. This was the home-taking.

The wedding party would lift the couple into the air and carry them to their new home, where the families and guests would celebrate the nuptials for as many as seven days.

It was during the betrothal period—between the vows and the home-taking—that Jesus was conceived by the Holy Spirit in Mary's womb. Luke's account records the story as it relates to her.

> Now in the sixth month [of Elizabeth's pregnancy] the angel Gabriel was sent from God to a city in Galilee called Nazareth, to a virgin engaged to a man whose name was Joseph, of the descendants of David; and the virgin's name was Mary.
>
> Luke 1:26–27

In referring to Mary, both Luke and Matthew employ the Greek term *parthenos*, which means "virgin." Some have argued that this merely points to a girl who is young and eligible for marriage, not necessarily one untouched by a man. But the ancient Greeks took this term quite literally. For instance, Artemis, the goddess whose temple in Ephesus is considered one of the seven ancient wonders of the world, was emphatically virginal. She was thought to protect chaste young men and women, and she symbolized the cultic power of virginity, representing "young and budding life and strict innocence."[3] Consequently, a young, unmarried woman was called a *parthenos*. To be anything other than a virgin before her wedding would have been unthinkable!

Sometime during Mary and Joseph's betrothal period, life became very complicated for the young couple. Perhaps as she went about her chores, Mary dreamed of the home-taking and the grand celebration Joseph was preparing—when a voice interrupted her solitude. "Greetings, favored one! The Lord is with you" (Luke 1:28).

The greeting completely confused her. A peasant girl? Highly favored by God? Why? Teenage girls occupied a very low status in ancient times. Before she could question him, the angel continued,

> "Do not be afraid, Mary; for you have found favor with God. And behold, you will conceive in your womb and bear a son, and you

shall name Him Jesus. He will be great and will be called the Son of
the Most High; and the Lord God will give Him the throne of His
father David; and He will reign over the house of Jacob forever, and
His kingdom will have no end."

Luke 1:30–33

Mary would not have missed the significance of the angel's words. For as
long as anyone could remember, prophets foretold the coming of a larger-
than-life King who would claim the throne, destroy Israel's enemies, inaugu-
rate an unprecedented time of peace and prosperity, and ultimately rule over
the whole earth. And every Jew anticipated the arrival of the Messiah in his
or her own way. The rich and powerful hoped He would not come in their
lifetime, because that would end their personal claims to wealth and status.
The poor and downcast longed for Him to come and break their yoke of
oppression.

After centuries of what undoubtedly felt like God's silence, Mary learned
that she would be the mother of the Messiah. Thousands of Hebrew women
for more than a dozen centuries had hoped to be the one to bear Israel's
Savior. It was an honor too wonderful to describe, but the privilege would
require immense sacrifice.

Mary said to the angel, "How can this be, since I am a virgin?"

Luke 1:34

The literal Greek reads, "How will this be, since a man I do not know?"
Of course, she used the word *know* in the intimate sense, as the common
euphemism for sexual intercourse. Mary understood enough about sexuality to
know that she could not conceive a child until after her first night with Joseph.
So she asked the most logical question: *how can a* parthenos *conceive a child?*

The angel answered and said to her, "The Holy Spirit will come
upon you, and the power of the Most High will overshadow you;
and for that reason the holy Child shall be called the Son of God.
And behold, even your relative Elizabeth has also conceived a son in

her old age; and she who was called barren is now in her sixth month. For nothing will be impossible with God."

Luke 1:35–37

The angel used imagery that would have been familiar to any Jew. After Moses led the Hebrew people out of Egypt, the Lord directed him to construct a tabernacle—a portable house of worship. When it was complete, God overshadowed the tent, which the people saw as an eerie glow in the form of a cloud (Exodus 40:34–38; Numbers 9:15–16). The angel used this imagery when he said "the power of the Most High will overshadow you" to explain that God's spiritual presence would miraculously conceive a male child in her womb. While the child would be human in every respect, He would not have a human father. His father would be, quite literally, the Almighty God.

What a request to put before a teenage girl! Yet take note of her immediate response.

Mary said, "Behold, the bondslave of the Lord; may it be done to me according to your word." And the angel departed from her.

Luke 1:38

The Greek word translated "bondslave" describes a particular kind of servitude common throughout history. The term refers to someone who voluntarily sells himself or herself into slavery. God obviously chose this humble maiden for good reason, not the least of which was her complete submission to the will of her Creator. "Behold, the bondslave of the Lord." In other words, *I willingly commit myself to the unconditional service of my Lord.*

Luke and Matthew report two subsequent events, but we must use our imagination to determine which came first. Luke tells us that Mary "went in a hurry to the hill country" to visit Elizabeth (Luke 1:39). Matthew describes Joseph's struggle to accept Mary's story. In my book *A Bethlehem Christmas,* I imagined Mary's telling Joseph about the miraculous way in which she became pregnant and then retreating to Elizabeth's house. But it is just as likely that she hastily scratched a note to her betrothed husband and quickly departed in order to put off a difficult face-to-face conversation.

Either way, I can only imagine how difficult this time was for both of them. Mary must have sounded insane. A virgin conceiving a child without having intercourse? Unbelievable. How ironic that young Mary would be the bearer of the most wonderful secret in the history of humankind and yet suffer the consequences of a sinner. What a commentary on the spiritual dullness of her community that such a privilege would come at the cost of so much pain. And not for Mary only.

Joseph didn't receive an angelic visit until later. Imagine his private pain and confusion. Perhaps he's looking forward to another visit with Mary's family after a hard day's work, another evening in the company of the woman he loves, another time to relax and dream of their future together. Then, suddenly, she's gone. A hurried trip to the hill country of Judea.

Three months pass before Joseph receives word that she has returned. Upon first glance, he notices a slight bulge in her outer garment. He doesn't know much, only that life has suddenly become very complicated. Here's how I imagine Joseph recalling his experience:

> After describing a most unusual story, Mary revealed that she was pregnant.
>
> The words hit my chest like a boulder. I sat stunned as she continued with a preposterous, blasphemous story about conceiving the Messiah and the invisible God behaving in a manner that seemed to me like the deviant gods of Rome. A wave of questions flooded my mind. *Who was the father? Was she taken advantage of, or did she consent? How could I have been so wrong about someone I knew so well? Is she insane? Is she in love with him? Does she not love me? Why would she do this?*
>
> I looked across the table at Mary to find her gazing at me with obvious compassion, which outraged me. Was her delusion so complete as to believe what she said? Or, worse, her deceit so profound as to feign concern for the lives she destroyed? The room began to spin and I felt my stomach rebel. I had to get outside.
>
> I nearly tore the door off its hinges, ran into the night, and didn't stop until I stood on the ridge outside Nazareth. Exhausted, I sank to my knees

then sat for hours in the darkness, staring across the plain and into the night sky. When I was a child, I had found comfort in the vast expanse of stars, a symbol of God's power, permanence, and unchangeable character. So, I found the appearance of a new light—a bright dot high above the horizon—a little unsettling. But my anguish would allow no other thoughts for very long before the utter absurdity of my circumstances overtook me. Each time I recovered, a new dimension of this tragedy invaded my mind and brought with it another spasm of sobs.

As the horizon turned light blue and then pink, I made my way home. My parents, though grieved and bewildered by the turn of events, advised me to delay making any decision regarding Mary. It was wise advice. One moment I wanted to rush to her side, the next I wanted to wash my hands of her. But one constant remained through all of my pain and confusion: an unrelenting love for Mary.[4]

According to Jewish law, Joseph had the right to demand a public stoning, which would not only salve his wounded honor, but would also clear his name in the community. But he was too honorable for that.

> And Joseph her husband, being a righteous man and not wanting to
> disgrace her, planned to send her away secretly.
>
> Matthew 1:19

What a remarkable man! What a tactful stand he took! He had every reason to believe that Mary had been unfaithful. And to marry an unfaithful woman who clung to such an outlandish story would have been irresponsible. Nevertheless, Joseph planned to deal with her mercifully. He would pursue a quiet divorce. He could get on with his life. She could remain with her family, who would care for Mary and the child. It was a logical, wise decision.

Then Joseph had a supernatural encounter of his own.

> But when he had considered this, behold, an angel of the Lord
> appeared to him in a dream, saying, "Joseph, son of David, do not

be afraid to take Mary as your wife; for the Child who has been conceived in her is of the Holy Spirit. She will bear a Son; and you shall call His name Jesus, for He will save His people from their sins." Now all this took place to fulfill what was spoken by the Lord through the prophet: "Behold, the virgin shall be with child and shall bear a Son, and they shall call His name Immanuel," which translated means, "God with us."

Matthew 1:20–23

Though surprised by it, Joseph undoubtedly appreciated the full significance of the angel's message. First, the angel revealed that the child was conceived by God's Holy Spirit, which made Him the literal Son of God. Second, the angel announced that the child would be the long-awaited Messiah. To a Jew, this news would have been breathtaking. Unquestionably, it was the most significant announcement in the history of Israel. And on a personal level, the angel confirmed Mary's innocence, which had to have come as a great relief to the heartbroken young groom.

The visit gave Joseph the personal peace he needed to move forward with their marriage plans. However, he must have appreciated the difficulty these circumstances would present him. Let's face it, at best life with Mary and her child in and around Nazareth would be messy. The great blessing given to Mary also brought a significant number of complications, and becoming·her husband would be more than most men could bear. Nazareth was a tiny town and none of the other people living there received an angelic visit. As far as they were concerned, Joseph's wedding party would be carrying an illegitimately pregnant bride back to his house.

According to rabbinical law, Joseph could only divorce Mary if her child was not his own. The law strictly forbade his ending the marriage merely because he had fathered her child before the home-taking. Therefore, under any other circumstance, to bring her home was to admit that the child was his. In other words, Joseph voluntarily subjected himself to any misunderstanding the community would have had about Mary's pregnancy.

And if that weren't enough, Matthew tells us that Joseph "kept her a virgin until she gave birth to a Son" (Matthew 1:25). He married her, took her home, and lived with her for several months in a close, warm, loving relationship. Despite the obvious temptation to enjoy what was rightfully theirs, Joseph denied himself any sexual gratification because of his conviction that Mary should deliver the Messiah in the same state in which He was conceived.

What a model of selfless grace. Joseph understood the risks, counted the cost, set aside his own rights, and willingly accepted Mary's difficulties as his own.

A PICTURE OF JESUS

Theologians call the birth of Jesus the "incarnation." The word is taken from a Latin term meaning "to enter into or become flesh." One Bible dictionary defines the *incarnation* as "that act of grace whereby Christ took our human nature into union with his Divine Person, and became man."[5]

Paul the apostle later described the incarnation of Jesus and used this supreme act of grace to challenge his readers. In a letter to the Christians living in the Macedonian city of Philippi, he wrote,

> You should have the same attitude toward one another that Christ Jesus had,
> who though he existed in the form of God
> did not regard equality with God
> as something to be grasped,
> but emptied himself
> by taking on the form of a slave,
> by looking like other men,
> and by sharing in human nature.
> He humbled himself,
> by becoming obedient to the point of death
> —even death on a cross!
>
> Philippians 2:5–8 NET

The word for "slave" in this passage is the very same word used by Mary when she submitted to the will of God, saying, "Behold, the bond-slave of the Lord" (Luke 1:38).

In the previous chapter, we considered the bold claim of Jesus that He was God. Stop for a moment and reflect on the implications. Stretch your imagination and put yourself in His position. You are the supreme power over everything. You are beyond the need for food or safety, you do not feel pain, you cannot suffer death, you exist in a realm beyond the confines of time and three-dimensional space, and you are entirely content. As the almighty Creator of everything, you spoke the universe into existence, established a perfect habitat for living creatures, fashioned people to reflect your image, and then breathed life into them, only to have them rebel and make a mess of your world.

For reasons we may never completely understand, the almighty Creator loves the people He made so much that He devised a plan to save us from this mess. And that plan called for the Creator to become a human being. In the person of the Son, the timeless, all-powerful God voluntarily exited eternity and stepped into time to become a helpless human being; the Creator became as a creature to suffer the same pains we suffer, to endure the same heartaches and disappointments, struggles and temptations that afflict us, to bear the same injustices that plague human existence, and even to subject Himself to the awful consequences of sin.

I find Joseph's willingness to share Mary's circumstances to be a wonderful illustration of the humility and sacrifice of the incarnation. Joseph was a righteous man who wanted little more than to enjoy an uncomplicated existence with the woman he loved. But, as is often the case, obedience to God requires great sacrifice. As Mary unjustly suffered the scorn of her community, Joseph willingly set aside his own desires to share her burden. Her injustices would be his. Any misunderstanding she suffered, he would suffer. Before a watching, judging world, his wedding party carried an obviously pregnant bride through the narrow streets of their narrow-minded community back to his home, where he received her as his wife, allowing everyone to think whatever he or she chose to imagine. As we will discover later, this is a foreshadowing of the injustice that the innocent Son of God would endure on our behalf.

In some way or another, each life is a stage on which the drama of Nazareth plays out. We justly and unjustly suffer the consequences of a world given over to wrongdoing. It treats us unfairly and we too often respond by committing our own unjust deeds, thus adding to the sin of the world. Then, collectively and individually, we all reap the terrible consequences of unwise and immoral choices. *What a mess!*

Fortunately, God didn't leave us to suffer alone. In His grace, He voluntarily became one of us in the person of Jesus. And He did this in order to share our burden and, ultimately, provide a permanent solution for the mess we've made—the problem of evil.

Chapter Three

Deity in Diapers

On the Ides of March, 44 BC, Julius Caesar died at the hands of the same men who had declared him a god just two years earlier. All of the dictator's wealth and power then became the birthright of his adopted son and sole heir, Gaius Octavius, who over a twenty-year span transformed himself from a callow nineteen-year-old into the unrivaled leader of the Roman Empire. Eventually, he held the titles of *Princeps*, "leading citizen," *Pontifex Maximus*, "high priest," and ultimately, *Augustus*, "supreme ruler," all the while playing himself off as a humble, reluctant leader. But when Halley's Comet painted a blazing stripe across the night sky in the fall of 12 BC, Caesar Augustus made the most of it, claiming it was the spirit of Julius entering heaven. The superstitious Romans barely flinched when Augustus suggested that he too should be worshiped. He was, after all, the son of a god.

Historians call this period of time the *Pax Romana*, "the peace of Rome," but it was a brutal peace. The Romans cared most about two things: submission to Rome and the steady flow of wealth into Roman coffers. As long as no one rebelled or disturbed the trade routes, they really didn't care what

happened on a local level. Chuck Colson paints the picture well in his book
Kingdoms in Conflict:

> Two thousand years ago Palestine was (as it is today) a land in
> turmoil, its two and a half million inhabitants bitterly divided by
> religious, cultural, and language barriers. An unlikely mix of Jews,
> Greeks, and Syrians populated the coastal towns and fertile valleys of
> the ancient land, and tensions among them often erupted in bloody
> clashes. Rome did little to discourage this volatile bitterness. As long
> as the people's passions were spent on each other, they weren't being
> vented on their conquerors.
>
> Among these disparate groups, the Jews alone had hope for the future,
> for they clung to the promise that a Messiah, sent from God, would one
> day come to set them free. According to the Scriptures, this savior would
> bring swift judgment to Israel's oppressors and triumphantly reestablish
> the mighty throne of the great King David.[1]

During these paradoxical days of severe oppression and safe travel,
Caesar Augustus declared that his entire realm should be subject to a census
just as Rome had been for many hundreds of years. The Gospel of
Luke describes the event.

> Now in those days a decree went out from Caesar Augustus, that a
> census be taken of all the inhabited earth. This was the first census
> taken while Quirinius was governor of Syria.
>
> Luke 2:1–2

Some scholars have debated Luke's facts, pointing out that Quirinius
did not become the governor of Syria until 6 AD and that Herod the
Great died in 4 BC. But archeological evidence strongly suggests that
Quirinius had been in Syria on a military mission for Augustus from 10–7
BC and that, with Herod's increasing madness, the emperor was preparing
the region for direct Roman control. Therefore, this would have been the
"*first* census taken while Quirinius was governor."

"In those days"—that is, days of economic oppression by a corrupt aristocracy, political tyranny under a mad dictator, and increasing terrorism by impetuous zealots—families had to report to their ancestral towns in order to give an accounting of their lives to a "censor." The venerable *Encyclopaedia Britannica* describes the basic role of a censor as,

> a magistrate whose original functions of registering citizens and their property were greatly expanded to include supervision of senatorial rolls and moral conduct. Censors also assessed property for taxation and contracts, penalized moral offenders by removing their public rights, such as voting and tribe membership, and presided at the lustrum ceremonies of purification at the close of each census.[2]

Soon after Augustus took complete control of Rome, the role of the censor became the emperor's responsibility. In the provinces, he empowered magistrates called *censitores*. Much like we know the term today, a censor evaluated the character and conduct of others as a part of his tax-gathering duties, which gave him and his delegates wide latitude for corruption. So imagine the personal affront this became to good Jews. The order of Augustus required Jewish men, whose only king was the creator God, to stand before a Roman official to give an accounting of their moral fitness. Certainly for a first-century Jew, the kingdoms of Augustus and God stood in sharp conflict. Nevertheless, the betrothed couple of Nazareth was compelled to journey ninety miles south to Bethlehem, the city of David, their ancestral capital.

> And everyone was on his way to register for the census, each to his own city. Joseph also went up from Galilee, from the city of Nazareth, to Judea, to the city of David which is called Bethlehem, because he was of the house and family of David, in order to register along with Mary, who was engaged to him, and was with child.
>
> Luke 2:3–5

Bethlehem, which means "house of bread," sits 2,350 feet above sea level, surrounded by some of the most fertile land in the world. Fig trees, olive groves, and vineyards covered the hillsides while vast flocks grazed the surrounding valleys. Though only five miles south of Jerusalem, it was five miles by foot over rugged terrain, which gave it the kind of rural simplicity you would expect in a farming community. But the decree of Augustus changed all that. Lots of men could legitimately trace their roots to David, so hundreds—perhaps even thousands—converged on the little town of Bethlehem all at once.

> While they were there, the days were completed for her to give birth. And she gave birth to her firstborn son; and she wrapped Him in cloths, and laid Him in a manger, because there was no room for them in the inn.
>
> Luke 2:6–7

Ancient Near Eastern rules of hospitality required the local inhabitants to open their homes to the visitors, but the sheer numbers would have overwhelmed the poor people of Bethlehem very quickly. So Mary and Joseph would have sought out an "inn."

Thanks to the charming little children's pageants presented in churches each Christmas, we typically think of the "inn" as an ancient version of Motel 6—clean beds for folks on a budget. We imagine the hapless couple vainly wandering the streets of Bethlehem searching for a vacancy.

In reality, "inns" were seedy little establishments run by shady characters, and they offered only a slightly better alternative to sleeping in the open fields. They were more like a truck stop than a motel, providing trade caravans modest room and board, as well as relative safety from robbers. They were not the kind of place a man would want to take his wife and children, and definitely not the ideal place to give birth. Nevertheless, even these were filled to capacity.

I have often wondered why Mary made the trip with Joseph knowing that she would likely deliver her child before returning home again. Perhaps he thought they could make the trip, conclude their business, and return in time. Maybe she delivered early or they miscounted the weeks. I happen to think they intended to stay with relatives, found Bethlehem overrun with travelers, and were surprised to find that the registration process took much

longer than anyone anticipated. It really doesn't matter, though. The decisions of men only served to accomplish the sovereign plan of God. Centuries
before the birth of Augustus, a Jewish prophet named Micah wrote,

"But as for you, Bethlehem Ephrathah,
Too little to be among the clans of Judah,
From you One will go forth for Me to be ruler in Israel.
His goings forth are from long ago,
From the days of eternity."
Therefore He will give them up until the time
When she who is in labor has borne a child.
Then the remainder of His brethren
Will return to the sons of Israel.
And He will arise and shepherd His flock
In the strength of the LORD,
In the majesty of the name of the LORD His God.
And they will remain,
Because at that time He will be great
To the ends of the earth.

Micah 5:2–4

Caesar Augustus thought this exercise of power would give him greater
control over the world, but in the end, all he did was run an errand for
God. Joseph and Mary lived in Nazareth, but the prophecy said the Messiah
would be born in Bethlehem. Furthermore, we dare not forget that God is
omniscient as well as sovereign. He was not taken by surprise when people
from all over the realm packed into Bethlehem just before Joseph and Mary
arrived. This would precipitate just one of many ironies, all of which would
serve a divine purpose.

A VERY SPECIAL BIRTH

As I pointed out in the first two chapters, the baby in Mary's womb was
no ordinary child. John, perhaps Jesus' closest friend on earth, described
His birth this way:

In the beginning was the Word, and the Word was with God, and the Word was God. . . . And the Word became flesh, and dwelt among us, and we saw His glory, glory as of the only begotten from the Father, full of grace and truth.

John 1:1, 14

In the weakness of human flesh, the almighty Creator of the universe came to earth. However, when God became a man in the person of Jesus Christ, He did not cease to be God, nor did He lose His divine attributes, such as omnipresence and omnipotence. He merely laid them aside for a time. Theologians call this choice *kenosis*, which derives from a Greek term meaning "to empty." Perhaps the best way to illustrate the concept is to tell the story of Thomas Mott Osborne.

In October 1914, Osborne entered Auburn Prison in upstate New York, and like all the other prisoners, he was photographed, fingerprinted, stripped of his possessions, issued a set of prison grays, and led to a cell, four feet wide by seven and a half feet long and seven and a half feet tall. The only difference between prisoner 33,333x and the other 1,329 inmates was the issue of freedom. On his command, he could leave the prison anytime he desired.

After his appointment to Governor Sulzer's State Commission on Prison Reform, Osborne made it his mission to live as one of the inmates, study their experience, and emerge as their advocate. He voluntarily laid aside his freedom to experience life behind bars. He slept in a dank, drafty cell just like theirs. He ate their food and labored as they did. He even endured their most dreaded punishment, a night in "the box." While he could order his own release at any time, he was nevertheless confined. He wrote, "I am a prisoner, locked, double locked. By no human possibility, by no act of my own, can I throw open the iron grating which shuts me from the world into this small stone vault. I am a voluntary prisoner, it is true; nevertheless even a voluntary prisoner can't unlock the door of his cell."[3]

Just as Osborne was at once free yet confined to prison, Jesus was omnipotent yet helpless as an infant, dependent upon His mother's milk for survival. He set aside His rightful entitlements of deity to become the least privileged of people—born among the poorest of the poor. This humble entrance into the world would characterize the rest of His days on earth and illustrate the difference between His kingdom and the world's idea of power, authority, riches, and privilege.

A NEW LIGHT

In 586 BC, long before Jesus was born, Babylon successfully overwhelmed the city of Jerusalem, which put an end to the kingdom of God on earth—at least for a time. Then Nebuchadnezzar did what most conquerors did in his day: he razed the city walls, looted the palaces and holy places, tortured the men who had resisted him, and set up a new government.

But unlike other empire builders, Nebuchadnezzar recognized the power of education and educated men. He carefully selected the most promising students from every conquered nation and relocated them to the capitol, thus building a university in the truest sense of the word. Their purpose was to gather knowledge from astronomy and astrology, science and metaphysics, philosophy and religion—any credible source of information they could find—in order to advise their king.

The best and brightest from Judah included a young boy named Daniel, who outshined them all. After several encounters with Nebuchadnezzar, he became a favored wise man and trusted adviser, eventually becoming a high-ranking official in the Babylonian government. Daniel also became a powerful prophet, predicting the rise and fall of the next four major empires of the world with astounding accuracy. In fact, his predictions were so accurate and so detailed that many scholars view them as clever forgeries written later in history.

Among his predictions, Daniel wrote that the Persian Empire would eventually overtake Babylon and the new king would grant the nation of Judah permission to rebuild the walls of Jerusalem. Sixty-nine "weeks of years"—or sixty-nine seven-year periods—from that event, the Messiah would appear (Daniel 9:24–25). On March 5, 444 BC, Artaxerxes Longimanus gave Nehemiah permission to repair the walls of Jerusalem (Nehemiah 2:1–8).[4]

So 483 Jewish lunar years after this event, any serious student of the Hebrew Bible would have been looking for the Messiah to appear.

The school of wise men, of which Daniel was a member, took great care to chart the heavens, hoping to determine the future from the constellations. Could it be that Daniel was able to mathematically forecast the positions of certain stars and planets at the time of Jesus' birth? (I can imagine his leaving clues for future generations of seers rolled up in papyrus manuscripts alongside the pagan ramblings of his colleagues.)

Matthew records that a group of these "magi" from the East—remnants of the old Babylonian and Persian schools of wise men—saw "His star" in the sky and knew what it signified, perhaps from information provided by Daniel. Regardless of how they came by their clues, the men undertook an expedition to find the great king. Their journey from the other side of the Arabian Desert would have taken several weeks if not months. Take special note of their purpose.

> Now after Jesus was born in Bethlehem of Judea in the days of Herod the king, magi from the east arrived in Jerusalem, saying, "Where is He who has been born King of the Jews? For we saw His star in the east and have come to worship Him."
>
> Matthew 2:1–2

As wise men from the East began their westward trek to find the Son of God and worship him, Mary delivered her child and "laid Him in a manger" (Luke 2:7). The ancient reader would not have missed the point of Luke's detail. Mary laid deity in diapers in a feeding trough, which is to say that the place of His birth—a stable—was even more humble than the detested inn.

Phillip Keller, in his fine work entitled *Rabboni*, offers this imaginative depiction of that night:

> The sheep corral, filthy as only an Eastern animal enclosure can be, reeked pungently with manure and urine accumulated across the seasons. Joseph cleared a corner just large enough for Mary to lie down.

Birth pains had started. She writhed in agony on the ground. Joseph, in his inexperience and unknowing manly manner, did his best to reassure her. His own outer tunic would be her bed, his rough saddlebag her pillow. Hay, straw, or other animal fodder was non-existent. This was not hay- or grain-growing country. Stock barely survived by grazing on the sparse vegetation that sprang from that semidesert terrain.

Mary moaned and groaned in the darkness of the sheep shelter. Joseph swept away the dust and dirt from a small space in one of the hand-hewn mangers carved from soft limestone rock. He arranged a place where Mary could lay the newborn babe all bundled up in the clothes she had brought along.

And there, alone, unaided, without strangers or friends to witness her ordeal, in the darkness, she delivered her son. It was the unpretentious entrance, the stage entrance of the Son of man—the Son of God, very God in human form—on earth's stage.[5]

RESPONSES

As Mary gave birth to Jesus, the small band of Eastern mystics followed the ominous light in the sky, fully expecting it to lead them to a great king. Naturally, they thought they would find Him in the capital city (Matthew 2:1), no doubt somewhere in the royal palace and surrounded by great celebration. The birth of royalty has always been cause for rejoicing, especially the birth of a firstborn son.

In Japan, the arrival of Prince Hisahito in 1996 was probably the most anticipated royal birth in recent history. The imperial family hadn't produced a male heir to the Chrysanthemum Throne in more than forty years, which caused no small amount of hand wringing among the more conservative members of that male-centered society. So upon his birth, Hisahito received a welcome like few in our time. I am also reminded of the births of Prince William and Prince Henry, the sons of the celebrated Charles and Diana in Great Britain.

Jesus, however, the rightful heir to the throne of Israel, quietly entered the world in a stable on the outskirts of little Bethlehem, beneath notice of the wealthy, the educated, and the elite. His arrival was not completely ignored, though.

> In the same region there were some shepherds staying out in the fields and keeping watch over their flock by night. And an angel of the Lord suddenly stood before them, and the glory of the Lord shone around them; and they were terribly frightened. But the angel said to them, "Do not be afraid; for behold, I bring you good news of great joy which will be for all the people; for today in the city of David there has been born for you a Savior, who is Christ the Lord. "This will be a sign for you: you will find a baby wrapped in cloths and lying in a manger."
>
> Luke 2:8–12

Shepherds were the social outcasts of their day, a necessary yet ostracized caste without whom the temple could not function. While they tended the animals required for ritual sacrifice, the conscientious Jew—ever concerned with purity—spurned shepherds as too unclean to stand among other worshipers. Imagine the reception a dirty migrant worker would receive at the door of a sophisticated country club, and you will understand where the shepherd ranked in Hebrew society.

While the rich and powerful in Jerusalem formed factions, alternately resisting and sweet-talking the Romans, blissfully unaware of the momentous event taking place in the countryside, angels appeared to the people most likely to understand what was happening. Imagine how the outcast shepherds felt when they heard their king's palace was a stable and His cradle was a feeding trough. At last, they had a king who shared their low station, who would care about the things that mattered to them. Perhaps this king would value His subjects more than conquests and the acquisition of more and more wealth.

The shepherds immediately left their livelihood to graze unattended in order to find their newborn king.

> When the angels had gone away from them into heaven, the shepherds began saying to one another, "Let us go straight to Bethlehem then, and see this thing that has happened which the Lord has made

known to us." So they came in a hurry and found their way to Mary and Joseph, and the baby as He lay in the manger. When they had seen this, they made known the statement which had been told them about this Child. And all who heard it wondered at the things which were told them by the shepherds.

Luke 2:15–18

I take it that the shepherds had to do some searching once they reached Bethlehem. I imagine their wandering through the town, talking with huddled groups of travelers from all over the region, asking who might have heard the cries of a baby in a feeding trough. Naturally, this would have prompted questions, which then led to a vivid story about angels and a quest to find the Messiah somewhere close to town. Once they found their Savior just as the angels had indicated, they told the story again, this time in the hearing of Joseph and Mary.

The Bible says that everyone who heard it "wondered at the things which were told" (Luke 2:18). The broadest meaning of the Greek word for "wondered" "has first the sense of astonishment, whether critical or inquisitive, then admiration, with a nuance of awe or fear at what is unusual or mysterious."[6] The descendants of David, gathered in the city of David for the purpose of giving an accounting of their lives to Augustus, were taken aback by what they saw and heard. But take note of Mary's response:

But Mary treasured all these things, pondering them in her heart.

Luke 2:19

The Greek word for "treasure" means "to protect, to preserve, to guard, or keep watch over something." The companion verb for "ponder" literally means "to throw together" or "to bring together," not unlike what someone would do with the pieces of a jigsaw puzzle. Everything that had happened to Mary: the angelic announcement, the crises it caused Joseph, the timing of the census, the birth of God-in-flesh in a stable, the worship of shepherds—discrete pieces of a giant, complex puzzle—floated about loosely in her mind, challenging her to arrange them into some kind of order.

The main verbs in Luke 2:18–19 form an interesting contrast, and I think Luke intended it deliberately. The people who witnessed the birth and heard the shepherds' story stood in slack-jawed astonishment, not at all sure they were able to trust what they were seeing and hearing, even a little unwilling to accept what they knew in their hearts to be true. They had so long anticipated the arrival of the Messiah that when He finally arrived, they were incredulous. Mind you, these are the same people who had witnessed the remarkable events surrounding the birth of John, the son of Zacharias and Elizabeth. When the forerunner of the Messiah was born, Luke's account says of them,

> Fear came on all those living around [Zacharias and Elizabeth]; and all these matters were being talked about in all the hill country of Judea. All who heard them kept them in mind, saying, "What then will this child turn out to be?" For the hand of the Lord was certainly with him.
>
> Luke 1:65–66

Mary, on the other hand, was not "astonished." She knew the event could be trusted as authentic, even if she couldn't completely understand it at the time.

A NEW WAY OF THINKING

Giving birth to God in human flesh would naturally challenge the new mother's previous concepts of motherhood. Let's face it, the idea of a God-man walking the earth challenges a lot of ideas. But we need to keep our minds open as we observe His life, even if we don't fully comprehend His words and works. His purpose was, and still is, the reconciliation of two worlds separated by two very different ways of thinking: the kingdoms of God and humanity, each of which finds a representative in the person of Jesus. However, this reconciliation is not merely a blending of philosophies. The ways of earth and heaven are entirely incompatible.

The world was not always what it is now. "In the beginning, God created the heavens and the earth" (Genesis 1:1), filled the universe with truth, gave it order, and called it "good." (The Lord declared His creation was "good" no fewer than seven times in the creation account: Genesis 1:4, 10, 12, 18, 21, 25, 31.)

But then something awful happened. The first man and woman dis obeyed the simple command of God.

> "From any tree of the garden you may eat freely; but from the tree of the knowledge of good and evil you shall not eat, for in the day that you eat from it you will surely die."
>
> Genesis 2:16–17

This changed everything. Theologians refer to this event as "the fall," the moment sin began its cascading corruption of the world, transforming it from the "good" God had created into a menacing perversion of it. The earth now produces crops hampered by weeds and thorns. Work has become grinding toil. The joy of childbirth comes at the expense of enormous pain and anguish. Even our very nature as people—created to bear the very image of God—has been twisted by sin so that much of the good we do is laced with selfishness. Evil now corrupts every good as if to insult the Creator. And sin brought with it the ultimate affront to God: death, the termination and decay of everything He created to be good.

God didn't become human merely to add His good to offset our evil. No, the birth of Jesus was an invasion, a benevolent takeover whereby everyone and everything in the world must be transformed. So we will have to remind ourselves often that, while Jesus was a flesh-and-bone man, He was no ordinary man. And His teaching will be, quite literally, out of this world. He will sometimes sound cryptic, even evasive with His answers, but rather than write off His words as nonsense or try to squeeze them into old categories, I challenge you to see with different eyes. Open yourself up to the possibility that what He said, did, and taught was intended to create a very different world than the one you presently occupy. In fact, you might even find that the truth He brought is intended to create a very different *you!*

Nonsense or life-changing truth? As we will soon see, how people received the words and deeds of Jesus depended greatly upon how they chose to respond to Him personally.

Wait. That seems to be backwards, doesn't it? Shouldn't that be the other way around?

Chapter Four

Eight days after the birth of Jesus, Joseph and Mary presented the boy for the *b'rit milah*, "the covenant of circumcision," a rite that identified Him as a genuine son of the covenant between God and Abraham. And, as custom dictated, they made his name official: *Yeshua*, "Yahweh saves." Then, in keeping with the law of Moses, they waited until Mary had completed her ritual purification before making the five-mile journey to the temple in Jerusalem. There, Joseph and Mary would offer a sacrifice for themselves and dedicate the boy to God.

As they made their way across the Court of Women, an elderly worshiper, a seer named Simeon, approached them—perhaps a little more boldly than they expected of a stranger. He had been roaming the temple precincts for some time—maybe years—looking for couples with newborn children in their arms, for he was a careful student of the Scriptures, and God had promised him that he would not pass from this world until he had laid eyes on the Messiah. And with this promise, the Lord gave Simeon the eyes to see, the ability to recognize the Promised One with a mere glance.

As he looked into the eyes of the long-awaited king, he exclaimed,

"Now Lord, You are releasing Your bond-servant to depart in peace,
According to Your word;
For my eyes have seen Your salvation,
Which You have prepared in the presence of all peoples,
A light of revelation to the Gentiles,
And the glory of Your people Israel."

Luke 2:29–32

After pronouncing a blessing on Joseph and Mary, the seer's voice grew serious. "Listen carefully: This child is destined to be the cause of the falling and rising of many in Israel and to be a sign that will be rejected. Indeed, as a result of Him the thoughts of many hearts will be revealed—and a sword will pierce your own soul as well!" (Luke 2:34–35). In other words, *This boy has a very special purpose, and as He pursues His call, the destiny of each person who encounters Him will be unveiled for all to see.*

The oracle would prove to be genuine sooner than later; how much later, we cannot say for sure. But sometime before Joseph and Mary had decided to return to Galilee, the magi arrived in Jerusalem looking for the "King of the Jews." Herod the Great, already mad with paranoia, took great interest in their quest, though obviously not for the same reason. After reviewing the prophecies concerning the Messiah and interviewing the magi, Herod encouraged the wise men, "Go and search carefully for the Child; and when you have found Him, report to me, so that I too may come and worship Him" (Matthew 2:8).

Upon finding the genuine King of the Jews, the mystics worshiped Him as God and laid their offerings before the manger-altar. Then, having been warned in a dream to avoid Herod, the magi returned home without reporting to Jerusalem as requested. Their choice of a different route stirred the rebellious heart of Israel's illegitimate king—with tragic results.

When Herod saw that he had been tricked by the magi, he became very enraged, and sent and slew all the male children who were in Bethlehem and all its vicinity, from two years old and under, according to the time which he had determined from the magi.

Matthew 2:16

To avoid the slaughter, Joseph and Mary escaped to Egypt and remained there until Herod died, which the historian, Josephus, described as the result of an intestinal infection of some kind.

> But now Herod's distemper greatly increased upon him after a severe manner . . . His entrails were also ex-ulcerated, and the chief violence of his pain lay on his colon; an aqueous and transparent liquor also had settled itself about his feet, and a like matter afflicted him at the bottom of his belly.[1]

According to Matthew, all of these events had a purpose in the sovereign plan of God. "He remained [in Egypt] until the death of Herod. This was to fulfill what had been spoken by the Lord through the prophet [Hosea]: 'Out of Egypt I called My Son'" (Matthew 2:15). As if to retrace the steps of the Exodus, Jesus left Egypt for the land that God had promised to Israel. Indeed, Jesus would be the Israel God longed to call "son." But they chose to worship false gods and suffered repeated invasions until finally exiled from the Promised Land. When restored to their home, they worshiped God outwardly while worshiping wealth in their hearts. To judge that sin, He withdrew His protection, gave them over to corrupt leaders, and stopped speaking to them. Then, by the time of Herod four hundred years later, the religious leaders of Israel had erected a new idol to stand alongside that of wealth: their own self-righteousness.

It was in this centuries-long wandering from God that Jesus would come to Israel. As Joseph and Mary reentered the Promised Land, perhaps only weeks after leaving, they discovered that Jesus' throne was still occupied. Herod the Great was dead, but his son Archelaus, a man even more brutal and erratic than his father, reigned in his place. So they set aside their expectation that their Messiah would reign anytime soon and returned to their home in the forgotten little town of Nazareth. Sometime during the eleven years that followed, the memories of their adventure in Bethlehem faded, washed out by the humdrum of daily existence. Simeon told them, but they forgot. Jesus was a boy with a destiny, and His destiny would affect everyone He touched.

DIGGING OUT FROM UNDER THE RUBBLE

The Gospels of Matthew, Mark, Luke, and John—the only accounts of Jesus' life that were unanimously accepted by the people who knew Him—offer no information about what happened to Him during those eleven years. History is silent. Luke alone offers this tidbit: "The Child continued to grow and become strong, increasing in wisdom; and the grace of God was upon Him" (Luke 2:40). Between the ages of one and twelve, we know nothing about Jesus' life.

Leave a blank space in history and, before long, someone will try to fill it. Many decades after the last eyewitnesses had died, several new documents emerged containing fanciful stories of Jesus' childhood. They first appeared in the second century, but none of them was considered remotely plausible by the gatherings of believers at the time. Recently, novelists and a few conspiracy theorists have claimed that "the church" and the Roman emperor Constantine colluded to squelch the truth of these documents because they threatened to undermine their power. It makes for a compelling adventure story, but as history it's comical.

Before Constantine rose to power as Roman emperor and made Christianity legal in AD 313, there was no single organization that governed Christendom like the Roman Catholic Church would later. Christianity was illegal, and Christians were frequently persecuted. Churches remained largely underground cell groups that struggled to survive in hostile areas and kept a low profile in the more tolerant corners of the empire. During the second and third centuries, churches were in no position to strong-arm anyone. They did, however, communicate. And they agreed that these alleged accounts of Jesus' life were fraudulent. The newer accounts weren't believable because they disagreed with the genuine documents they had possessed for decades. Consequently, the communities of believers scattered across the empire didn't bother to reproduce or preserve these later documents.

We don't know much about what Jesus was like as a child. What we do know comes from one story in the Gospel of Luke, probably because Luke interviewed Mary as a part of his research.

At thirteen, a Jewish boy was called a *bar mitzvah*, a "son of the commandment." In preparation for His thirteenth birthday, Jesus might have undergone a rigorous program of instruction and preparation for this passage into manhood. But the modern bar mitzvah ceremony and celebration evolved from Jewish customs in the Middle Ages, so we can only speculate as to what first-century Jews did. Regardless, one year prior to officially becoming a man, Jesus accompanied His family's caravan to the Holy City to celebrate the Passover Feast and the Feast of Unleavened Bread. These back-to-back celebrations spanned eight days, a time taken together as the Passover.

After the celebration came to a close, Joseph and Mary began the journey north to Galilee along with hundreds of other pilgrims, including dozens of friends and extended relatives. Perhaps thinking Jesus had joined His cousins farther back, the couple discovered only later that He was not in their number at all. Immediately, Joseph and Mary turned again for Jerusalem and retraced their steps. After three days of searching, they finally found Jesus in the temple, surrounded by the nation's foremost experts in Jewish law.

> Then, after three days they found Him in the temple, sitting in the midst of the teachers, both listening to them and asking them questions. And all who heard Him were amazed at His understanding and His answers.
>
> Luke 2:46–47

The Greek word used to describe the response of the religious leaders is intriguing for two reasons. First, "amazed" literally means "'to remove oneself,' figuratively 'to lose one's wits,' 'go out of one's mind,' 'be terrified out of one's wits.'"[2] We would say, "They were beside themselves." Thus, "amazed" doesn't capture the utter astonishment and excitement that seized Israel's most gifted teachers. It's the kind of reaction we might have if we were to see a four-year-old play Rachmaninov's 3rd Piano Concerto perfectly from beginning to end. They had discovered a prodigy. The Greek terms indicate that Jesus was able to put things together and come up with insights that should have been far beyond His grasp at age twelve. He could go to the heart of an issue like no one they had seen.

A second reason the choice of terms is remarkable: the Greek translation of the Old Testament used the same word to describe the reaction of people who had seen a manifestation of God. Of all the words he could have chosen, Luke chose the most theologically loaded term available. And his readers undoubtedly would have noticed.

As Joseph and Mary entered the scene, they were dumbstruck to find Him in the temple. They probably worried that He was dead in a gutter. (That's usually the place a parent's mind goes when his or her child can't be found.) So, naturally, they spoke to Jesus like any parent would upon finding a lost child. Remember, they had been searching for Him for three days.

> When they saw Him, they were astonished; and His mother said to Him, "Son, why have You treated us this way? Behold, Your father and I have been anxiously looking for You." And He said to them, "Why is it that you were looking for Me? Did you not know that I had to be in My Father's house?"
>
> Luke 2:48–49

Upon first glance, Jesus' answer might appear a tad sassy, but we can't hear the inflection of His voice in print. He was genuinely confused by their searching for three days before looking in the temple. If they had remembered His beginnings or recalled the words of Simeon, the temple should have been their first place to look upon returning to Jerusalem. Where else would the Son of God be but in the house of God? Nevertheless, Joseph and Mary didn't connect the dots. "They did not understand the statement which He had made to them" (Luke 2:50).

I find the irony of this episode absolutely priceless. Joseph and Mary, firsthand witnesses to angelic announcements, shepherd and magi worship, and prophetic oracles, didn't have the eyes to see Jesus' divine purpose emerging. Jesus, however, knew what was happening to Himself. He understood His purpose, His call, His divinely appointed mission.

Tragically, most people don't discover their purpose until late in life. Some never find it. As Os Guinness writes,

50

To be sure, calling is not what it is commonly thought to be. It has to be dug out from under the rubble of ignorance and confusion. And, uncomfortably, it often flies in the face of our human inclinations. But nothing short of God's call can ground and fulfill the truest human desire for purpose.[3]

I sometimes wonder how and when Jesus discovered His purpose. Because He had set aside His omniscience, He started like anyone else, as an infant having no knowledge of anything. His purpose had to be "dug out from under the rubble of ignorance and confusion" just like any other human.

When did Jesus first become aware of His true identity? Did He put it all together by reading about the Messiah in Scripture? Did He hear a sermon in the synagogue near Nazareth that caused it to click in His mind? Was it an innate understanding that slowly emerged with Him because of the Spirit of God within Him?

No one can say for certain. We only know that He understood His divinely ordained purpose by His twelfth birthday. Even with this knowledge, He remained humble and silent until the proper time.

> He went down with [Joseph and Mary] and came to Nazareth, and He continued in subjection to them; and His mother treasured all these things in her heart. And Jesus kept increasing in wisdom and stature, and in favor with God and men.
>
> Luke 2:51–52

CALLING ALL COMERS

Numerous people claimed to be the Christ in first-century Israel, so when the son of Zacharias and Elizabeth prophesied in the wilderness of Judea, he appeared to be nothing more than another flash-in-the-pan fanatic. But John, known as "the Baptizer," didn't claim to be the Messiah—only the forerunner, sent by God to prepare the people for the promised King's appearance. He called Israel to repentance and administered the traditional Jewish rite of baptism, whereby converts to Judaism were ceremonially cleansed as they became, as it were, adopted sons of the covenant. John's baptism of repentance called Jews to admit they had forsaken their covenant with God and to approach Him as if for the very first time. By submitting to John's baptism, they were essentially starting over with God.

The rite of baptism also had another meaning that would be important to Jesus. It was the rite of priests who were purified by the washing of water just prior to representing the people before God in the Most Holy Place.

In AD 29, eighteen to twenty years after Jesus became a son of the covenant, He presented himself to John for baptism. At first, John refused, saying, "I have need to be baptized by You, and do You come to me?" (Matthew 3:14). He mistakenly thought Jesus was submitting Himself to the prophet's baptism of repentance, but Jesus had something else in mind. He was about to give the symbol of immersion in water a new meaning and change the rite of baptism forever.

Jesus entered the waters of the Jordan River to be immersed and, with a host of John's disciples and other witnesses looking on, welcomed the affirmation of His Father. As the Spirit of God appeared as a dove descending upon Jesus, a booming voice shook the crowd: "This is My beloved Son, in whom I am well pleased" (Matthew 3:17). That day, Jesus officially began a journey that would lead to His ultimate destiny. His ritual cleansing publicly announced the beginning of His ministry—the pursuit of His call. And His first act was to make baptism a symbolic doorway to a new kind of life, through which He would be the first to walk.

Two of John the Baptizer's disciples, John the son of Zebedee and Andrew, found this new doorway too intriguing to ignore and, upon hearing the forerunner call Jesus "the Lamb of God," left to follow Him home (John 1:35–37). I can only imagine the conversation that took place that afternoon and evening as Andrew and John listened to Jesus' dinner talk. But it obviously had a profound impact on Andrew, who left early the next morning to find his brother and bring him to meet the rabbi.

One of the two who heard John speak and followed Him, was Andrew, Simon Peter's brother. He found first his own brother Simon and said to him, "We have found the Messiah" (which translated means Christ). He brought him to Jesus. Jesus looked at him and said, "You are Simon the son of John; you shall be called Cephas" (which is translated Peter).

John 1:40–42

Cephas derives from an Aramaic word meaning "rock." Simon was a fisherman by trade and powerfully built after years of throwing nets and hauling up loads of fish. The winsome rabbi probably put a hand on Simon's shoulder while greeting him and decided the nickname "Rocky" or "Rock-man" was fitting. Of course, Jesus intended a double meaning, which would only become clear later. And so the name stuck: Cephas— *Petros* to the Greeks, Peter in English.

As the small group of men enjoyed the presence and words of Jesus, Peter began to realize that Andrew was right. The men had found the Messiah and very much wanted to become His disciples. But discipleship in the first century was no small matter. Disciples, through the teaching of their mentor, were to become reproductions of their master. If they failed to learn or did something publicly embarrassing, critics would look past the pupil to condemn the teacher. So, naturally, teachers took great care to choose disciples who not only had promise, but would completely submit to their instruction. A person could ask a rabbi to become his mentor, but the relationship didn't begin until the teacher extended an invitation.

After Jesus bade farewell to His house guests, He began preparations for a teaching expedition through Galilee. Another potential disciple named Philip lived in Judea, perhaps with extended family in the little town of Emmaus, seven miles or so from Jerusalem. Jesus knew him to be from Bethsaida, "house of fish," a fishing village on the northern banks of the Sea of Galilee that had recently been built into a city to honor the daughter of Caesar Augustus. Furthermore, not coincidentally, it was also the hometown of Andrew, Peter, and John. Upon finding him, Jesus extended a mentor's invitation: "Follow Me." Philip responded positively and invited his brother Nathaniel to meet Jesus. After a short discourse, Jesus was impressed with his straightforward manner and Nathaniel, too, became a disciple.

We don't know what happened then to Simon, Andrew, and John. Perhaps they thought Jesus had no interest in them as disciples and returned to their normal routines at home and on the sea. All we know for certain is that sometime later—days, perhaps weeks—they had returned to their trade along the shores of the Sea of Galilee. Soon, their paths crossed again. However, the reunion was anything but chance.

Jesus had been teaching and healing His way through the countryside of Galilee when He began preaching to a crowd along the banks of the sea. During a break in His morning lessons, He noticed a group of fishermen cleaning their nets on the shore, something they typically did just before returning home. Jesus knew one of the men to be Peter and decided to make the most of the moment.

> [Jesus] got into one of the boats, which was Simon's, and asked him to put out a little way from the land. And He sat down and began teaching the people from the boat. When He had finished speaking, He said to Simon, "Put out into the deep water and let down your nets for a catch." Simon answered and said, "Master, we worked hard all night and caught nothing, but I will do as You say and let down the nets." When they had done this, they enclosed a great quantity of fish, and their nets began to break; so they signaled to their partners in the other boat for them to come and help them. And they came and filled both of the boats, so that they began to sink.
>
> Luke 5:3–7

I would love to know what Jesus taught the people from Simon's boat. A lesson on discipleship? Trusting God for provision? I like to think He spoke about the joy of fulfilling one's destiny, following one's call. Peter was reluctant at first but, calling Jesus "Master," he begrudgingly had his men lower the nets, despite having spent all morning cleaning them. In Peter's mind, it was a fool's errand just to appease the Rabbi. A few moments later, though, Peter tugged the nets and discovered the top line taut to the point of breaking. The scene from shore must have been comical as he frantically barked orders to the crew as they scrambled around the deck, trying to haul in the nets full of fish. When the deck of the first boat filled to capacity, and then the second, both vessels sat low in the water, nearly sinking under the load.

When the crews of both boats were able to secure the load of fish, the object lesson brought Peter to his knees. Luke wrote of the rock-solid fisherman, "stunning astonishment surrounded him," and Peter's next act reveals a dawning awareness that Jesus was no ordinary man: "He fell down at Jesus' feet, saying, 'Go away from me Lord, for I am a sinful man!'" (Luke 5:8).

Peter's exclamation is reminiscent of another man who found himself frozen with fear in the presence of God. Isaiah, the Old Testament prophet, said, "Woe to me! . . . I am ruined! For I am a man of unclean lips, and I live among a people of unclean lips, and I have seen the King, the LORD Almighty" (Isaiah 6:5 NIV). Both Isaiah and Peter understood the potential consequences of direct contact with God. Sinfulness cannot survive in the presence of divine glory. Because Peter understood himself to be a man tainted with sin, he feared Jesus.

As Peter, John, and John's brother James trembled before their Messiah, they heard the words that would forever change their lives: "Do not fear, from now on you will be catching men" (Luke 5:10).

THE MEANING OF LIFE

Peter was a man I can appreciate. He never did anything halfway. One day, he was in Judea sitting at the feet of the Messiah, ready to become His disciple. Then, when that didn't seem to pan out, he went back up to Galilee, back to his old life as a commercial fisherman, dutifully dropping his nets each day and consistently coming up empty.

It's a funny thing, pursuing a call. Once we begin the journey, we can never turn back. Something pulled Peter, Andrew, and John away from their nets and brought them to Judea in the first place. Andrew and John even became the disciples of John the Baptizer, who prophesied in the wilderness and lived off the land—an existence far removed from the upper-middle-class life they once enjoyed. And when the men finally came face-to-face with the Christ, they thought they had found their calling. Indeed they had, but Jesus knew they didn't have eyes to see it. At least not yet.

The call to fulfill one's purpose doesn't come from within; existential-ists and self-help gurus are wrong about that. I learned years ago that fol-lowing a call—fulfilling one's purpose—isn't that complicated and it isn't as mysterious as it sounds. It begins with a realization that God has cre-ated each person with a unique design and a special purpose. The ancient Hebrew poet-king put it this way:

> For You formed my inward parts;
> You wove me in my mother's womb.
> I will give thanks to You, for I am fearfully and wonderfully made;
> Wonderful are Your works,
> And my soul knows it very well.
> My frame was not hidden from You,
> When I was made in secret,
> And skillfully wrought in the depths of the earth;
> Your eyes have seen my unformed substance;
> And in Your book were all written
> The days that were ordained for me,
> When as yet there was not one of them.
>
> Psalm 139:13–16

Unfortunately, sin and selfishness make fulfilling that purpose impossible. Sin creates a barrier between our divine design and our ordained path, creating a tension that can be excruciating. Life becomes meaningless; a drab, colorless, pointless existence in which even pleasure and success bring no satisfaction. But that gnawing hunger for meaning can also create the opportunity and means for God to heal our sin-sick souls and put us on the right path.

Os Guinness, in his fine book *The Call*, tells this moving story about Martin Luther:

> Painfully climbing up the steps of a medieval cathedral tower in the dark, he reached for the stair rope to steady himself and was amazed to hear a bell ring out above him—he had inadvertently pulled on the bell rope and woken up the whole countryside.

> Far from a man with a comprehensive vision of reform and a well-calculated plan for carrying it out, Luther struggled painfully for salvation before God and was surprised to set off the cataclysmic sixteenth-century movement that we now call simply the Reformation.[4]

Luther struggled for salvation because none of his piety, none of his good deeds, none of the penance he paid or the rituals he followed would satisfy his longing to be justified before God. That hunger led him to discover from his reading of Scripture that a right relationship with God cannot be earned or deserved because we can never work enough or become good enough to earn His favor. Only God, who gave us a design and a purpose, can ease the tension between them by removing the problem of sin.

As Peter, Andrew, and John labored all night in vain to fill their nets with fish, they came to realize that life apart from their calling would always come up empty. They had left on a journey to dig out their calling "from under the rubble of ignorance and confusion" and discovered they could never turn back. But neither could they ease the tension between design and purpose by merely switching careers or chasing religious knowledge or fighting for the right cause. There, on the shores of the Sea of Galilee, the men lived in a gray twilight of limbo.

Fortunately, Jesus didn't leave them—or any of us—without hope or direction. Where we fail, Jesus has succeeded. The only One who was able to recognize and follow His purpose from the beginning was Jesus. He alone was able to obey consistently and please God completely. And His divine mission was to make a way for each of us to do the same.

Jesus has prepared the way and has made following our destiny possible, whereas we are helpless by ourselves. We can find and fulfill our purpose by responding to the clear, simple call of Jesus Christ: "Follow Me." He is the doorway to fulfilling our destiny, where our divine design and God-ordained purpose live in perfect harmony.

The disciples' unprecedented haul of fish that day didn't prompt them to invite Jesus to become a senior partner in the business. They understood the principle Jesus was teaching: *with Me, you can do all things; without Me, everything you touch will come to nothing.* When they were ready to accept this truth, they had eyes to see and ears to hear the call of God to pursue their purpose. Peter, Andrew, John, and his brother James immediately dropped their nets, left everything behind, and responded to the call of Jesus.

Part Two

The Rabbi

Chapter Five

Life . . . as God Intended It

The story of Jesus and the kingdom He came to establish has deep roots in the soil of Israel's history. For centuries, the strip of land between the eastern side of the Mediterranean Sea and the western boundary of the Arabian Desert has been—and continues to be—ground zero for an ongoing conflict between good and evil. The conflict is—and will be—cosmic, not political. Therefore, it is no accident that Jesus was born there or that His destiny was so intricately intertwined with the future of Israel's throne.

When God originally brought the descendants of Abraham out of Egypt to settle them in the Promised Land, He established a covenant that read, in summary, *If you obey Me, you will enjoy abundance; if you disobey Me, you will suffer famine, pestilence, poverty, and foreign invasion.* It was His way of saying that material abundance must build upon a strong spiritual foundation—at least for God's people. And for a very brief time, they appeared to keep their end of the agreement. But a little compromise here and little tolerance there, and God's specially chosen nation soon looked like their idol-worshiping neighbors. The consequences of disobedience kept Israel in poverty and struggling to survive for centuries until God chose a young shepherd named David to lead them.

King David's devotion to God quite literally put Israel on the map. He quickly defeated all of Israel's enemies in the region, and by the end of his life forty years later, he had increased Israel's territory tenfold. As David systematically destroyed the handmade deities of Israel's neighbors and led his people in the exclusive worship of the one true God, Israel entered its golden age. Secure borders and wise diplomacy brought untold wealth from around the world. Fields produced bumper crops of wheat and vegetables; the hillsides teemed with livestock; orchards hung heavy with figs, dates, pomegranates, and olives; winepresses overflowed. And for a time, it seemed the Hebrew nation would finally claim all land the Lord had promised them and enjoy the abundance He longed for them to have.

God called David "a man after His own heart" (1 Samuel 13:14) because David understood the unique relationship the Lord had initiated with the descendants of Abraham and painstakingly led his people to be faithful in their calling. He composed hymns and used the power of the throne to call Israel to worship. Moreover, David empowered the priesthood to make the worship of God top priority. All the while, he dreamed of building the Lord a great temple in Jerusalem. And to that end, he collected the finest materials from around the world and located the most gifted artisans in Israel. David's devotion to God was second to none.

David's faithfulness did not go unnoticed. In keeping with His earlier covenant, the Lord caused the fledgling world power to flourish. Furthermore, He renewed His commitment to the descendants of Abraham by establishing a new covenant with the man He had chosen to shepherd them. Whereas His earlier covenant with the nation promised abundance in response to obedience, He made this new promise without conditions. The Lord promised David that the people of Israel would never vanish from the earth and that He would never remove the right of kingship from his lineage. Others may usurp the throne or occupy it illegitimately, but never with God's blessing or sanction . . . and never permanently.

To this very day, Jews call David their greatest king because of his faithfulness to God. David's immense power and extreme wealth didn't pollute his motives. His successes didn't erode his humility. His bravery never undermined his steady dependence upon God. But . . . (don't you hate that word?) mighty King David, for all his devotion and humility, could not completely escape the subtle, relentless pull of evil. The man who led his nation in the exclusive worship of God also collected wives like some people collect stamps. As women from all over the Eastern world took up residence in the royal palace, their gods found quarter in Israel. David's nonsensical compromise with temptation would have dire consequences for centuries to come.

Within a few generations, the spiritual foundation David had built was crumbling, and God's covenant with the shepherd-king appeared to be in jeopardy. The pride and hubris of David's grandson led to civil war, which divided the Hebrew people into two nations: the idolatrous rebel-kings of Israel in the north, and the seldom-faithful descendants of David, who ruled Judah in the south. By 722 BC, the Assyrian Empire had decimated Israel, leaving only a Hebrew remnant in Judah to bear God's covenants with Abraham and David. But, like the kings of Israel, the kings of Judah eventually led the people into rebellion against their God by worshiping images carved out of stone. And despite the weeping pleas of Jeremiah and the chilling warnings of Ezekiel, the people of Judah (who eventually came to be known as Jews) faced a long period of severe judgment.

Isaiah foresaw the desolation the Jews would face as a result of their unfaithful shepherds. But he also looked past their tribulation to describe a glorious future—a new kingdom under the leadership of a faithful descendant of David.

> Behold, a king will reign righteously
> And princes will rule justly.
> Each will be like a refuge from the wind
> And a shelter from the storm,
> Like streams of water in a dry country,
> Like the shade of a huge rock in a parched land.
> Then the eyes of those who see will not be blinded,
> And the ears of those who hear will listen.
> The mind of the hasty will discern the truth,
> And the tongue of the stammerers will hasten to speak clearly.

No longer will the fool be called noble,
Or the rogue be spoken of as generous.

Isaiah 32:1–5

Isaiah (and other prophets) predicted that this shepherd-king would lead God's people to a glorious future. His reign would launch an unprecedented period of agricultural and economic superabundance, he would free the nation from foreign tyranny, and he would expand his dominion to bring the entire world under his sovereign rule. Later generations would call this king the Messiah, the Christ, the Anointed One.

But hope is like a windowpane to the future. It's clear enough, but you can see only a reflection of what's behind you if your focus isn't right. The people of Judah made the mistake of thinking the Messiah would merely recapture the glory days of King David and merely turn the world into a Jewish empire. In other words, they hoped the Messiah would bring them the same power and prosperity they once enjoyed, only magnified and multiplied. Given their exclusive worship of God, that's not a bad wish, but compared to the reality that lay before them, it was a wispy, unsubstantial likeness of former glory. That was the old covenant; God had a new covenant in mind. The new would build upon the old in order to provide God's people much more than mere temporal power and material wealth. It would be a new kind of abundance.

THE MESSIAH'S RISE TO POWER

Before officially beginning His public ministry, Jesus would figuratively retrace the steps of the Hebrew people through the wilderness. There, in the rugged Judean hill country, He would also face the temptations that cause kings and their kingdoms to fail so miserably. After a brief time with some potential disciples, He departed for the desert for an extended period of solitude and fasting. Matthew states emphatically that Jesus went there specifically "to be tempted by the devil" (Matthew 4:1). The Greek verb rendered "tempt" means "to try to learn the nature or character of someone or something by submitting such to thorough and extensive testing."[1]

In other words, Jesus went into the desert to confront His enemy and throw down the gauntlet. He would prove Himself to be the legitimate shepherd of Israel by overcoming the temptations that had undone all of Israel's previous kings, including His mighty ancestor, King David.

After Jesus had spent forty days with only water to drink, Satan confronted Him with a proposition: "If You are the Son of God, tell this stone to become bread" (Luke 4:3). On the surface, it was a reasonable suggestion. The time had come for Jesus to break His fast, He was hungry, and the power of the Almighty was, after all, His to use. So why not use that power to meet a legitimate need? But Jesus came to earth to be the man all other men failed to be and to become the king Israel had always needed, a king who would depend upon God completely and serve Him consistently.

The crisis of physical hunger is essentially a crisis of faith. What or whom will you trust to meet your most basic needs? Will you trust the God who made human bodies, or will you seek your own way? The response of Jesus to this temptation recalls the words of Moses to the Israelites in the desert:

> You must keep carefully all these commandments I am giving you today so that you may live, increase in number, and go in and occupy the land that the LORD promised to your ancestors. Remember the whole way by which he has brought you these forty years through the desert so that he might, by humbling you, test you to see if you have it within you to keep his commandments or not. So he humbled you by making you hungry and then feeding you with unfamiliar manna. He did this to teach you that humankind cannot live by bread alone, but also by everything that comes from the LORD's mouth.
>
> Deuteronomy 8:1–3 NET

Where the Israelites failed, Jesus triumphed. And this bold declaration would become the first principle of the new kingdom: "Man does not live on bread alone, but on every word that comes from the mouth of God" (Matthew 4:4 NIV). Though His stomach growled after forty days of hunger, He enjoyed abundance. Jesus came to establish a new kingdom based upon complete trust and dependence upon God, not the kind of abundance that can be eaten for nourishment or traded for gain.

A prophecy in Malachi 3:1 stated the Messiah would "suddenly come to His temple." As Satan's attack on the integrity of the Messiah continued, he transported Jesus to the pinnacle of the Jewish temple in Jerusalem, either literally or in a vision, and challenged Him to leap to the crowded courtyard below. He cleverly twisted Psalm 91:11–12 to imply that that the Jews would immediately recognize the miracle and accept Him as the Messiah.

> For He will give His angels charge concerning you,
> To guard you in all your ways.
> They will bear you up in their hands,
> That you do not strike your foot against a stone.
>
> Psalm 91:11–12

Again Jesus responded with a quotation from the Old Testament Scriptures. He recalled the words of Moses to the Israelites, who refused to believe in God's protection without a miraculous sign: "You shall not put the Lord your God to the test" (Matthew 4:7). The Greek word for "test" in this verse is the same word rendered "tempt" earlier. To require God to prove that He is able and willing to fulfill His promises would be proof positive that one does not trust Him. The new kingdom will be one in which God's people trust Him completely and without reservation.

God's promise that this new kingdom would encompass the entire world became the focus of Satan's third and final attempt to corrupt Jesus during His time in the desert. Having shown Jesus the splendor of all the world's kingdoms, Satan said, "All these things I will give You, if You fall down and worship me" (Matthew 4:9). It was the same bargain he offered the corrupt kings of Israel—the unfaithful shepherds who sought material wealth at the expense of exclusive devotion to God and His people.

Jesus again responded with a quotation from the Old Testament. "Go, Satan! For it is written, 'You shall worship the Lord your God, and serve Him only'" (Matthew 4:10). In time, Jesus would indeed go to Jerusalem to present Himself in the temple as the Messiah, but not before proving Himself to be a king worthy of Israel's throne. As one commentator put it, "Before a king can rule others, he must prove that he can rule himself."[2]

NOT YOUR GRANDFATHER'S ABUNDANCE

Soon after His sojourn in the wilderness, Jesus began His itinerant ministry, traveling up and down the strip of land once ruled by David and Solomon. And as He addressed His Hebrew brothers and sisters in the synagogues, markets, hillsides, and byways, great multitudes began to dream of an abundant life under the leadership of a righteous king—perhaps *the* righteous King. Surely He would be the one to break the yoke of Rome and bring them more wealth, greater power, limitless freedom, and longer life. While Jesus was, indeed, the Messiah, His subjects failed to see the kind of abundance He came to bring. As they peered into the window to the future, they saw only what lay behind, not the superior kind of abundance Jesus wanted to bring them.

To describe His new kingdom, Jesus used a word picture that would have been very familiar to His audience. In wintertime, shepherds kept their sheep in a stone enclosure at night and led them to pasture the following morning.

> "I tell you the solemn truth, the one who does not enter the sheepfold by the door, but climbs in some other way, is a thief and a robber. The one who enters by the door is the shepherd of the sheep. The doorkeeper opens the door for him, and the sheep hear his voice. He calls his own sheep by name and leads them out. When he has brought all his own sheep out, he goes ahead of them, and the sheep follow him because they recognize his voice. They will never follow a stranger, but will run away from him, because they do not recognize the stranger's voice." Jesus told them this parable, but they did not understand what he was saying to them.
>
> So Jesus said to them again, "I tell you the solemn truth, I am the door for the sheep. All who came before me were thieves and robbers,

but the sheep did not listen to them. I am the door. If anyone enters through me, he will be saved, and will come in and go out, and find pasture. The thief comes only to steal and kill and destroy; I have come so that they may have life, and may have it abundantly."

John 10:1–10 NET

Great multitudes flocked to hear Jesus teach and have their ailments healed by Him. And from these multitudes of disciples, He chose twelve to form an inner circle of pupils, men He would prepare to become the first leaders of the new kingdom. When He called them to follow, they left everything behind. And while He promised abundance, I see no indication that He offered them anything by way of financial security or creature comforts. No retirement plan. No insurance coverage. Not even a guarantee of safety. In fact, He promised them quite the opposite. He said to His disciples,

"If anyone wishes to come after Me, he must deny himself, and take up his cross daily and follow Me. For whoever wishes to save his life will lose it, but whoever loses his life for My sake, he is the one who will save it. For what is a man profited if he gains the whole world, and loses or forfeits himself?"

Luke 9:23–25

Understand, Jesus was not preaching against wealth, per se. We must not forget that God's promise to Israel included material abundance. However, neither did Jesus preach a "plant-a-seed-of-faith-and-name-your-blessing" gospel of health and wealth. Christianity is not and never has been a greedy get-rich scheme.

A warning is in order. Reject any teaching that even suggests material wealth, physical health, or favorable circumstances have anything to do with the amount of faith you have or how pleased God happens to be with you. And beware those who teach that financial donations will unlock an endless abundance of God's blessings. They are false shepherds who will rob you of your money and destroy your relationship with God. The "faith" they proclaim is a toxic faith.

As far as Jesus was concerned, money and possessions are morally neutral and have no relation whatsoever to the new kingdom, except that they might distract us from what He considers important. He clarified the issue for His followers in a bold declaration followed by a searching parable.

> He said to them, "Beware, and be on your guard against every form of greed; for not even when one has an abundance does his life consist of his possessions." And He told them a parable, saying, "The land of a rich man was very productive. And he began reasoning to himself, saying, 'What shall I do, since I have no place to store my crops?' Then he said, 'This is what I will do: I will tear down my barns and build larger ones, and there I will store all my grain and my goods. And I will say to my soul, "Soul, you have many goods laid up for many years to come; take your ease, eat, drink and be merry."' But God said to him, 'You fool! This very night your soul is required of you; and now who will own what you have prepared?'"
>
> Luke 12:15–20

The prospect of death has a way of quickly putting things into perspective. When viewed through the lens of eternity, material wealth suddenly becomes infinitesimally small compared to the things that transcend death, things like relationships and the abundant life Jesus promised. The issue is not whether you have a lot of cash or material possessions, but do they have you? It's a matter of the heart. What role does the acquisition and preservation of "stuff" play in the major decisions of life? What priority do you give those pursuits compared to the important relationships in your life? To what or whom do you look to meet your needs? Do you live by physical sustenance alone or by the decrees and promises of God? Do you serve anything before Him?

God's great goal for His people is a holy life unencumbered by distractions.

ABUNDANCE FROM ABOVE

So if abundance is not cash, possessions, or comfort, what is it? Given that Jesus' inner circle of followers suffered persecution and died as martyrs, what kind of abundance did they receive? John, the disciple of Jesus, chose to open His narrative with this explanation:

> In the beginning was the Word, and the Word was with God, and the Word was God. He was in the beginning with God. All things came into being through Him, and apart from Him nothing came into being that has come into being. In Him was life, and the life was the Light of men. The light shines in the darkness, and the darkness did not comprehend it.
>
> John 1:1–5

Jesus is eternal and He is the Creator, so the kind of life He brings is not man-made, but God-made. It is a kind of life that didn't exist on earth before His coming. Moreover, the abundant life is so contrary to the thinking of this world that the world cannot comprehend it—not without help.

Nicodemus, one of Israel's great theological and philosophical minds, struggled to comprehend the kind of life Jesus offered. As a politician, Nicodemus cared about the crisis in Israel, for God's kingdom had become a province of Rome. As a teacher of Scripture, he cared about truth. As a religious man, he cared about morality and conduct that pleases God. As a man, he cared about himself, his future, and his standing before God. And he was probably sure of most of those things until Jesus spun Nicodemus on his heels with the words, "You must be born again" (John 3:7).

The expression "born again" has unfortunately become so overused that it has lost much of its meaning. It's even become something of a joke in our culture. But in the Greek language in which John wrote this story, the words are charged with multiple layers of meaning, all of which reveal a simple yet profound truth. It's an expression that invites us, as it did Nicodemus, to look deeper.

According to commentator Merrill Tenney, "Birth is our mode of entrance into the world and brings with it the potential equipment for adjustment to the world."[3] It is passing from one way of life and from one environment to another. Birth ushers one into a very different existence in an entirely new world. And in that new world, the person is almost entirely ill-equipped to survive. Yet he or she is filled with potential.

The Greek word *anōthen,* translated here as "again," can have several meanings. It's more commonly used as an adverb meaning "from above." Similarly, we might say of someone, "She received help from above," meaning that God helped her. This understanding is true of almost every other instance in which John uses the word. And as it is used here, the meaning works well to explain the truth that Jesus revealed to Nicodemus.

Tenney continues,

> To be born again, or "born from above," means a transformation of a person so that he is able to enter another world and adapt to its conditions. . . . To belong to the heavenly kingdom, one must be born into it.[4]

Birth is a work of God. Certainly the mother plays a necessary role and the doctor helps, but let's face facts: we call birth a miracle because God alone makes it happen. And what about the role of the baby? What does the baby contribute to his or her own birth? Nothing.

Birth from above, as with physical birth, is not something that can be earned, deserved, or worked for. You can't pray long and hard to receive it. You can't clean up your life enough to make it possible. And you don't join a church to be born from above. All of that is just as nonsensical as a baby saying that he decided to form himself within his mother's womb.

When Nicodemus heard Jesus use the odd phrase "must be born *anōthen,*" he deliberately focused on the "again" aspect of the word. Perhaps with tongue in cheek, he asked,

> "How can a man be born when he is old? He cannot enter a second time into his mother's womb and be born, can he?"
>
> John 3:4

71

At first glance, Nicodemus's challenge appears to be either completely obtuse or very sarcastic. But remember, this is no dullard sitting across from Jesus. This is a master teacher addressing someone he suspects to be an upstart. This was his way of suggesting, "What a ludicrous proposition!"

Teachers in that day—including Nicodemus—called Gentile converts to Judaism "newborn children." It was a lovely way of affirming that a person had begun life anew by establishing a relationship with the God of Abraham. This process involved circumcision for men and whole-body baptism in water for both women and men. So the old teacher thought Jesus was referring to Gentile converts. His second mistake was in thinking of the "kingdom" only as the earthly, physical kingdom of Israel under the future Jewish Messiah. In other words, Nicodemus interpreted Jesus to be saying, "Only Gentile converts can take part in the coming earthly kingdom under the Messiah."

Of course, that's not what Jesus was teaching. Though he was extremely intelligent, Nicodemus's thinking was two-dimensional. He could only think in the horizontal plane. Nicodemus, like many today, thought that the world can be discovered only by physical evidence combined with human reasoning—that which can be touched, perceived by the senses, tested in a lab, proven mathematically, or weighed and decided upon in court. So his natural response was, in effect, *Now I'm being told there's a kingdom that I'm not a part of, and to be a part of that kingdom, I have to somehow go back and be born a Gentile. And besides, this kingdom sounds very different from the kingdom I've been looking forward to. What kind of abundance is this?*

Nicodemus was looking intently, but he could not see. But rather than chide the old teacher, Jesus took him deeper. To our culture, His explanation appears more cryptic than before, but He deliberately chose terms and concepts that Nicodemus would understand.

Jesus answered, "Truly, truly, I say to you, unless one is born of water and the Spirit he cannot enter into the kingdom of God."

John 3:5

When Jesus referenced both water and Spirit, he acknowledged the water cleansing (baptism), which Jews associated with repentance, while highlighting the necessity of spiritual birth. By differentiating between these terms, Nicodemus would know that *anōthen* meant "from above" as spiritual rebirth while alluding to a favorite Old Testament, messianic promise:

> "I will take you from the nations and gather you from all the countries; then I will bring you to your land. I will sprinkle you with pure water and you will be clean from all your impurities. I will purify you from all your idols. I will give you a new heart, and I will put a new spirit within you. I will remove the heart of stone from your body and give you a heart of flesh. I will put my Spirit within you; I will take the initiative and you will obey my statutes and carefully observe my regulations. Then you will live in the land I gave to your fathers; you will be my people, and I will be your God."
>
> Ezekiel 36:24–28 NET

Nicodemus was looking for the Messiah to rescue Israel from Rome and bring them fabulous abundance . . . horizontal thinking. By saying that one must be born of water (repentance) and spirit ("from above"), Jesus tried to give Nicodemus's vision of the kingdom a more vertical dimension. "Spirit" is unseen, completely invisible. It's the inner cleansing and renewal of a person that the Spirit of God brings when that person is "born from above"—or "born again." This is the work of the Spirit of God within someone who, alone, cannot grasp spiritual truth. Jesus continued:

> "That which is born of the flesh is flesh, and that which is born of the Spirit is spirit."
>
> John 3:6

By now, Nicodemus's jaw must have been on his chest. Jesus continued:

> "Do not be amazed that I said to you, 'You must be born again.' The wind blows where it wishes and you hear the sound of it, but do not

know where it comes from and where it is going; so is everyone who
is born of the Spirit."

John 3:7–8

In other words, *Nicodemus, this is not something you can analyze or work
your way through. It involves the supernatural—the work of God inside a
person.* The work of the Spirit is like the wind. To outsiders, the Spirit is
invisible. He's silent. He's powerful. He moves wherever He wants. He can't
be controlled or contained by humans. Imagine trying to explain wind to
someone who has never experienced it. That's what it must have been like
for Jesus to explain the supernatural work of the Spirit to Nicodemus.
This brilliant religious scholar was clueless.

Finally, Nicodemus became vulnerable enough to admit his ignorance.
Perhaps with his hand to his head, leaning forward, searching Jesus' eyes
for an answer, he asked, "How can these things be?" (John 3:9). He was
the teacher in Israel and one of the most devout men serving in God's
temple, yet he had no awareness of this spiritual dimension of the kingdom and the kind of abundance its citizens would enjoy.

That should stand as a warning to anyone actively involved in church.
Someone may be the most faithful member in the building. He or she
may have the respect of the entire religious community, even be viewed
as an authority on divine truth. Yet neither theological intelligence nor
religious standing makes someone "born from above," "born again."

Jesus responded by going directly after the problem, and He did it with
three pointed statements:

You do not understand? (v. 10)

You do not accept. (v. 11)

How will you believe? (v. 12)

Jesus answered and said to him, "Are you the teacher of Israel and
do not understand these things? Truly, truly, I say to you, we speak
of what we know and testify of what we have seen, and you do not
accept our testimony. If I told you earthly things and you do not
believe, how will you believe if I tell you heavenly things? No one

has ascended into heaven, but He who descended from heaven: the
Son of Man."

John 3:10–13

Nicodemus's problem wasn't intellectual; it was volitional. He couldn't
see because he *wouldn't* see, a point Jesus chose to press: "you do not accept
our testimony" (v. 11).

As the conversation turned to focus on the work of the Holy Spirit,
their dialogue became very interesting. Because Nicodemus was a seasoned student of Moses, Jesus drew upon his knowledge of Hebrew history—specifically, an event recorded in Numbers 21:4–9.

As we reflect on Numbers 21, the Israelites had just experienced God's
miraculous deliverance from slavery in Egypt. They had witnessed the
ten plagues, experienced the parting of the Red Sea, and seen the pillar
of cloud and fire to lead them. Nevertheless they began to grumble and
complain. Ornery, disobedient, and unbelieving, they brought God to the
end of His tether. So He decided to discipline them. His discipline came
in the form of venomous snakes, from which a number of people died,
prompting Moses to intercede, saying, in effect, *If this keeps up, they're all
going to die.*

The Lord responded with a specific set of instructions: Fashion a
bronze snake and put it on a pole so that anyone who's bitten can look up
at it. Once a person sees the snake, the venom in his or her body will lose
its effectiveness (vv. 8–9). And just as the Lord promised, the plan worked.
Nicodemus was, of course, familiar with the story.

Therefore, Jesus used this episode in Israel's history as an analogy:

"As Moses lifted up the serpent in the wilderness, even so must the
Son of Man be lifted up."

John 3:14

To what was Jesus referring? The cross, of course! The cross, where He
paid the complete payment for all sin—sin past, sin present, sin future. All
sin. Yours, mine, all. When He was lifted up on that cross, He completely

satisfied the demands of a holy God, who said that sin must be punished. And in looking to Jesus, the venom of sin loses its effectiveness and we do not have to suffer eternal death. Whoever believes in Him will have His kind of life, participate in His kind of kingdom, and enjoy a new kind of abundance.

Verse 15 completes the thought of verse 14. Here is the complete statement. In light of all you know thus far, read it again slowly.

> "Just as Moses lifted up the serpent in the wilderness, so must the Son of Man be lifted up, so that everyone who believes in him may have eternal life." (NET)

Having stripped Nicodemus's mind of false notions, poor theology, and pride, and having given the old teacher a new dimension to his thinking, Jesus gave him a clear, direct statement of His divine mission:

> For this is the way God loved the world: He gave his one and only Son, so that everyone who believes in him will not perish but have eternal life.
>
> John 3:16 NET

The abundance Jesus offers is a spiritual abundance that transcends circumstances, like income, health, living conditions, and even death. The abundant life is eternal.

ABUNDANCE NOW

When Jesus spoke of abundance, He most likely spoke Aramaic. And when John told his story, he wrote in the common language of the Roman Empire, Koine Greek, using the word *perissos* to convey the idea of abundance. It means "to be present overabundantly or to excess."[5] Abundant life is not only eternal, but it is overwhelmingly, exceedingly ample life. And while abundant life has profound implications beyond the grave, Jesus gave every indication that it also has practical relevance here and now. As I reflect on the kind of life He offers, I find four tangible qualities.

Soaring. Life . . . as God intended it enables us to live above the drag of fear, superstition, shame, pessimism, guilt, anxiety, worry, and all the negativity that keeps people from seizing each day as a gift from Him. The abundant life allows a person to start the day by saying, "Lord, I'm Yours. Today is Yours. I give You all of my problems as I begin this new day. I know I'll struggle and grope, and I may even stumble, but I know You are with me and You will use every experience of my life to increase my ability to receive more and more strength from You."

Ignoring. Life . . . as God intended it causes us to refuse to take our cues from those who operate their lives from a purely human perspective. It's feeling secure in the truth while ignoring the majority opinion. It's daring to stand for what is right without fear of ridicule or persecution. Those who receive abundant life have no need to please people because they thrive in the pleasure of God.

Risking. Life . . . as God intended it dares us to attempt the impossible in the unwavering belief that all things are possible with Him. Because abundance is immaterial, not material, there's very little fear of loss. And we can live outside the trap of worrying about losing "stuff."

Releasing. Life . . . as God intended it loosens our grip on everything because security and contentment come from God. Money, possessions, status, and even relationships are but God's means of blessing us as we, in turn, bless others. Because He owns it all, we have no need to clutch and cling.

The abundant life has only one requirement: we must be willing to exchange our old life—our former way of living, choosing, thinking, and behaving—for a new life, a life crafted and directed by the Lord. The exchange begins with a decision, but runs its course over a lifetime. The abundant life is not something we claim; it's something we receive. And we begin to receive it as we become citizens of the Messiah's new kingdom.

And that starting point is when we are "born from above."

Do you understand?

Have you accepted?

Will you believe?

Chapter Six

Resting in Christ

Levi was a priestly name, not the name of someone you would expect to find behind a tax collector's table. But there sat Levi, using the power of the empire to extort money from his Jewish kinsmen, inflating their tax bill and lining his pockets with the excess. As far as his countrymen were concerned, this put him on the same level with harlots, who were equally guilty of selling themselves to foreigners.

No one can say for certain how Jesus came to know Levi. Perhaps like Nicodemus, Levi came to the rabbi under the cover of darkness for private instruction. Or maybe Jesus knew Levi's father, Alpheus. All anyone knows for sure is that one day, Jesus walked by Levi's booth and shocked everyone by calling him to be one of "the Twelve." The tax collector didn't seem surprised, though. He immediately shut down his enterprise, vowing never to open it again, and then hosted a giant party to celebrate his turning from sin.

> Then it happened that as Jesus was reclining at the table in the house, behold, many tax collectors and sinners came and were dining with Jesus and His disciples. When the Pharisees saw this,

they said to His disciples, "Why is your Teacher eating with the tax collectors and sinners?"

Matthew 9:10–11

Common sense would lead us to believe that the religious leaders in the community would have joined the celebration. After all, a former collaborator had seen the light and become a full-time follower of a prominent rabbi. But as tax collectors, harlots, and other sinners emerged from the social shadows to celebrate their friend's decision, a group of squint-eyed clerics stood across the courtyard talking in whispers.

THE POLITICS OF RELIGION

Religion has always been a favorite tool of kings and governments. All you need is a visible institution to embody the beliefs of the people you want to control and the credibility to determine who can be in and who should remain out. If someone believes you hold his or her eternal destiny in your hands, you can make him or her believe almost anything, want almost anything, do almost anything. Some of the world's greatest evils have been accomplished by people who believed that what they were doing—however horrific or inhuman—was good and right, based on their religion. A classic example is 9/11.

In first-century Israel, two primary groups vied for religious control over Israel, which kept them locked in a symbiotic, love-hate relationship with each other. The aristocratic Sadducees occupied the official positions of power, which included authority over Herod's magnificent temple, Israel's most visible institution. But their open collaboration with Rome made them very unpopular with the Jewish population, who wanted nothing less than a free nation. The nationalistic Pharisees maintained control over the Jewish masses by becoming conspicuously Jewish. And if obedience to the law of Moses made someone Jewish, they would remain kings of the moral hill at any cost.

While the Sadducees controlled the temple, they did so at the pleasure of Rome. They needed the religious clout of the Pharisees to control the Jewish people. While the Pharisees were extremely influential with the people, their pugnacious attitude toward Rome and lack of military might kept them from doing much more than chanting slogans. Rome needed the Sadducees to keep Roman interference to a minimum. Of the two things needed to manipulate people—a religious institution and religious authority—neither party had both. So they jealously guarded what they controlled.

LORDS OF THE SABBATH

To maintain moral superiority—or at least the impression of it—the Pharisees chose to emphasize the portion of God's law that suited their natural inclinations. For whatever reason, the fourth commandment became their favorite. According to the Law given to the Israelites through Moses,

> The seventh day is a sabbath of the LORD your God, in it you shall not do any work. . . . For in six days the LORD made the heavens and the earth, the sea and all that is in them, and rested on the seventh day; therefore the LORD blessed the sabbath day and made it holy.
> Exodus 20:10–11

Originally the seventh day was set aside to commemorate God's creation of the world and to celebrate His provision. In six days, He fashioned the earth and filled it with everything humankind would need. On the seventh, He stopped all activity. "Sabbath" is based on the Hebrew verb "to cease." God paused to declare His creation complete and good.

The Sabbath also commemorated the covenant He had established with the nation of Israel when He gave them the Promised Land. It was a day for feasting and singing, a time in which families delighted in their God and bonded with one another. Their respite from the grind of daily duties gave them the opportunity to celebrate God's provision and protection. But something curious happened when the armies of Babylon destroyed the temple in 586 BC and carried the Jews away from their land. Having been stripped of all that made them distinctly Hebrew, they looked to the law of Moses to restore their national identity and to bind them together as a people. Thus, the exile gave birth to Pharisaism, which made legalism the core value of Judaism and Jewish identity.

By the time of Jesus, the Pharisees had transformed the Sabbath into something very different from what God had ordained. To the simple command "rest," the Pharisees added a long list of specific prohibitions. And, just in case they overlooked something, they established thirty-nine categories of forbidden activity: carrying, burning, extinguishing, finishing, writing, erasing, cooking, washing, sewing, tearing, knotting, untying, shaping, plowing, planting, reaping, harvesting, threshing, winnowing, selecting, sifting, grinding, kneading, combing, spinning, dyeing, chainstitching, warping, weaving, unraveling, building, demolishing, trapping, shearing, slaughtering, skinning, tanning, smoothing, and marking.

How strange that resting should be so burdensome!

> The Pharisees, who carried religion like a shield of self-justification and a sword of judgment, installed the cold demands of rule-ridden perfectionism because that approach gave them status and control, while reassuring believers that they were marching in lock-step on the road to salvation. The Pharisees falsified the image of God into an eternal, small-minded bookkeeper whose favor could be won only by the scrupulous observance of laws and regulations. Religion became the tool to intimidate and enslave rather than liberate and empower. Jewish believers were instructed to focus their attention on the secondary aspect of the Sabbath—abstention from work.
>
> The joyous celebration of creation and covenant stressed by the prophets disappeared. The Sabbath became a day of legalism. The means had become the end. (Herein lies the genius of legalistic religion—making primary matters secondary and secondary matters primary.)[1]

No one dared to challenge the Pharisees' exclusive jurisdiction as police, judge, and jury over all matters related to the Sabbath. That is, until Jesus. One sunny afternoon, they observed Him and His disciples gleaning grain as Jewish Scripture allowed (Deuteronomy 23:24–25), but in violation of Pharisaic custom.

And it happened that He was passing through the grainfields on the Sabbath, and His disciples began to make their way along while picking the heads of grain. The Pharisees were saying to Him, "Look, why are they doing what is not lawful on the Sabbath?" And He said to them, "Have you never read what David did when he was in need and he and his companions became hungry; how he entered the house of God in the time of Abiathar the high priest, and ate the consecrated bread, which is not lawful for anyone to eat except the priests, and he also gave it to those who were with him?" Jesus said to them, "The Sabbath was made for man, and not man for the Sabbath. So the Son of Man is Lord even of the Sabbath."

Mark 2:23–28

In the mind of the Pharisee, the men were laboring on the Sabbath, for "plucking wheat from its stem is reaping, rubbing the wheat heads between one's palms is threshing, and blowing away the chaff is winnowing!"[2] Jesus rebuked the self-appointed guardians of morality with three important points.

First, *the Pharisees gave higher priority to the customs of men than the law of God.* In their effort to elevate themselves and dominate others, they overlooked the two most important commandments: "You shall love the Lord your God with all your heart, and with all your soul, and all your mind" and, "You shall love your neighbor as yourself" (Matthew 22:35–40).

Second, *God gave laws to His people to bless them, not to burden them.* Every rule either elevates the quality of human life or restores one's relationship with God after a breach. He makes no extraneous demands and He is never capricious.

Third, *because the Law came from God, it can never be greater than God.* "The LORD blessed the sabbath day and made it holy" (Exodus 20:11). Jesus' bold claim, "[I] the Son of Man am the Lord of the Sabbath" was intended to challenge the authority of the Pharisees, who had stolen it from God. In other words, *The Sabbath is not yours to control; it is Mine because I am God. Therefore, I am taking it back from you.*

A DIFFICULT REST AND AN EASY BURDEN

Jesus didn't come to earth to establish a new religion. He came to restore a broken relationship. He came to make the primary, primary again. The secondary activity of obedience to the law of God was always intended to serve the primary activity: to love God and enjoy Him forever. When that is primary, the secondary becomes a labor of love, a joyful, "easy" burden to bear. This is what Jesus meant when He said,

> "Come to Me, all who are weary and heavy-laden, and I will give you rest. Take My yoke upon you and learn from Me, for I am gentle and humble in heart, and you will find rest for your souls. For My yoke is easy and My burden is light."
>
> Matthew 11:28–30

Come to . . . what? Church? Temple? Ritual? Sacrifice? Poverty, penance, or pilgrimages? Good deeds? Spiritual enlightenment? Come to *religion*? No. Jesus beckoned, "Come to *Me*." Note that Jesus didn't say that the Sabbath was bad, nor did He discourage anyone from observing the Sabbath. There's nothing wrong with church, or church activities, or good deeds, or spiritual maturity—as long as they remain secondary to the invitation of God: "Come to *Me*."

In our culture, a written invitation has at least three pieces of information: From whom does the invitation come? To whom is it given? And what is being offered? Let's look at each of these as they relate to Jesus' invitation.

First, *from whom does the invitation come?* Just before Jesus issued this invitation, He declared, "All things have been handed over to Me by My Father; and no one knows the Son except the Father; nor does anyone know the Father except the Son, and anyone to whom the Son wills to reveal Him" (Matthew 11:27). We cannot find peace with God the Father except through Jesus Christ, His Son. Jesus would later declare, "I am the way, and the truth, and the life; no one comes to the Father but through Me" (John 14:6).

As bold as those claims appear, Jesus also described Himself as "gentle" and "humble of heart." Jesus spoke Aramaic, but Matthew recorded his story in Greek. In doing so, he chose two terms to convey Jesus' original thoughts.

The first is *praus*, which generally meant "mild," "friendly," or "pleasant," but readers of the Old Testament would know the verb as "to find oneself in a stunted, humble, lowly position."[3] It was a social and economic term for "'one who is in the position of a servant.' It describes the man who has no property and who has thus to earn his bread by serving others."[4] Old Testament prophets later picked up the term to describe those who were obedient to God and who bore their exile from the Promised Land with a quiet, hopeful trust in the Lord without a hint of anger. In other words, it describes a person who has absolutely no sense of entitlement.

Jesus said of the Pharisees, "They do all their deeds to be noticed by men; for they broaden their phylacteries and lengthen the tassels of their garments. They love the place of honor at banquets and the chief seats in the synagogues, and respectful greetings in the market places, and being called Rabbi by men" (Matthew 23:5–7).

The second, *tapeinos*, pictures someone bowing low and thus means "bowed down," "small," "insignificant in comparison to something else." In the Old Testament, it describes the posture of a righteous person before God. To illustrate His high opinion of this lowly term, Jesus told a story.

> "The Pharisee stood and was praying this to himself: 'God, I thank You that I am not like other people: swindlers, unjust, adulterers, or even like this tax collector. I fast twice a week; I pay tithes of all that I get.' But the tax collector, standing some distance away, was even unwilling to lift up his eyes to heaven, but was beating his breast, saying, 'God, be merciful to me, the sinner!' I tell you, this man went to his house justified rather than the other; for everyone who exalts himself will be humbled, but he who humbles himself will be exalted."
>
> Luke 18:11–14

Unlike the puffed-up, self-important Pharisees who had no genuine basis for pride and who deserved no exaltation for righteousness, Jesus deliberately identified Himself with the people He came to lift up. To help the lowly, He became low. He burdened Himself with the burdens of those He sought to set free.

Second, *to whom is Jesus' invitation given?* When Matthew recorded the invitation of Jesus to those who are "weary" and "heavy-laden," he used two very expressive Greek terms. The first, *kopos*, refers to "weariness as though one had been beaten . . . the proper word for physical tiredness induced by work, exertion or heat."[5] This term is usually used to describe the severe exhaustion of a soldier in battle or a messenger who had run several miles. Jesus also used the term to describe the affliction of worry (Matthew 6:28).

The second word, *phortizō*, is a shipping term meaning "to load." It pictures a ship or an animal heavily burdened by a great weight. A frugal merchant could maximize his profit by using a limited number of pack animals so that each was laden with as much cargo as it could bear. Jesus used this image to describe hypocritical religious leaders who "tie up heavy burdens and lay them on men's shoulders, but they themselves are unwilling to move them with so much as a finger" (Matthew 23:4). The first verb is active, the second, passive, picturing the "active and passive sides of human misery."[6]

The venerated commentator William Barclay observed,

> To the Jews, religion was a thing of endless rules. People lived their lives in an endless forest of regulations which dictated every action. They must listen forever to a voice which said, "You shall not."
>
> Even the Rabbis saw this. There is a kind of rueful parable put into the mouth of Korah, which shows just how binding and constricting and burdensome the demands of the Law could be. "There was a poor widow in my neighborhood who had two daughters and a field. When she began to plow, Moses [i.e. the law of Moses] said: 'You must not plough with an ox and an ass together.' When she began to sow, he said: 'You must not sow your field with mingled seed.' When she began to reap and make stacks of corn, he said: 'When you're reaping or harvesting in your field, and have forgotten a sheaf in the field, you shall not go back and get it' [Deuteronomy 24:19],

and 'you shall not reap your field to its very border' [Leviticus 19:9]. She began to thresh, and he said, 'Give me the heave-offering, and the first and second tithe.' She accepted the ordinance and gave them all to him. What did the poor woman then do? She sold her field, and bought two sheep, to clothe herself from their fleece and to have profit from their young. When they bore their young, Aaron [i.e. the demands of the priesthood] came and said: 'Give me the first-born.' So she accepted the decision, and gave them to him. When the shearing time came, and she sheared them, Aaron came and said: 'Give me the first of the fleece of the sheep' [Deuteronomy 18:4]. Then she thought: 'I cannot stand up against this man. I will slaughter the sheep and eat them.' Then Aaron came and said: 'Give me the shoulder and the two cheeks and the stomach' [Deuteronomy 18:3]. Then she said: 'Even when I have killed them I am not safe from you. Behold they shall be *devoted.*' Then Aaron said: 'In that case they belong entirely to me' [Numbers 18:14]. He took them and went away and left her weeping with her two daughters."[7]

The Jews of first-century Israel labored under a man-made burden of religiosity, an endless list of rules that governed virtually every aspect of life—all of them based on laws handed down by God, but twisted and inflated to serve the desire of one group of people to dominate another. Earnest Jews were spiritually demoralized and incapable of meeting further demands. They needed to find relief. In a word, they needed *rest.*

Finally, *what is being offered in Jesus' invitation?* The word translated "rest" comes from a Greek verb meaning "to cause to stop" or "to put an end to something." It is closely akin to the Hebrew verb *shabat,* from which derives the word "Sabbath." Every Friday evening at sundown, faithful Jews put an end to work until sunset the following day. What religiosity had perverted, Jesus promised to restore. Religion says, *Work more. Try harder. Do this. Don't do that. Give until you have no more. God isn't yet pleased with you. Push, push, harder, longer!* Jesus looked into the hearts of exhausted, overburdened, anxious, stressed-out people and offered a better way.

Jesus' metaphor "Take My yoke upon you and learn from Me" has an obvious connotation to servitude that He clearly intended, but it also involves much more. A yoke is a carved, wooden beam that rests across the shoulders of a pair of beasts (usually oxen or mules), allowing them to pull a plow or other machinery in tandem. In the Old Testament, a yoke was a symbol of burden or servitude (Genesis 27:40; Deuteronomy 28:48; 1 Kings 12:4–14; Isaiah 9:4; 10:27; Jeremiah 27:8–12; 28:2–4; Lamentations 1:14; Ezekiel 34:27). In other areas of Scripture, a yoke may symbolize close alliance or union (Numbers 25:3–5; 2 Corinthians 6:14). And in later Jewish literature, a yoke represented the totality of moral obligations that every good Jew was to take upon his shoulders ("yoke of the Torah," "yoke of the commandments," and so on).

Jesus clearly intended to invoke this imagery in an ironic twist. Indeed, *slavery* to Christ is the greatest *freedom* a person can experience. However, the phrase "and learn from Me" suggests He intended more. In the first century, Jewish rabbis used the phrase "take the yoke of" to mean "become the pupil of" a particular teacher. Unfortunately, the rabbis had become notoriously harsh and hypocritical.

> Because of their misinterpretation, alteration, and augmentation of God's holy law, the yoke which Israel's teachers placed upon the shoulders of the people was that of a totally unwarranted legalism. It was the system of *teaching* that stressed salvation by means of strict obedience to a host of rules and regulations. Now here in [Matthew] 11:29 Jesus places his own teaching over against that to which the people had become accustomed.[8]

Jesus said, in today's terms, "Are you tired? Worn out? Burned out on religion? Come to me. Get away with me and you'll recover your life. I'll show you how to take a real rest. Walk with me and work with me—watch how I do it. Learn the unforced rhythms of grace" (Matthew 11:28–29 MSG).

Jesus described His yoke as *chrestos,* which means "excellent," "serviceable," "useful," "adapted to its purpose," "good."[9] Frequently, a carpenter was commissioned to custom-carve a yoke to perfectly fit a particular animal. With a *chrestos* yoke, an ox or donkey could pull a plow for many hours without chafing or blistering. Furthermore, Jesus promised that His "burden" (based on the same term as "heavy-laden" in verse 28), would be light, or easy to bear.

Jesus' "yoke" illustration conveys an invitation with three parts:

- He invites us to exchange the tiresome burden of legalism ("strict obedience to a host of rules and regulations") for a lifelong Sabbath of the soul.
- He invites us to accept Him as our teacher so that we might learn how He coped, how He managed stress, how He faced the pressures of the world with tact and grace, how He forgave, how He ministered to others, and how He remained connected to the Father.
- He invites us to reject slavery to religiosity, wealth, status, relationships, or anything else that burdens us so that we might become a slave to Him.

The best word to describe servitude to Jesus Christ is *refreshment.*

THE GIFT OF HUMILITY

Of the four Gospel writers, Matthew seemed to understand this paradox better than anyone. In fact, he was the only one to have recorded this particular invitation of Jesus. I suspect it's because he remembered the yoke of sin, especially the heavier-than-average burden borne by harlots and tax collectors, strippers and drug dealers, runaways, addicts, and other objects of public distain. In addition to the weight of private shame carried by all people, they bear the yoke of public disgrace.

I suspect Matthew also understood what it felt like to don the leathery emotional hide worn by the desperately down-and-out who need no reminder that good people consider them undesirable. They hide their shame behind a steely, hollow gaze and dare the world to judge their only trustworthy companion: sin. They would seek help among the righteous, but nicely dressed church people appear sanctimoniously superior and profess a religion that merely promises to exchange one burden for another.

Almost nothing can penetrate the emotional armor worn by those who have been beaten down by the morality of the righteous. Almost nothing. Jesus, the only thoroughly righteous man, knew the secret. He knew the only way to penetrate the sheath of calloused emotions was to extend grace.

Grace has to be the loveliest word in the English language. It embodies almost every attractive quality we hope to find in others. Grace is a gift of the humble to the humiliated. Grace acknowledges the ugliness of sin by choosing to see beyond it. Grace accepts a person as someone worthy of kindness despite whatever grime or hard-shell casing keeps him or her separated from the rest of the world. Grace is a gift of tender mercy when it makes the least sense.

The Old Testament Hebrews knew grace as *chesed*, which described God's unrelenting, overabundant love for people, despite their unfaithfulness. The ancient Greeks understood grace, or *charis*, as "that which brings delight, joy, happiness, or good fortune."[10] Grace begets grace, and Jesus radiated this quality. His invitation, "Come to Me, all who are weary and heavy-laden," attracted the very worst elements of society while repelling the most self-righteous. And it won the shunned rabbi a following of fiercely loyal disciples, whom He shamelessly defended.

As the city's moral down-and-outers celebrated with Levi and his new Master, the Pharisees voiced their reproach. "Why do you eat and drink with the tax collectors and sinners?" (Luke 5:30). The relationship between God and His creatures was the least of their concerns. The Pharisees had a moral caste system to maintain and political territory to defend. It never occurred to them that God might not be pleased with them.

As Brennan Manning noted, "Paradoxically, what intrudes between God and human beings is our fastidious morality and pseudo-piety. It is not the prostitutes and tax collectors who find it most difficult to repent: it is the devout who feel they have no need to repent."[11] That's why Jesus sent word to the Pharisees outside the house, "It is not those who are well who need a physician, but those who are sick. I have not come to call the righteous but sinners to repentance" (Luke 5:31–32).

Levi was just the kind of sinner Jesus wanted in a disciple. One honest enough to admit he was deathly ill with the disease of sin and wanted to be healed of it. After Jesus restored Levi's moral health, He invited him to become one of the Twelve and gave him a new name. From then on, the former Roman collaborator would be known as Matthew, "gift of God."

Chapter Seven

It Is Best to Rest

The life of a "striver" is typically characterized by dogged, relentless struggle and fueled by a volatile mixture of pride, perfectionism, and self-sufficiency. We have lots of names for the striver: the self-made man, the driven woman, firebrand, visionary, revolutionary, high-roller, type-A, mover and shaker. We also know strivers as those who are angry, depressed, frustrated, unsatisfied, greedy, power hungry, turbulent, or quite often overanxious. Some strivers we celebrate; some we shun. And what keeps the striver in a state of perpetual motion—much of it purposeful and even productive—is something author Robert Wise calls the "churning place."

> You discover it in the early years of your life. It seems to be located either near the pit of your stomach or at the base of your neck, where every muscle tightens. When it begins to turn and pump like an old washing machine, you find that every other area of your life marches to its lumbering, dull, paralyzing beat. . . .
>
> In adulthood our needs only become more sophisticated. The problems loom larger and the consequences appear more final. Yet we

have the same churning place we discovered at age four. Now, however, the ghosts are real people who are quite willing to betray our confidences and manipulate our decisions. All the insecurities of love and money seem to give an endless prospect to the churning. . . .

Nothing exempts us from the relentless process created by haunting memories and bankrupt expectancies. As universal as the human heart and head, the existence of the churning place cannot be denied.

And it is not a constructive place. Positive thoughts lead to action and results, but the churning place is a tank that fills with anxieties that just settle into a stagnant infection.[1]

Eventually strivers discover that no amount of expended energy—even in the pursuit of noble ends—will ever drain the tank. Near the end of his days, wise, old Solomon called his pursuits "a striving after wind" (Ecclesiastes 1:14).

This is not the abundant life that God intends for His people. This is the *opposite*. God never asked us to meet life's pressures and demands on our own terms or by relying upon our own strength. Nor did He demand that we win His favor by assembling an impressive portfolio of good deeds. Instead, He invites us to enter His rest.

Because the Sabbath rest is so quintessentially Jewish, we will never comprehend Jesus—a thoroughly Jewish man—without an appreciation for this divine institution. But more significantly, Jesus presented Himself as the personification of the Sabbath. To understand God's invitation to us to "enter the Sabbath rest" is to understand the ministry and mission of His Son.

AN AGES-OLD INVITATION

The concept of the Sabbath is as old as creation. In six days, God created the world, gave it order and purpose, and then imbued it with life and everything needed for it to flourish. Then, on the seventh day, He ceased all activity to survey His handiwork and declare it "good." It was complete. Nothing remained undone. Humankind needed nothing more than to tend the abundance God had created, which included the opportunity to enjoy an intimate relationship with Him.

The concept of "rest" involves much more than a day away from the job. It transcends the calendar. The Sabbath rest embodies everything the Creator intended for humankind to enjoy from the very beginning of time. And despite how often we complicate something so good, simple, and pure, He relentlessly adapts His creation and invites us, *Come to Me, and I will give you rest.*

When God heard the cries of His covenant people languishing in servitude to godless masters, and when the time was right, He sent a prince-turned-shepherd named Moses to lead them out of Egypt into the land He had promised their ancestor, Abraham. Throughout their journey, God referred to the Promised Land as "the resting place" and their "rest,"[2] a place in which they could live in security and enjoy God's abundance without toil, "a good and spacious land . . . a land flowing with milk and honey" (Exodus 3:8). But when they approached the border of the Promised Land, they recoiled. Enormous and intimidating people lived there in fortified cities. Nevertheless, two of the contingent of Hebrew reconnaissance scouts boldly declared, "We should by all means go up and take possession of it, for we will surely overcome it" (Numbers 13:30). But the majority of ten complained,

> "We are not able to go up against the people, for they are too strong for us. . . . The land through which we have gone, in spying it out, is a land that devours its inhabitants; and all the people whom we saw in it are men of great size. There also we saw the Nephilim (the sons of Anak are part of the Nephilim); and we became like grasshoppers in our own sight, and so we were in their sight."
>
> Numbers 13:31–33

In response, the minority pleaded, "The LORD is with us; do not fear them" (Numbers 14:9); but their cowardly, faithless kinsmen failed to believe God. Therefore, the Lord declared the nation would not enter their rest but wander the desert as nomads for forty years. During that time, the faithless lived out the balance of their lives, traveling with no destination, subsisting on God's daily provision of manna and quail, and living like grasshoppers while giants consumed the abundance God set aside for His people.

Centuries later, a Hebrew poet memorialized the event.

> Come! Let's bow down and worship!
> Let's kneel before the LORD, our creator!
> For he is our God;
> we are the people of his pasture,
> the sheep he owns.
> Today, if only you would obey him!
> He says, "Do not be stubborn like they were at Meribah
> ["place of proving"],
> like they were that day at Massah ["contention"] in the wilderness,
> where your ancestors challenged my authority,
> and tried my patience, even though they had seen my work.
> For forty years I was continually disgusted with that generation,
> and I said, 'These people desire to go astray;
> they do not obey my commands.'
> So I made a vow in my anger,
> 'They will never enter into the resting place I had set aside for them.'"
>
> Psalm 95:6–11 NET

After the unbelievers among the older generation had passed away, Israel again stood on the border of the Promised Land and received a sober warning.

> "Then it shall come about when the LORD your God brings you into the land which He swore to your fathers, Abraham, Isaac and Jacob, to give you, great and splendid cities which you did not build, and houses full of all good things which you did not fill, and hewn cisterns which you did not dig, vineyards and olive trees which you did

not plant, and you eat and are satisfied, then watch yourself, that you
do not forget the LORD who brought you from the land of Egypt, out
of the house of slavery."

Deuteronomy 6:10–12

But the Israelites did forget their God. They conquered, and settled,
and grew complacent. In time, they failed to trust Him; they failed to worship Him exclusively; they failed to obey Him. Consequently, they inhab-
ited the Promised Land but never quite entered their rest. God pleaded
and wooed and warned, but to no avail. After centuries of wind chasing,
the prophet Jeremiah lamented the stubbornness of his people.

Thus says the LORD,
"Stand by the ways and see and ask for the ancient paths,
Where the good way is, and walk in it;
And you will find rest for your souls.
But they said, 'We will not walk in it.'"

Jeremiah 6:16

The history of the Sabbath rest reminds me of the old cowboy prov-
erb, "You can lead a horse to water, but you can't make him drink." The
Promised Land was a tangible representation of God's ultimate desire for
His people, but they failed to comprehend His gift for at least three reasons: It was unconditionally promised, it was outrageously generous, and
it was absolutely free. None of those make sense in the world as we know
it . . . a world overrun with "strivers."

AN AGES-OLD WARNING

Of all the people who should understand the Sabbath rest, you would
think it would be Hebrew followers of Jesus Christ. But they struggled
the same as anyone else, which only proves that rich heritage and biblical
knowledge can lead someone to the border, but . . .

Knowledge doesn't necessarily lead to action. The first generation of

Christ's followers hadn't passed from the scene before one of the apostles penned a stern letter chiding them for repeating the sins of their fathers.

> Therefore we must be wary that, while the promise of entering his rest remains open, none of you may seem to have come short of it. For we had good news proclaimed to us just as [the Israelites] did. But the message they heard did them no good, since they did not join in with those who heard it in faith. For we who have believed enter that rest, as he has said, "As I swore in my anger, 'They will never enter my rest!'" And yet God's works were accomplished from the foundation of the world. For he has spoken somewhere about the seventh day in this way: "And God rested on the seventh day from all his works," but to repeat the text cited earlier: "They will never enter my rest!" Therefore it remains for some to enter it, yet those to whom it was previously proclaimed did not enter because of disobedience. So God again ordains a certain day, "Today," speaking through David after so long a time, as in the words quoted before, "O, that today you would listen as he speaks! Do not harden your hearts." For if Joshua had given them rest, God would not have spoken afterward about another day. Consequently a Sabbath rest remains for the people of God. For the one who enters God's rest has also rested from his works, just as God did from his own works. Thus we must make every effort to enter that rest, so that no one may fall by following the same pattern of disobedience.
>
> Hebrews 4:1–11 NET

The author of Hebrews used the Greek term *sabbatismos*, "Sabbath rest," in three distinct yet interrelated ways. He wrote of the historic sabbath rest as it related to the Promised Land. He wrote of the theological Sabbath, which God ordained upon the creation of the world and then required of His covenant people. And he wrote of a personal Sabbath into which the people of God are invited to enter.

Admittedly, God's invitation uses an odd pairing of words. "Enter" is not the verb we expect to be paired with "rest." We typically think in terms of enjoying rest, having rest, giving rest, or even pursuing rest, but *entering* rest? God's rest is available, but entering will not come naturally or occur automatically. Perhaps because we don't know how.

The word *enter* usually applies to a space, such as a building, a house, or a car. And it's different inside the space than it is outside. When we enter a building, we leave the weather, the noise, and the traffic outside. And usually the space we enter has a certain character or ambiance that's unlike any other space. We might even think of that interior space as a shelter from all that is outside. God presents the Sabbath rest as a shelter we can enter.

The author of Hebrews expressed his fear that those who had heard the "good news" would end up like the faithless Israelites, wandering around somewhere outside the threshold of rest but never crossing it. This implies a close connection between hearing the good news and entering rest.

The Greek term translated "good news" is a form of the noun *euangelion*, from which we derive the English word *evangelism*. It's the same root word used by the angel in Luke 2:10, when he announced the arrival of Jesus to the shepherds: "I bring you good news of great joy which will be for all the people." The *euangelion* is essentially the story of Jesus and His mission on earth.

The word "rest" in the last part of the invitation comes from the Greek word *katapausis*. The prefix, *kata*, means "down" and the noun, *pausis*, means "a ceasing." Think of *katapausis* as what life is like after "quitting down." We might call it "down time." Greek has another word for rest, but the emphasis of *katapausis* "is more upon the cessation of activity resulting in rest rather than upon the mere restorative character of rest."[3]

So then, believing the good news allows us to find shelter in the process of ceasing. The question is, ceasing what?

The warning in Hebrews 4:2–8 points to *unbelief* as the primary reason the Israelites recoiled at the border of the Promised Land, and that unbelief threatens to keep us from entering our Sabbath rest as well. As the nation of Abraham's descendants faced the challenge of giants occupying their land, the believing and unbelieving factions perceived the situation very differently. Whereas the believers said, "The LORD is with us; do not fear them"

(Numbers 14:9), the pathetic whine of the unbelievers explains why they failed to claim their inheritance. "All the people whom we saw in it are men of great size. . . . And we became like grasshoppers *in our own sight*, and so we were in their sight" (Numbers 13:31–33; emphasis added).

At least one indication of unbelief is the tendency to measure life's challenges against our own adequacy instead of God's promises. To enter our Sabbath rest, we must put an end to self-reliance—trusting in our own abilities to overcome difficulties, rise above challenges, escape tragedies, or achieve personal greatness. We must cease striving and trust God to provide what He thinks is best and in whatever time He chooses to make it available. But this kind of trusting doesn't come naturally. It's a spiritual crisis of the will in which we must choose to exercise faith.

THE FORMULA OF RESTING

Some have attempted to define faith as belief without the support of evidence. Or, as the Mark Twain character Pudd'nhead Wilson put it, "Faith is believing what you know ain't so."[4] Many in the scientific community see faith as holding a belief that either contradicts or ignores reason. But that's not what I call faith. That's stupidity!

Faith does not run contrary to evidence; faith goes beyond evidence. Faith doesn't ignore reason, but faith doesn't wait upon it either. Faith is merely a choice to trust, something we do every day. Go to the airport and at any given moment you'll see a group of people board an aircraft—eighty tons of metal and wire assembled by the lowest bidder, maintained by people they've never seen, and flown by people they don't know. Yet they buckle up and settle in by the thousands each and every day. They trust the reservation system, they trust the ground crew and pilots, they trust the aircraft, and they trust the laws of aerodynamics. They are literally flying by faith.

However, suppose a man noticed a crack forming between the engine and the wing. If he boards the aircraft with a shrug, then the object of his faith may fall out of the sky. Faith doesn't change reality, and it will not keep the man in the air. Only a trustworthy airplane will do that. Faith itself cannot accomplish anything, yet without faith, no one can fly.

The same is true of entering the Sabbath rest. According to the author of Hebrews 4:1–11, one must hear the story of Jesus Christ and His mission, and then believe it. In other words, resting has a formula.

HEARING + BELIEVING = RESTING

Belief in God—that is, the exercise of faith in Him—involves two essential elements: the correct knowledge and a right attitude.

Correct knowledge. Someone can believe in the wrong thing with the sincerest conviction and end up no better off than he or she began. Suppose a woman wanted to fly to Chicago. She receives the flight information from her assistant and on the appointed day, drives to the airport. Once she arrives, she must go to the correct gate by a certain time. The sincerity of her belief won't change the fact that if she stands at the wrong gate, she will either be turned away or will board the wrong plane.

It's not enough merely to believe there is a God. You must believe in the God who is there.

Furthermore, you must know what He has said. What would you think of the woman flying to Chicago if she drove to the airport without knowing which airline, which flight, and the scheduled time of departure? She has a reserved seat waiting for her, but without the right knowledge, what good is her belief that her seat exists?

Proverbs 14:12 says, "There is a way which seems right to a man, but its end is the way of death."

Right attitude. Someone can believe in the right thing with the sincerest conviction, and still end up no better off than he or she began. Correct knowledge must be coupled with the right attitude. According to Hebrews 4:6–11, the Sabbath rest remains available, but only those who submit to this truth and respond in obedience will enter. Belief cannot be genuine without action, and, in this case, the action to which we are called is ceasing.

Therein lies the paradox. Our churning place would propel us forward, ever faster, in an attempt to accomplish for ourselves what God has already provided. To enter our Sabbath rest, we must come to God in humble submission to His truth and in complete dependence upon Him.

In order to cease our striving, we must transfer our trust away from our own abilities, our own accomplishments, our own strength, and place it on His provision.

In six days, God created the world, gave it order and purpose, and then imbued it with life and everything needed for it to flourish. Then, on the seventh day, He ceased all activity to survey His handiwork and declare it "good." It was complete. Nothing remained undone. Humankind needed nothing more than to tend the abundance God had created, which included the opportunity to enjoy fellowship with Him. Entering this Sabbath rest has both temporal and eternal significance. Transferring trust away from our own capacity to earn a place in heaven and placing it upon God's provision is the essence of salvation.

Entering our Sabbath rest also has temporal significance. It takes faith in our sovereign Creator to respond with hope to a disturbing report from the doctor. It takes faith in God's provision to avoid stress over a tight deadline or a challenging sales quota. It takes faith to find personal significance in your relationship with God rather than how much money you earn, how beautiful you look, how many toys you own, how many trophies you collect, or how much territory you conquer and control.

REST FOR TODAY

God's invitation to enter the Sabbath rest didn't end with creation, nor was it intended for Israel alone. As Moses described the beginning of everything, he punctuated his account with a repeated phrase.

> God created light and divided it into night and day.
> "And there was evening and there was morning, one day."
>
> Genesis 1:5

> God created the earth's atmosphere and divided it into layers.
> "And there was evening and there was morning, a second day."
>
> Genesis 1:8

God separated the seas from the dry land and populated the land with
vegetation.

"There was evening and there was morning, a third day."

Genesis 1:13

God created the heavenly bodies and set them in regular motion.

"There was evening and there was morning, a fourth day."

Genesis 1:19

God created the sea life and birds.

"There was evening and there was morning, a fifth day."

Genesis 1:23

God created the land animals and, lastly, man and woman in His own
image.

"And there was evening and there was morning, the sixth day."

Genesis 1:31

Then Moses declared,

Thus the heavens and the earth were completed, and all their hosts.
By the seventh day God completed His work which He had done,
and He rested on the seventh day from all His work which He had
done. Then God blessed the seventh day and sanctified it.

Genesis 2:1–3

Notice that nothing marks the conclusion of the seventh day. The
Sabbath has never ended. Disobedient people have denigrated the Sabbath,
self-reliant people have ignored the Sabbath, and self-righteous people
have twisted the Sabbath into something burdensome; nevertheless, God
has kept it open.

> So there remains a Sabbath rest for the people of God. For the one
> who has entered His rest has himself also rested from his works, as
> God did from His.
>
> Hebrews 4:9–10

God has reserved each one of us a seat in His banquet room, where
He wants to fill our deepest longings and supply our every need. This
invitation forms the basis of God's command to His covenant people, the
Israelites.

> Remember the sabbath day, to keep it holy. Six days you shall labor
> and do all your work, but the seventh day is a sabbath of the LORD
> your God; in it you shall not do any work, you or your son or your
> daughter, your male or your female servant or your cattle or your
> sojourner who stays with you.
>
> Exodus 20:8–10

And it is this invitation He extends to us. "Let us be diligent to enter
that rest, so that no one will fall, through following the [Israelites'] example
of disobedience" (Hebrews 4:11).

ENEMIES OF THE SABBATH REST

Lurking within each of us are at least three attitudes that feed the churning
place and threaten to keep us perpetually wandering and striving instead
of contentedly resting. These enemies of the Sabbath rest are presumption, panic, and pride.

Presumption. Presumption is the notion that we understand exactly
what we need and how to get it or the precise nature of our problem and
how to solve it. In fact, we typically know far less than we think we do.
We don't even know ourselves very well, which is why we do nonsensical
things like turn to work, food, alcohol, sex, or worse to ease emotional
pain. We feed our hunger for significance by chasing relationships, pursuing positions of power or fame, or exhausting all our resources in support

of some noble cause. We create and nurture the illusion of security by filling the bank account, fretting over every new medical report, manipulating our relationships, or avoiding them altogether.

How much energy do we expend trying to meet our own needs for significance and security only to find none of our own provision satisfying?

Panic. Panic is the tendency to react to needs or difficulties impulsively. Very often we leap into action and apply a familiar fix without considering unseen issues or lasting consequences.

The next time a financial emergency pops up and you're short on cash, think about this tendency before you reach for the credit card or ask for a loan. Could it be that you're denying God the opportunity to provide for you in His way and at a time He deems appropriate? What if you were to pray and present your need to Him in humble submission . . . and then *wait?*

Pride. Pride is the feeling of self-sufficiency or adequacy to fulfill one's own need or to solve one's own problem without God's assistance. We feel the least need for God when we have full bank accounts, perfect health, strong relationships, impressive abilities, and a bright future. But should any one of those suffer, we're quick to drop to our knees and ask for help. As we enter the Sabbath rest, we acknowledge that all good things come from God and we are powerless to face the difficulties of life without Him.

These three enemies of God's rest share a common cause: *unbelief.* When we presume to know the right course of action, we believe we are as smart or as able as God. When we panic, we instinctively turn to our own internal resources because we doubt Him. And when we feel adequate for a task, our belief in self has diminished our view of the Almighty.

On the other hand, if we see God as He is—omnipotent, unfailingly good, and interested in us—we will not hesitate to take every matter to Him, no matter how trifling. And the degree to which we have entered God's rest can be measured by the shrinking size of the issues we release into His capable hands.

Strivers have a very small god. Does this describe you? If so, he lives in the pit of your stomach or at the base of your neck—in the churning place. You look to this god to have your longings satisfied, your problems solved, your insecurities soothed, and your worth affirmed. With such pitiful resources, it's no wonder you strive so hard.

There is a better way. Remember? The entrance to it remains open. And the invitation is still yours to accept. "There remains a Sabbath rest" for you to enjoy.

Because it is best to rest in Jesus Christ, why strive?

Chapter Eight

The Astonishing Power of Jesus

S tories of miraculous events drew visitors from every part of the Roman Empire to Sais, Egypt, to see the magnificent temple dedicated to Minerva, the Roman goddess of crafts, poetry, and wisdom. Having paid their oaths, wealthy pilgrims gathered around the centerpiece of worship, an enormous gilded altar, around which a bronze snake wound its body in order to look down upon the surface. On one side stood Bacchus, god of the vine; on the other, Diana, the mother goddess. Each dutifully held a pitcher over the altar, patiently waiting their cue to offer libations of wine and milk to Minerva.

At the appointed time, Minerva's priests entered the sanctuary, prepared a second altar, and set it ablaze. As fire consumed the wood, the smell of incense permeated the room and then wafted slowly up through the open roof, presumably into the nostrils of the goddess. Then, as if eager to join the ceremony, Bacchus and Diana spontaneously poured out their drink offerings. As wine and milk flowed from their pitchers and mingled on the gilded altar, the bronze serpent hissed in loud approval. It was the miracle the worshipers had traveled so far and paid so dearly to experience.

Religion was big business in the Roman world. A temple could put a city on the map if the miracles were impressive enough or the supernatural displays sufficiently believable. And people craved an encounter with the supernatural so much that city leaders sent delegates to the library of Alexandria to solicit the services of miracle workers. We would call them architects and engineers, but men like Philon, Ctesibius, and Heron could make temples do the impossible. Fluid mechanics dispensed holy water, opened doors, and caused engraved figurines to dance and spin. Cleverly designed pitchers with hidden chambers and tubes created the illusion of turning water into wine. Steam caused snakes to hiss and great organs to moan like a satisfied god. Thanks to a clever blend of ancient technologies, worshipers heard rain, wind, and rolling thunder accompanied by flashes of lightning. Temple magicians even astonished the worshipers of Serapis by causing an iron chariot to rise and float, perhaps by means of a giant lodestone mounted in the temple ceiling.

Naturally, the excitement and wonder experienced in pagan temples became a source of tension for first-century, monotheistic Hebrews. In terms of architecture and sheer size, Herod's temple complex was the envy of the ancient world, but the Jews worshiped a silent, invisible God, who declined to amuse visitors. Even His name was too holy to pronounce. Nevertheless, the prospect of experiencing the supernatural proved irresistible. False prophets commonly won a hearing outside the temple through sleight-of-hand tricks and carefully crafted illusions. In fact, so common was the use of magic that audiences came to expect a show. No sooner would an orator begin teaching than someone would ask, "What sign do you give?" after which the would-be prophet had to impress his hearers with something astonishing or lose them.

Fewer people would be fooled today. The modern mind has been conditioned to presume a perfectly valid, scientific explanation behind every mystery. However, we cannot afford to become guilty of what historians call "temporal arrogance." This is the notion that ancient people were habitually superstitious and automatically looked for a supernatural explanation for anything that baffled them. They viewed the world differently, but they were neither stupid nor easily deceived.

Today, reasonable people exist in an uncomfortable tension between the dogma of science, which denies the existence of the supernatural, and the fanaticism of some television evangelists who peddle it for donations. And for those unwilling to suspend belief, the supernatural exhibitions of faith healers aren't very convincing. They perform their illusions in very controlled environments, and the "healings" are either limited to mild improvements or they claim results that are difficult to verify.

Faith healers and skeptics notwithstanding, another realm transcends what we can experience with our senses and, on rare occasions, God allows us to see and touch. However, miracles don't happen every day. "If they did," a colleague of mine once noted, "we'd call them 'regulars.'" While they appear common in the Bible, miracles are in fact extremely rare in history. God reserves them for brief, remarkable periods of time just prior to His making a major change in how He interacts with His creation. For example, after four hundred years of silence, God astonished the Egyptians and the Hebrews with a series of miraculous events as He prepared His covenant people for the Promised Land.

To avoid any confusion, let me first define what I mean by the term *miracle.* When God created all things out of nothing, He also devised laws of nature, such as gravity and thermodynamics, to give order and purpose to everything in the universe. However, this is not to suggest He is a watchmaker God who assembled the cosmos, wound it up, and is allowing it to wind down with no further involvement from Him. While God, for the most part, allows this cosmos to work according to the laws of nature, there is never a time when He is not directly and personally involved in every detail of life. Nevertheless, His interaction with creation rarely involves a miracle.

Sometimes, however, God dramatically defies the laws of nature in order to validate an event as divinely ordered. He parts the waters of a sea to make a dry path from one side to the other (Exodus 14:22). He causes a donkey to speak like a human (Numbers 22:28). He causes an axe head to float (2 Kings 6:6). He allows three young men to enter a blazing fire and emerge without singeing a hair (Daniel 3:23–27). And, as we read earlier, He allows a virgin to conceive a child without a human father. *These* are authentic miracles—dramatic, undeniable acts of God in which

He demonstrates indisputable authority over the universe He created and continues to rule. And they usually remedy problems that are "impossible" within the normal framework of life. Miracles remind us—as the angel reminded Mary—"Nothing will be impossible with God" (Luke 1:37).

CONFRONTING THE IMPOSSIBLE

After Adam and Eve chose to disobey God in the Garden of Eden, the world changed. As if to mimic the rebellion of the first couple, creation chose to go its own way. The world God created to be our perfect home now afflicts us with misfortune, disappointment, hunger, chaos, disease, and the ultimate affront to God's creation, death. Because people have chosen to sin—and continue to choose it—we frequently face humanly impossible situations. But Jesus came to earth so that sin will not have the last word in the cosmic conflict between good and evil. God became one of us, and now we have an advocate. We now have hope to carry us through and beyond our afflictions. That hope can transform our mindset. *Because of Jesus, we can view life as a series of great opportunities brilliantly disguised as impossible situations.*

Power over the trivial. Soon after beginning His public ministry, Jesus attended a wedding celebration—a lavish, weeklong feast hosted by the groom's parents and attended by dozens of family and friends. As any event planner can testify, no wedding is exempt from Murphy's Law. Groomsmen faint. Bridesmaids trip. Ring bearers pick their noses. Cakes fall. And, in the case of this family in Cana of Galilee, someone failed to order enough wine—a humiliating faux pas in that day and culture. When Jesus' mother discovered the problem, she alerted her son without hesitation. And after a brief exchange, she left the impossible situation in His care. She instructed the servants, "Whatever He says to you, do it," and then returned to the party.

> Jesus told the servants, "Fill the water jars with water." So they filled them up to the very top. Then he told them, "Now draw some out and take it to the head steward," and they did. When the head steward tasted the water that had been turned to wine, not knowing where it

came from (though the servants who had drawn the water knew), he called the bridegroom and said to him, "Everyone serves the good wine first, and then the cheaper wine when the guests are drunk. You have kept the good wine until now!" Jesus did this as the first of his miraculous signs, in Cana of Galilee. In this way he revealed his glory, and his disciples believed in him.

John 2:7–11 NET

Turning water into wine was, by the time of Jesus, a hackneyed temple illusion that would have caused any Jew to roll his eyes, not unlike pulling a rabbit out of a top hat today. Like the familiar children's illusion, the trick required a special apparatus prepared ahead of time and demanded a great willingness to suspend belief.

Jesus could have remedied the shortage of wine by any number of means, but, perhaps with a wink and a smile, He chose to do in reality what pagan conjurors in heathen temples could only simulate. And no one could dispute the miracle. While Jesus stood back, the servants chose the vessels and filled them with water to the very top. Then, somewhere between the stone jar and the wine steward, the miraculous transformation took place. No dramatic announcement, no "voilà," no tricks, no applause. Jesus simply and quietly exercised His divine prerogative and transformed an embarrassing situation into a social triumph for the groom's family. No one would have suffered greatly if He had not acted; the issue at stake was not of monumental importance—some might have even called it trivial. Nevertheless, the impossible predicament of His friends was important to Him.

Interestingly, John chose to call the event a "sign." Upon seeing Jesus use His power to accomplish a simple act of kindness, His disciples' faith grew deeper.

Power over distance. Sometime later, Jesus and His disciples were again in Cana. The city of Capernaum, where Peter, Andrew, James, and John once operated their fishing enterprise, lay on the north shore of the Sea of Galilee about twenty miles away—no less than an eight-hour journey on foot. Jesus had become very well known by this time, so word of His return spread quickly. When a wealthy aristocrat—a Sadducee, no doubt—heard the news, he traveled from his home in Capernaum on an urgent matter. His son lay dying.

The Sadducees were a peculiar breed of Jew. Conservative by Jewish standards—some would say conveniently so—they accepted no teaching or tradition beyond what could be found in the Pentateuch, the first five books of the Old Testament and the only Scripture to have come from the hand of Moses. They did not believe in life after death or resurrection or angels or spirits. They believed God to be ineffably remote, leaving each person free to craft his or her own fate with no prospect of eternal reward or punishment. Therefore, the Sadducees believed punishment for sin to be the duty of men and that it should be both merciless and severe.[1] The Jewish historian Josephus described them as contentious with everyone, including their own, and even "think it an instance of virtue to dispute with those teachers of philosophy whom they frequent."[2]

Sadducees were the deists of their day—vehemently skeptical of anything supernatural and fatalistic to the core. They believed each person creates his own fate; therefore, he deserves whatever fate he receives, including sickness, poverty, misfortune, and even his manner of death. So to have a Sadducee standing before Jesus, pleading for a miraculous divine intervention, was a poignant stroke of irony.

> So Jesus said to him, "Unless you people see signs and wonders, you simply will not believe." The royal official said to Him, "Sir, come down before my child dies." Jesus said to him, "Go; your son lives."
>
> John 4:48–50

Note the aristocrat's singular concern. Perhaps on another day, he would have disputed Jesus or made sport of His lecture by demanding a magic show. On other occasions, Sadducees delighted in word games and crafted ludicrous scenarios to demonstrate the absurdity of any teaching that transcended experience in the here and now. *Faith* was not in the Sadducees' vocabulary. But the man standing before Jesus was no longer a Sadducee or a wealthy aristocrat or a powerful official in the royal court. He was the anxious father of a dying son. And his vulnerability gave Jesus a unique opportunity to brush aside the man's superficial skepticism and teach him gently about mercy and faith.

Note also Jesus' response. How much more reassuring it would have been for the father if He had stood to face Capernaum and shouted, "Be healed!" Even better if He had extended His arms as if to thrust His healing power over the great distance. Instead, He quietly stated, in effect, "Go home; he'll be fine."

> The man believed the word that Jesus spoke to him and started off. As he was now going down, his slaves met him, saying that his son was living. So he inquired of them the hour when he began to get better. Then they said to him, "Yesterday at the seventh hour the fever left him." So the father knew that it was at that hour in which Jesus said to him, "Your son lives"; and he himself believed and his whole household.
>
> John 4:50–53

Jesus kept it simple. The lesson wasn't complicated. *I speak; you believe My word; your son will be fine.* We complicate what God has made simple by seeing the world through human eyes. We want to see in order to believe and presume that our limitations are His. John also called this event a "sign." The aristocrat and his household discovered that omnipotence and omnipresence are not limited by trifling things like distance—twenty miles or twenty thousand, it's all the same.

Power over time. We also tend to think that the longer something is true, the more difficult it is to change—perhaps because time has a way of cementing reality in our minds and forming an impenetrable barrier against hope. Traditions and superstitions become cemented over several generations and can have the same mind-numbing effect.

> Now there is in Jerusalem by the Sheep Gate a pool called Bethzatha in Aramaic, which has five covered walkways. A great number of sick, blind, lame, and paralyzed people were lying in these walkways.
>
> John 5:2–3 NET

This complex of two pools surrounded by five colonnades lay just below the northeast corner of Herod's temple and appears to have been a religious sanitarium, called an *asclepieion*. The Greeks believed Asclepius, the god of medicine and healing, to be a kind, gentle savior to the infirm.

> In the temple dedicated to [Asclepius's] service there were spacious halls in which the sick lay to rest and received healing as they slept. This sleep in the temple was known as the *incubatio*. As they slept, the sick people would dream that they were being healed by the intervention of Asclepius, so that the following morning they would wake in good health. The lame could walk again, the dumb speak, the blind see. Many people experienced miraculous healing and in gratitude donated gold or silver images of the limbs which had been healed or brought offerings to the temple. Asclepius was lauded as the god of healing and as a saviour who came to the aid of human beings and cared for them.[3]

When Jesus arrived in Jerusalem to celebrate one of the Jewish feasts, He visited the local sanitarium. John didn't explain why, but we can guess. Jesus frequently went places that made the religious leaders feel uncomfortable. During His visit, Jesus came upon a man who had been debilitated by disease for nearly four decades—a lifetime in those days.

> When Jesus saw him lying there and when he realized that the man had been disabled a long time already, he said to him, "Do you want to become well?" The sick man answered him, "Sir, I have no one to put me into the pool when the water is stirred up. While I am trying to get into the water, someone else goes down there before me."
>
> John 5:6–7

Apparently, superstition promised that the stirring of the waters brought special healing to those who could make their way in. But the man was alone, and in a cruel twist of irony, the race for a spot in the pool went to the able-bodied first. Of all the hopeless cases in the sanitarium, none rivaled his. How many nights did the man plead for a visit from Asclepius in his dreams? How many days did he lay there in the shadow of the temple, helplessly watching for the stirring of superstitious waters?

Again, without fanfare, without crowd-pleasing predictions, Jesus simply instructed the man, "Stand up! Pick up your mat and walk." Immediately, atrophied bones and muscles grew strong and lifted the man to his feet for the first time in decades. Time may have cemented his fate in the mind of the community and they certainly had relegated him to the sanitarium, so his striding into the temple later that day must have come as a shock to everyone.

By this time, the temple leaders were beginning to take notice. This was no mere upstart rabbi from the backwaters of Galilee.

Power over insufficiency. As Jesus continued His ministry of healing and teaching, the miracles increased in size and complexity as if to reveal His power by degrees. Some months later, Jesus had been teaching throughout the region of Galilee when He decided to take His disciples away from the crowds to enjoy the solitude of the hill country northeast of the Sea of Galilee.

But His fame had grown far and fast. As He taught His inner circle of pupils, a multitude began to gather on the hillside. People—thousands of them—followed their Messiah into the wilderness and had given no thought to provision. They quite possibly expected that He would provide for them. After all, they remembered what He had taught them in a sermon on another hillside:

> "I tell you, do not worry about your life, what you will eat or drink, or about your body, what you will wear. Isn't there more to life than food and more to the body than clothing? Look at the birds in the sky: They do not sow, or reap, or gather into barns, yet your heavenly Father feeds them. Aren't you more valuable than they are? And which of you by worrying can add even one hour to his life? Why do you worry about clothing? Think about how the flowers of the field grow; they do not work or spin. Yet I tell you that not even Solomon in all his glory was clothed like one of these! And if this is how God clothes the wild grass, which is here today and tomorrow is tossed

into the fire to heat the oven, won't he clothe you even more, you
people of little faith? So then, don't worry saying, 'What will we eat?'
or 'What will we drink?' or 'What will we wear?' For the unconverted
pursue these things, and your heavenly Father knows that you need
them. But above all pursue his kingdom and righteousness, and all
these things will be given to you as well. So then, do not worry about
tomorrow, for tomorrow will worry about itself. Today has enough
trouble of its own."

Matthew 6:25–34 NET

Eventually five thousand men and their families had gathered on the
hillside. Jesus tugged on Philip's sleeve and asked, "Where can we buy
bread so that these people may eat?" (John 6:5 NET). The question, of
course, was the beginning of a lesson. Jesus had chosen the Twelve and
had been training them to assume leadership in the new kingdom. Like a
true mentor, He was gently pushing His men to the forefront and allowing them to meet the challenges of ministry. Unfortunately, learning often
comes on the heels of failure.

Now Jesus said this to test him, for he knew what he was going to do.
Philip replied, "Two hundred silver coins worth of bread would not
be enough for them, for each one to get a little."

John 6:6–7 NET

Every group of leaders has a statistical pessimist, the one who approaches
each challenge with a detailed accounting of what he lacks instead of what
God promises to provide. Philip should have known by this time that
God never calls His people to accomplish anything without promising to
supply their every need. A correct response to Jesus' question would have
been, "I don't know yet, Lord, but I know You'll think of something!"

Jesus patiently waited as Philip tallied the people and estimated the
cost of bread. His mental calculator kicked in. *Let's see . . . five thousand
men and some of them have their families, we'll call it eight thousand for the
sake of argument. One loaf of bread per person should run about . . . carry the*

two, and . . . Wow! The way I figure it, Lord, if we had the equivalent of eight months' wages, we'd barely have enough to give each person a snack!

Meanwhile, Andrew had been looking around to see what food might be on hand when a young boy offered his sack lunch. The disciple probably felt foolish even mentioning it, but, ever the cautious optimist, he said, "Here is a boy who has five barley loaves and two fish, but what good are these for so many people?" (John 6:9 NET).

Perhaps with a twinkle in His eye and a reassuring nod, Jesus said, "Have the people sit down" (John 6:10 NET). The disciples divided the multitude into groups and arranged an efficient distribution plan as Jesus gave thanks for the provision and began breaking the bread and pulling off pieces of fish . . . again and again and yet again. For hours, He multiplied the humble offering of the little boy and passed the abundance to a brigade of disciples.

As the requests for food dwindled to nothing, Jesus gave His students another task. "Gather up the broken pieces that are left over, so that nothing is wasted" (John 6:12 NET). Each of the disciples took a wicker basket called a *kophinos*—typically used to carry one person's provision of food on a journey—and collected enough uneaten scraps to fill the stomachs of each of the twelve.

At the end of the day, the lesson should have been clear. The size of a challenge should never be measured in terms of what we have to offer. It will never be enough. Furthermore, provision is God's responsibility, not ours. We are merely called to commit what we have—even if it's no more than a sack lunch. As we consider the staggering need of the world, God's invitation is simple: *You take care of the addition; I'll be in charge of the multiplication. The mission I've called you to fulfill will be abundantly accomplished.*

At the end of the day, each disciple held in his hands enough surplus food for a journey.

Power over nature. After this "sign," the multitude rose up and began discussing how they could remove the present government and make Jesus their king. Because Jesus disapproved of their plan and rejected their motives, He commanded the crowd to disperse. He quickly withdrew further into the hill country. Meanwhile, His disciples prepared the boat as He had commanded and set sail for Capernaum.

As Jesus enjoyed a few hours of solitude, the frenzy of the crowd died down, which allowed Him time to relax and reflect. But by that time, a fierce squall had descended on the sea. One commentator described the scene: "The Sea of Tiberias or Galilee is a deep gouge in the Jordan rift surrounded by hills so that winds frequently sweep down and stir the waters into a frenzy. Even today the situation is similar. Power boats periodically are warned to remain docked as the winds whip the water into foamy white caps."[4]

The men had been rowing against the wind and straining at the oars for more than three miles when Jesus decided to rescue them. He walked down the mountain to the shore and straight across the top of the water. As He approached the ship, the men quite naturally didn't know what to make of the figure coming toward them.

> When they saw him walking on the water they thought he was a ghost. They cried out, for they all saw him and were terrified. But immediately he spoke to them: "Have courage! It is I. Do not be afraid." Then he went up with them into the boat, and the wind ceased. They were completely astonished, because they did not understand about the loaves, but their hearts were hardened.
>
> Mark 6:49–52 NET

A person with a "hard heart" in the disciples' day and culture didn't mean he was unkind or cruel, but that his reasoning and emotions had become resistant to development. We might say, "They were hard-headed." Even after witnessing Jesus perform the astonishing miracle on the hillside earlier that day, the disciples failed to put all the clues together.

Jesus walked on the very sea that threatened to pull the disciples under. He commanded the wind that tossed their boat around like a toy. He spoke a word and the storm instantly ceased its fury. Who but God can control the weather?

Power over tragedy. The Pharisees and Sadducees regarded any misfortune to be the direct result of someone's sin, even when a child came into the world with a debilitating disease or birth defect or developmental disability. As Jesus left the temple in Jerusalem, He came upon a man who had been blind from birth. This man could feel the warmth of the sun but had never seen a sunrise. He had heard the pounding of waves, but had never seen the foamy turbulence of the seashore.

Upon seeing the blind man, a disciple asked Jesus, "Rabbi, who committed the sin that caused him to be born blind, this man or his parents?"

> Jesus answered, "Neither this man nor his parents sinned, but he was born blind so that the acts of God may be revealed through what happens to him. We must perform the deeds of the one who sent me as long as it is daytime. Night is coming when no one can work. As long as I am in the world, I am the light of the world." Having said this, he spat on the ground and made some mud with the saliva. He smeared the mud on the blind man's eyes and said to him, "Go wash in the pool of Siloam" (which is translated "sent"). So the blind man went away and washed, and came back seeing.
>
> John 9:3–7 NET

Imagine the scene. The man was well known in his community because of his blindness. His begging for alms had made him a notable figure around the temple for years, perhaps decades. Pharisees judged him, Sadducees ignored him, some worshipers showed compassion, while others clutched their purses and tiptoed by. Then, one day, this man strode into the temple without his stick and beggar's basket, his eyes feasting on the splendor of God's house and savoring every detail. Worshipers in the temple courtyard noticed the familiar face but struggled to make sense of what they saw. "Is this not the man who used to sit and beg?" "This is the man!" "No, but he looks like him." All the while he kept insisting, "I am the one!"

> So they asked him, "How then were you made to see?" He replied, "The man called Jesus made mud, smeared it on my eyes and told me, 'Go to Siloam and wash.' So I went and washed, and was able to see." They said to him, "Where is that man?" He replied, "I don't know."
>
> John 9:10–12 NET

At this point in the story, I would expect someone to make plans for a huge celebration. But the Pharisees, upon discovering the man had been healed on the Sabbath, nitpicked, grumbled, and debated. "'This man [Jesus] is not from God, because he does not observe the Sabbath.' But others said, 'How can a man who is a sinner perform such miraculous signs?'" (John 9:16 NET).

The Pharisees had, as usual, failed to see the big picture. Their blindness would be comical were it not so tragic and their example so influential. On another occasion, Jesus warned His followers, "Leave them! They are blind guides. If someone who is blind leads another who is blind, both will fall into a pit" (Matthew 15:14 NET).

As soon as Jesus finished correcting the theology of His disciples, He declared, "I am the light of the world," and then He gave the man sight. In this one act, Jesus exercised power over disabilities, sin, bad theology, the temple, the Sabbath, and the skeptics—especially the self-absorbed Pharisees who opposed Him. He had this opportunity because a baby came into the world without the ability to see. The man was not blind because he or his parents sinned. He was blind because he was born into a world that has been twisted by sin. And all of us suffer the affliction of evil in varying degrees because of it. Furthermore, God gave the baby's congenital disability a divine purpose before the world ever began.

Power over death. The greatest enemy of life is also the greatest affront to God's creative act. He did not fashion our bodies for death, nor did He intend them to rot in a grave. But as the apostle Paul wrote, "Sin entered the world through one man [Adam] and death through sin, and so death spread to all people because all sinned" (Romans 5:12 NET). Collectively, humankind inherited the penalty of Adam's rebellion, which is death. Individually, we deserve death because each of us has ratified Adam's decision by adding our own sin to his. Nevertheless, God has promised something wonderful. And Jesus would take the most impossible situation of all as an opportunity to reveal it.

As Jesus ministered in Galilee, a very close friend named Lazarus contracted a fatal illness and lay dying in his home at Bethany, a town near Jerusalem in Judea. The man's sisters, Martha and Mary, sent a messenger to Jesus to let Him know that His friend was very sick, but He waited for days before starting out. By the time He reached Bethany, Lazarus had been in the grave four days. Martha bitterly complained, "Lord, if you had been here, my brother would not have died. But even now I know that whatever you ask from God, God will grant you" (John 11:21–22 NET). Jesus then responded with a bold reassurance. "I am the resurrection and the life. The one who believes in me will live even if he dies, and the one who lives and believes in me will never die" (John 11:25–26 NET).

Shortly thereafter, He stood before the burial cave that held the body of His friend. Without hesitation, He commanded, "Take away the stone."

> Martha, the sister of the deceased, replied, "Lord, by this time the body will have a bad smell, because he has been buried four days." Jesus responded, "Didn't I tell you that if you believe, you would see the glory of God?" So they took away the stone. Jesus looked upward and said, "Father, I thank you that you have listened to me. I knew that you always listen to me, but I said this for the sake of the crowd standing around here, that they may believe that you sent me." When he had said this, he shouted in a loud voice, "Lazarus, come out!" The one who had died came out, his feet and hands tied up with strips of cloth, and a cloth wrapped around his face. Jesus said to them, "Unwrap him and let him go."
>
> John 11:39–44 NET

What a remarkable reunion that must have been! As Jesus stood back and watched the family embracing, weeping with joy, surely He smiled. His silence is eloquent. In the words of an old gospel song, it was "a foretaste of glory divine."

As Lazarus's family and friends celebrated his return from the dead, they enjoyed a brief taste of a future feast Jesus promised to bring the world. Sin may have the power to kill and destroy, but God is the creator of life. He can create it from nothing, and He can restore it from death. The reassurance Jesus gave Martha is the same promise He extends to the world: "I am the resurrection and the life. The one who believes in me will live even if he dies, and the one who lives and believes in me will never die" (John 11:25–26 NET).

WHY JESUS DID MIRACLES

Ancient conjurors created the illusion of miracles to keep their followers coming to them with money. They mimicked the supernatural to position themselves in the minds of others as those with special access to a realm that exercised dominion over the world and determined the fate of those who hope to pass from here to there. They trafficked in the fear of the unknown.

Jesus performed miraculous signs for a very different purpose. His miracles provided relief from pain and fear, and taught of a God who cares deeply about the suffering of people and who heals for free. Jesus performed many more miracles than are described in the Gospels (John 20:30), and His motivation for them was nothing more than compassion.

Viewing His miracles as a whole, the astonishing power of Jesus should be a source of comfort. The matters we or the world might consider trivial, He cares about and wants to remedy. He longs to relieve our worries and has promised to supply our most fundamental needs. He has taken dominion over illness, tragedy, chaos, and death. And His power is not limited by time, distance, superstition, prejudice, or even the forces of evil. He taught by way of His miracles of resurrection that evil may win a few skirmishes on earth, but only He wields everlasting power. The fleeting seventy to eighty years in these bodies of disease and eventual death are but a twinkling compared to the magnificent and endless delights He has promised those who believe.

Jesus' closest friend on earth, the disciple John, wrote near the conclusion of his Gospel,

> Many other signs Jesus also performed in the presence of the disciples, which are not written in this book; but these have been written so that you may believe that Jesus is the Christ, the Son of God; and that believing you may have life in His name.
>
> John 20:30–31

Having read of these authentic miracles Jesus performed, you are left with an opportunity to respond to the one who performed them. His miracles have been recorded "so that you may believe" that He is, in fact, the Son of God.

Have you? Will you? Do you?

Chapter Nine

The Ultimate Healer

Jesus, the healer, had come to town. As a throng of people pressed and pushed and elbowed and jostled, the din of voices calling His name deafened the disciples. They locked arms and formed a circle around their Master and vainly pushed against a crush of diseased and disabled people who were hoping for just a few seconds of His attention. By this time in Jesus' ministry, everyone knew that one touch could change everything. Hundreds, perhaps thousands had experienced the surge of healing power coursing through their bodies, causing maladies of every conceivable kind to vanish with sudden finality.

As the disciples pushed the swell of people backward and Jesus inched His way toward the town, a familiar, authoritative voice shouted something from the direction of the synagogue and distracted the mob for an instant—but only for an instant. The frenzy swelled again with renewed urgency. Then, another shout from up the road caused the crowd to part as if a giant, invisible wedge had forced a clear pathway to Jesus. Such was the respect for the ruling elder of the synagogue.

The mob fell silent as the elder submissively sank to his knees and dropped his face to the ground. "Please, Lord, my daughter lies dying of . . . something, we don't know. Her hold on life grows weaker by the minute, and it will slip from her fingers any moment. In fact, she might be dead even as I speak. Please, please come. If You touch her, she will recover completely."

Jesus reached down, lifted the man to his feet, and after reassuring him, motioned His disciples to fall in behind the elder and follow him.

During this brief exchange, a woman on the fringes of the crowd decided to seize her only opportunity. Weak from the loss of blood—a perpetual flow from her womb that left her little strength to spare—and habitually pushed to the periphery of society, she had little chance ever to reach Jesus again. With everyone's attention focused on the wailing leader, she crouched low and crawled between the bodies to steal a touch.

As she stretched out her hand, Jesus moved and the crush closed around Him again, but a last, desperate lunge allowed her fingers to graze the hem of His robe. And that's when she felt it. A tingling rush of vitality. A warm glow from the center of her body that radiated to each limb and caused her face to glow. And most important of all, no more blood seeping from her body. Healed at last. A dozen years of chronic anemia and baffled doctors and disapproving neighbors . . . ended!

Jesus felt the surge of healing power too. He whirled around with startling speed and asked, "Who touched My garments?" His disciples looked at one another and then their master. "Lord, You must be joking! With all of these people pushing and grabbing, who *hasn't* touched You?"

Jesus remained stone-still, peering through the cluster of legs at a trembling figure lying on the ground. One by one, each person moved out of His line of sight and followed His gaze until no one stood between them. With her face to the ground, the woman explained everything. How she had suffered for so long, how she tried in vain to reach Him through the crowd, how she knew beyond any doubt that one touch from Him would make her whole.

"Daughter, take courage."

She raised her head to meet His eyes and found His expression filled with gentleness.

"Your faith has made you well."

After her encounter with the healing power of Jesus, the woman's disease never returned.

The walk into the city did not go quickly, but eventually Jesus and His entourage approached the home of Jairus, the leader of the synagogue. The walls of the house reverberated with the anguished cries of mourners, who lined the great room and spilled out the front entrance into the courtyard. Some threw their arms around Jairus, who struggled to retain his composure.

As Jesus made His way through the gathering funeral party, He reassured them, "Why make a commotion and weep? The child has not died, but is asleep."

Some laughed through their tears. Others who didn't know the girl very well chided the rabbi. For people in those days, death was as common as birth. They knew a dead body when they saw one. The girl had been weak with fever. She did indeed fall asleep. But everyone knew that people in her limp and lifeless condition don't wake up.

Jesus glanced at Peter, James, and John, who then politely ushered everyone out of the house, leaving only themselves, Jesus, and the girl's parents. The Healer then took the cold, ashen hand of the child and spoke softly to her. "Little girl, arise!"

When her eyes fluttered and she sat up, her parents fell on her with hugs and kisses mingled with tears of joy. Jesus smiled. "Get her something to eat. She'll be hungry" (Matthew 9:18–25; Mark 5:22–43; Luke 8:40–55).

PREYING HEALERS

I hope you don't mind my imaginative retelling of that story, but when I turn on the television and see the mockery that some have made of divine healing, I sometimes have to remind myself that neither Jesus nor His disciples were like that. "Word-faith" healers cleverly couch their money-making schemes in pious-sounding theology while claiming to be instruments of God's power and grace. How insulting! In reality, they prey upon those made vulnerable by the pain of illness; they have perfected the fine art of balancing hope and guilt in order to convert suffering into profit. Make no mistake—it has nothing to do with compassion and everything to do with cash.

Let me be clear from the start, I absolutely and unreservedly believe in divine healing. Divine healers, however, are nothing more than a modern-day version of the temple tricksters I described in the previous chapter. And more than two thousand years later, their methods have changed but their motivation remains the same. Money.

Some Christian denominations hold a particular theology that makes their members more susceptible to becoming victims of faith healers' greed. They tend to be more expressive and dramatic in their belief and practice. Many claim that if someone does not possess a supernatural ability—often called a "gift of the Holy Spirit"—he or she either cannot claim to be a Christian or does not exercise enough faith. Though not always articulated, many followers come to believe that if God doesn't respond to their earnest prayer, it's because they haven't prayed long enough or approached God with enough faith. Or perhaps they have not lived as worthy followers of Jesus Christ, so their prayers are ineffective. Furthermore, a number of people formerly associated with these denominations confess that their desire for an encounter with the supernatural was so strong that they became willing participants in a shared delusion that is sustained and honored as genuine spirituality by their peers.

During the time following the resurrection of Jesus Christ and before the final piece of New Testament Scripture had been completed, God did indeed give some believers miraculous power over illness and other afflictions. However, their use of this power looked nothing like that of today's alleged healers.

To better understand the *true* nature of divine healing, we must understand and accept two important aspects of God's nature. First, God is all-powerful, which means He is able to do anything He chooses to do. He made the world and everything in it, and He can alter it at any time.

Hebrew Scripture affirms:

> For I know that the LORD is great
> And that our LORD is above all gods.
> Whatever the LORD pleases, He does,
> In heaven and in earth, in the seas and in all deeps.
>
> Psalm 135:5–6

King Nebuchadnezzar ruled most of the known world as the supreme ruler of the Babylonian Empire, and the power of his position quickly went to his head. One morning, he woke up, stood on his terrace overlooking the splendor of his capital, and said, "Is this not Babylon the great, which I myself have built as a royal residence by the might of my power and for the glory of my majesty?" (Daniel 4:30).

Within moments of his boast, God announced that he would become subject to a mental disorder that would cause him to think he was a wild beast instead of the greatest of men. When his long ordeal came to an end years later, the great King Nebuchadnezzar wrote,

> I, Nebuchadnezzar, raised my eyes toward heaven and my reason returned to me, and I blessed the Most High and praised and honored Him who lives forever;
>> For His dominion is an everlasting dominion,
>> And His kingdom endures from generation to generation.
>> All the inhabitants of the earth are accounted as nothing,
>> But He does according to His will in the host of heaven
>> And among the inhabitants of earth;
>> And no one can ward off His hand
>> Or say to Him, "What have You done?"
>
> Daniel 4:34–35

Darius the Mede, who ruled the Medo-Persian Empire, also acknowledged God's supreme power.

> "I make a decree that in all the dominion of my kingdom men are to fear and tremble before the God of Daniel;
>> For He is the living God and enduring forever,
>> And His kingdom is one which will not be destroyed,
>> And His dominion will be forever."
>
> Daniel 6:26

As rulers of vast empires, both of these men understood the concept of sovereignty, the right of a monarch to do as he pleases without having to answer to anyone. This points to the second aspect of God's nature that we must understand and accept. Because He is all-powerful, He is also utterly sovereign. God has the right to do whatever He chooses, for whomever He chooses, and whenever He chooses to do it. He answers to no one.

Ancient men and women believed their pagan gods to be as capricious and depraved as humans, only more powerful. To coax blessings out of their gods, worshipers were required to bring lavish sacrifices or go to extreme lengths to demonstrate their devotion. They believed that if their gods were sufficiently impressed, their crops would grow, their enemies would fail, and their children would be healthy. However, the God of the Bible has always distinguished Himself as wholly distinct from the false gods of humankind's imagination. He cannot be coerced, tricked, manipulated, or bribed into doing anything. He freely chooses to act (or not) at His own inclination, though His actions are always consistent with His unchanging, holy character.

Keep these two fundamental truths in mind as we examine a genuine supernatural healing in the book of Acts.

Jesus eventually charged His disciples with the privilege of making disciples and teaching others how to be Christian. And for a time, His disciples were given the ability to heal just as He did. During this period, Peter and John were making their way to the temple to worship and teach. As they neared one of the gates, a man paralyzed in his legs from birth called to them begging for money.

> But Peter, along with John, fixed his gaze on him and said, "Look at us!" And he began to give them his attention, expecting to receive something from them. But Peter said, "I do not possess silver and gold, but what I do have I give to you: In the name of Jesus Christ the Nazarene—walk!" And seizing him by the right hand, he raised him up; and immediately his feet and his ankles were strengthened. With a leap he stood upright and began to walk; and he entered the temple with them, walking and leaping and praising God.
>
> Acts 3:4–8

Naturally, the healed man responded by praising God, but he also embraced Peter and John as though they were responsible for his healing. The people in the temple recognized the man who had begged for alms most of his life, and they wanted to know who had this healing power. Peter set the matter straight.

> When Peter saw this, he replied to the people, "Men of Israel, why are you amazed at this, or why do you gaze at us, as if by our own power or piety we had made him walk? . . . It is the name of Jesus which has strengthened this man whom you see and know; and the faith which comes through Him has given him this perfect health in the presence of you all."
>
> Acts 3:12, 16

Three crucial observations will help us recognize a miraculous healing from God:

- The healing was instantaneous and permanent.
- The healing was obvious and comprehensive.
- The healing was neither directly nor indirectly the work of people.

The "healings" of the word-faith hucksters always leave you wondering why they don't heal paraplegics or people blind from birth or victims of cerebral palsy. Furthermore, faith healers typically give God all the credit for the healings that occur at their rallies, saying they are merely conduits of God's healing power, but their humility is superficial. Their words say one thing, but their theatrics and appeals for money make it very clear that in order to receive healing, one must come to them. Curiously, they do not appear in hospital rooms, healing one sick person after another.

THE FIVE LAWS OF HEALING

While modern-day healers are fraudulent, please understand that to this day God does heal people. While these healings are sometimes dramatic and frequently unexplained, they rarely involve a miracle—that is, an obvious, contrary-to-the-laws-of-nature event that can only be explained as divinely ordered. Nevertheless, God does intervene on behalf of people and very often in conjunction with the prayers of others.

To better understand the nature of divine healing today, consider the following five laws derived from the Bible.

Law 1: There are two categories of sin: original and personal. Theologians call Adam's disobedience "original sin," because it was the first incidence of sin, and all sinfulness in all people throughout all time can be traced back to his tragic choice (Genesis 3:17–19). Each of us has inherited a diseased nature that is bent toward wrongdoing, so much so that we cannot resist the temptation to sin. In this sense, sin is universal. When, individually, we choose to disobey, sin has become personal.

Law 2: Original sin introduced suffering, sickness, disease, and death. As a result of sin, God's creation became a distorted version of what He had originally made perfect. The Lord didn't create the human body for the purpose of suffering and decay. He created the world to be a harmonious, nurturing environment for our bodies, and He created us for the purpose of intimate fellowship with Him. Now, because of sin, there's something wrong with everything and everyone, including our bodies, which are susceptible to sickness and death.

Law 3: Sometimes sickness and death are the direct result of personal sin. Obviously, illegal drug use destroys the body and extramarital sex can expose us to disease, but some afflictions are supernaturally allowed for the purpose of chastisement (1 Corinthians 11:27–30). The Lord may, as a loving act of severe mercy, allow physical affliction to steer a person away from behavior that is destructive to himself or others.

Law 4: Sometimes sickness and death are not related to sin at all. Of the man born blind in John 9:1–3 (NET), Jesus said, "Neither this man nor his parents sinned, but he was born blind so that the acts of God may be revealed through what happens to him." The man's blindness was the result of birth into a world that is distorted by evil; nevertheless, God gave his affliction a divine purpose even before speaking the universe into existence.

We are tiny creatures with a limited lifespan, moving about in a vast universe measured in eons and light-years. It is easy to forget there's more going on than what happens to us. We're shortsighted and impatient. We want our software to download instantly, we want our coffee prompt, fresh, and hot, and we want answers to all our cosmic questions *now*!

But God doesn't work on our timetable. He has a plan that He will execute perfectly and for the highest, greatest good of all, and for His ultimate glory. Confusing and mysterious though that may seem, He commandeers every random cruelty of evil for His own divine purpose.

Law 5: It is not God's will that every illness be healed. This is probably the most counterintuitive principle to accept. It runs contrary to *our* idea of what a good God should do. For sure, it flies in the face of the health-wealth theology that keeps the applause coming and the crowds increasing. According to the word-faith preachers, God wants you to be healthy, wealthy, and blissfully unaware of anything sad. And make no mistake about it, the reason you're not healthy and wealthy is *you*—not enough faith, too much sin.

By the time of the apostle Paul's death, much of the New Testament had poured forth from his pen as the Holy Spirit communicated divine truth to him and through him. Furthermore, he was initially responsible for the spread of Christianity through the western Roman Empire and for the stability of the churches there. Certainly, if anyone had enough faith and favor with God to receive divine healing, it was Paul. Yet the man struggled with illness during most of his years in ministry. Of one particular bout with physical affliction, he wrote,

> So that I would not become arrogant, a thorn in the flesh was given to me, a messenger of Satan to trouble me—so that I would not become arrogant. I asked the Lord three times about this, that it would depart from me. But he said to me, "My grace is enough for you, for my power is made perfect in weakness." So then, I will boast most gladly about my weaknesses, so that the power of Christ may reside in me. Therefore I am content with weaknesses, with insults, with troubles, with persecutions and difficulties for the sake of Christ, for whenever I am weak, then I am strong.
>
> 2 Corinthians 12:7–10 NET

Alfred Plummer, a reliable New Testament scholar, writes of this thorn, "It's a very vivid metaphor for intense physical suffering." Bishop Lightfoot characterized the expression *thorn in the flesh* as "a stake driven through the flesh." William Barclay writes,

> By far the most likely thing is that Paul suffered from chronically recurrent attacks of a certain virulent fever which haunted the coast of the eastern Mediterranean. The natives of the country, when they wished to harm an enemy, prayed to their gods that he should be "burnt up" with this fever. One who has suffered from it describes the headache that accompanies it like "a red-hot bar thrust through the forehead." Another speaks of "the grinding, boring pain in one's temple—the phantom wedge driven in between the jaws," and says that when the thing became acute it "reached the extreme point of human endurance."[1]

No one can say for certain what afflicted Paul. All we know is that it was excruciating . . . so much so that he prayed no fewer than three times for divinely provided relief. Despite Paul's close relationship with God and the great things he accomplished in ministry, God, in His immeasurable wisdom, considered that Paul was better off with "the thorn" than without it. And who can argue? Clearly, Paul was a better preacher, a more insightful teacher, and writer with greater compassion because of his continuing afflictions.

As I read the New Testament, I find that all of the miraculous healings are immediate, comprehensive, permanent, and *free*. While Jesus often affirmed a person's choice to believe in Him, He never suggested that the person's depth of spirituality or the sincerity of his or her faith had anything to do with His choice to bring about healing.

GENUINE FAITH HEALING

The New Testament writer James explained how believers can respond to a person's illness. He never intended this to be the only response, nor was it the one-and-only requirement for God to heal someone. James wrote his book to urge Christians to give practical application to the spiritual truths they were learning. This included doing more than merely hoping the sick would recover. Pay close attention to the following words:

> Is anyone among you suffering? He should pray. Is anyone in good spirits? He should sing praises. Is anyone among you ill? He should summon the elders of the church, and they should pray for him and anoint him with oil in the name of the Lord. And the prayer of faith will save the one who is sick and the Lord will raise him up—and if he has committed sins, he will be forgiven. So confess your sins to one another and pray for one another so that you may be healed. The prayer of a righteous person has great effectiveness.
>
> James 5:13–16 NET

The Greek word translated "suffering" is *kakopathe*, a broadly applied term meaning "to suffer distress," which can include physical, mental, emotional, financial, relational, even spiritual anguish. James prescribed prayer as the first response to any kind of suffering. However, he does not specify the content of prayer, nor does he promise delivery from the affliction as a result of such praying. In fact, the best prayers often come after we have exhausted our pleas for deliverance.

Soon after learning that cancer had returned to his body, former White House Press Secretary Tony Snow wrote an article for *Christianity Today* titled, "Cancer's Unexpected Blessings." In that marvelous piece, he wrote,

> Picture yourself in a hospital bed. The fog of anesthesia has begun to wear away. A doctor stands at your feet; a loved one holds your hand at the side. "It's cancer," the healer announces.
>
> The natural reaction is to turn to God and ask him to serve as a cosmic Santa. "Dear God, make it all go away. Make everything simpler." But another voice whispers: "You have been called." Your quandary has drawn you closer to God, closer to those you love, closer to the issues

that matter—and has dragged into insignificance the banal concerns that occupy our "normal time."

There's another kind of response, although usually short-lived— an inexplicable shudder of excitement, as if a clarifying moment of calamity has swept away everything trivial and tiny, and placed before us the challenge of important questions.[2]

While it may not be God's will to heal every sickness, He nonetheless cares deeply for everyone's suffering—so much that He sent His own Son to bear the worst of it with us and for us. Moreover, He has called His people to nurture the suffering. James outlined a practical, three-step process to give comfort—and should God choose, quite possibly healing—to people enduring physical affliction.

Step 1: Call the elders of the church. "Is anyone among you sick? Then he must call for the elders of the church . . ." (James 5:14).

Unlike the other term, *kakopatheō*, the Greek word translated "sick" is *astheneō*, which means "to be without strength, to be debilitated, feeble in body." It refers to someone debilitated by a physical malady. This person is encouraged to notify the leaders of his or her church. Suffering may not be relieved or end quickly, but no one should suffer alone.

Step 2: Elders respond by providing medical help. ". . . and they are to pray over him, anointing him with oil in the name of the Lord" (James 5:14).

At the risk of appearing pedantic, I need to point out an important nuance in the Greek that is very important, yet frequently overlooked. The main verb in this command is "pray," with "anointing" as a supporting participle. Very often, the translation of this arrangement of verbs would be "Having anointed him with oil in the name of the Lord, they are to pray for him." Most versions choose to depict the verbs as simultaneous actions: "They are to pray over him, *while* anointing him with oil." Either way, the point is the same. Neither the praying nor the anointing should be overlooked.

But, equally important, what does James mean by "anointing with oil"? Some religions take it to mean a type of ritual. They carry little vials of oil when they visit the sick, and they pour oil or splash oil on the person. The practice of "extreme unction" found its roots in this particular passage, even though they use it for those who have died or are very close to death.

The Greek language has two words that apply to the customary use of oil in the ancient world, *aleiphō* and *chirō*. The latter most commonly refers to the ceremonial anointing used to signify God's special blessing upon someone. For instance, the word *Christ*, which means "anointed one," comes from *chirō*. James could have chosen this term, but he elected to use *aleiphō*. This particular term has more to do with the pragmatic, therapeutic use of oil, such as rubbing or massaging with it for medicinal purposes. Various herbs and extracts were added to olive oil in ancient times. The mixture was applied to the body to aid with a number of afflictions.

In the first century, this was the best medicine available. To say that the elder believers were to rub the sick with oil was to say that they were to help the physically afflicted receive medical attention. Today, in applying these instructions, elders should be certain the sick person is receiving the best available medical help.

James's point is simple and obvious. Don't substitute prayer for medical assistance. Following the advice of a medical professional, using medications wisely, and applying medical procedures appropriately does not suggest that a person lacks faith in God. He gave medical knowledge to humankind as an act of grace. He has given some men and women a greater ability to understand and apply that knowledge. And while He has called these men and women to be the means of His healing, God alone is the healer.

Step 3: Submit the illness to God's will in prayer. ". . . and they are to pray over him" (James 5:14).

The process of caring for the physically afflicted must include prayer. The literal translation of James 5:15 reads, "And the prayer of faith will save the weary one." Express your sincere desire for the complete restoration of the suffering. Pray that he or she will experience less pain and will avoid the debilitating effects of fear. Pray that the illness will yield surprising, unexpected benefits. But submit your requests to the sovereign care of God in complete confidence that He is impeccably good and unfailingly right. As Jesus Himself prayed in the Garden of Gethsemane, "Not My will, but Yours be done" (Luke 22:42).

FIVE PRINCIPLES REGARDING DIVINE HEALING

The anguish and confusion of physical suffering can be overwhelming and can cause even the most level-headed person to seek relief in the most unlikely places and from the most unreliable sources. That's why faith healing is such big business. Five simple principles, each coupled with an exhortation, will help keep us focused on the true source of healing as we ignore the peddlers who promote a false hope.

The will of God is paramount; respect it. God's will is sometimes difficult to understand from our limited, earth-bound perspective. It is even more difficult to accept when it involves great suffering. Even as we pray, we must remember that God is right in all His ways, including our afflictions. However, our suffering is deeply felt by Him, and for those who are His, all suffering will become the means by which He brings greater blessing later (Romans 8:26–28; 1 Peter 5:10).

Medical assistance is imperative; seek it. Prayer was never intended to replace competent medical care. God's grace to all people—not just to those who have answered His call—includes the gift of medical science. In fact, God may choose to answer your prayer for healing through the hands of an unbelieving physician (Luke 10:33–35).

Intercessory prayer is God's commandment; obey it. As we do everything within our power to bring healing, hope, and encouragement to others, we do so under the providence of God. He invites us to give all matters over to Him because He cares deeply for those who hurt (Philippians 4:6). We can trust Him to do what is right (Matthew 7:7–11).

Confession of sins is healthy; practice it. Not all sickness is related to the personal sins of the one who is afflicted; however, we cannot always rule it out. Confession and repentance of sins—even those we consider insignificant—are never inappropriate. Even if the sin has nothing to do with the illness, confession and repentance keep our relationship with the Lord free of distracting issues (James 5:16; 1 John 1:8–9).

All healing is of God; celebrate it. Whenever someone's health has been restored, whether by the expertise of a medical professional or through direct, supernatural intervention, God deserves the credit. We are never mistaken to praise God and thank Him for healing and sustained health (James 1:17; 1 John 5:14–15).

Again, divine healing must be understood in the context of God's nature. He is all-powerful, so He can heal any illness. And He is sovereign, which means that He will act in the best interest of each person according to His unfailing goodness, even if, in our estimation, it doesn't seem very good at the moment.

ULTIMATE HEALING

Let's return to an episode in the life of Jesus (John 11:18–26) for another look at something He said. When a messenger brought Jesus word that His friend Lazarus lay dying, He deliberately tarried. After two days, He started out for Bethany, knowing that Lazarus had died.

He arrived to find Martha waiting for Him on the outskirts of town. "Lord, if You had been here, my brother would not have died," she said.

Martha and her sister, Mary, had earnestly requested healing from Jesus, whom they trusted completely. Even as their brother lay cold in a tomb, Martha still rested in the sweet assurance that whatever Jesus chose to do was right. Indeed, He chose to honor their request in His way and in His time. "Your brother will rise," He said.

Martha recalled His earlier teaching and replied, "I know that he will rise again in the resurrection on the last day."

Jesus clarified the teaching for her. "I am the resurrection and the life; he who believes in Me will live even if he dies, and everyone who lives and believes in Me will never die." He then asked a most important question—one that goes to an issue of far greater importance than temporary relief from the pangs of illness. "Do you believe this?"

Martha understood the full significance of the question and declared her faith in unambiguous terms. And with that, Jesus presented her with a token of His ultimate promise by performing the ultimate healing, by reversing the death and decay of Lazarus.

Jesus, the healer, did not come to prolong our earthly existence or even to make it more pleasant—at least not pleasant in the selfish, pampered way we would prefer. He came to give us healing from the disease that threatens eternal life, and to give us joy, which surpasses mere happiness by eons and light-years.

He healed Lazarus of death and decay, but healing of that kind is only temporary. Lazarus eventually died again. Even if we were to receive complete healing from every challenge to our health, we must eventually face death. It is an unavoidable consequence of sin. Jesus, the healer, however, will not allow death to win the final victory. Because of Him, we can look forward to an ultimate healing that is permanent.

As Tony Snow reflected on his bout with colon cancer, he included this reminder:

> Most of us have watched friends as they drifted toward God's arms not with resignation, but with peace and hope. In so doing, they have taught us not how to die, but how to live. They have emulated Christ by transmitting the power and authority of love.
>
> I sat by my best friend's bedside a few years ago as a wasting cancer took him away. He kept at his table a worn Bible and a 1928 edition of the Book of Common Prayer. A shattering grief disabled his family, many of his old friends, and at least one priest. Here was a humble and very good guy, someone who apologized when he winced with pain because he thought it made his guest uncomfortable. He retained his equanimity and good humor literally until his last conscious moment. "I'm going to try to beat [this cancer]," he told me several months before he died. "But if I don't, I'll see you on the other side."
>
> His gift was to remind everyone around him that even though God doesn't promise us tomorrow, he does promise us eternity—filled with life and love we cannot comprehend—and that one can in the throes of sickness point the rest of us toward timeless truths that will help us weather future storms.
>
> Through such trials, God bids us to choose: Do we believe, or do we not?[3]

Chapter Ten

Abiding in Christ

For many months, storm clouds had been gathering over Jerusalem. Jesus focused His attention on Galilee during the early part of His ministry, but He regularly traveled to the Holy City in Judea to celebrate the more than half-dozen Jewish feasts throughout the year. And each visit intensified the growing tension between Jesus and the religious establishment—the Sadducees, with their control of the temple, and the Pharisees, who had a grip on the people.

The disciples could sense the danger mounting. So when Jesus announced that they would travel to visit Martha and Mary in the village of Bethany, just two miles from Jerusalem, Thomas turned to the other disciples and shrugged. "Let us also go, so that we may die with Him" (John 11:16). The disciples' fear was not unfounded. On their last visit, an angry mob sought to stone their Master.

After Jesus raised Lazarus from the dead, He won a new assembly of followers. However, several friends of the Pharisees saw His growing popularity as a threat and scurried to Jerusalem with the news.

So the chief priests [Sadducees] and the Pharisees called the council together and said, "What are we doing? For this man is performing many miraculous signs. If we allow him to go on in this way, everyone will believe in him, and the Romans will come and take away our sanctuary and our nation."

Then one of them, Caiaphas, who was high priest that year, said, "You know nothing at all! You do not realize that it is more to your advantage to have one man die for the people than for the whole nation to perish."

John 11:47–50 NET

With that, the plot to kill Jesus began.

The religious leaders would have to be crafty. They didn't dare seize Him in public for fear that the ever-growing multitude of His followers would turn on them and revolt. And nothing would bring down the wrath of Rome quicker than insurrection. When Marcus Licinius Crassus defeated the runaway slave Spartacus and his six thousand rebels, he crucified them at regular intervals along the highway leading to Spartacus's hometown. The general never issued the order to have the bodies or the crosses removed, so for years—perhaps decades—the macabre wooden memorials warned would-be revolutionaries, *This could be you.*

HAIL, KING JESUS!

Imagine the seething consternation of the religious authorities when Jesus arrived in Jerusalem to celebrate the Passover feast. He deliberately chose to ride a humble foal of a donkey, not only a recognized symbol of peace, but a glaring reference to the messianic prophecy of Zechariah.

Rejoice greatly, O daughter of Zion!
Shout in triumph, O daughter of Jerusalem!
Behold, your king is coming to you;
He is just and endowed with salvation,

Humble, and mounted on a donkey,
Even on a colt, the foal of a donkey.
I will cut off the chariot from Ephraim
And the horse from Jerusalem;
And the bow of war will be cut off
And He will speak peace to the nations;
And His dominion will be from sea to sea,
And from the River to the ends of the earth.

Zechariah 9:9–10

The religious rulers clearly understood the message this sent. It said, in effect, *I'm coming in peace as your Messiah, Israel's promised priest-king. Yield your authority to Me, and let's begin building the new kingdom.* Thousands of Jesus' followers responded to the gesture by giving Him a welcome reserved for royalty. They lined the road leading into the city, cheered His name, and paved His path with their cloaks and cut palm branches. They shouted, "Hosanna!" which means, "Save us now!"

Everyone knew the tradition. For hundreds of years, Jews had recited Psalm 118 in anticipation of this day.

The stone which the builders rejected
Has become the chief corner stone.
This is the LORD's doing;
It is marvelous in our eyes.
This is the day which the LORD has made;
Let us rejoice and be glad in it.
O LORD, do save, we beseech You;
O LORD, we beseech You, do send prosperity!
Blessed is the one who comes in the name of the LORD;
We have blessed you from the house of the LORD.
The LORD is God, and He has given us light;
Bind the festival sacrifice with cords to the horns of the altar.

Psalm 118:22–27

On previous occasions, Jesus worshiped in the temple and taught willing hearers. When challenged by the religious elite, He responded, but never at the expense of His mission of teaching and preaching. He taught against the corruption He saw there and even disrupted their business more than once. But this time was different. This time He came to claim authority over the temple and to take His stand against the organized crime of Annas, the power broker behind the office of high priest.

At one point during the tumultuous week after His arrival, Jesus sat to teach in the temple. As a large group of followers and conspirators gathered around the daring rabbi to hear a parable, He captured their attention with His opening words: "There was a landowner who planted a vineyard and put a wall around it and dug a wine press in it, and built a tower . . ." (Matthew 21:33).

Most of the images in Jesus' teaching drew upon the common experience of Jews living in the first century: shepherd and sheep, sower and seed, wine and wineskins, master and servants. But no metaphor touched the Hebrew soul like the picture of the vinedresser and his vineyard. Because this image so poignantly illustrated God's special care for the nation of Israel, the prophet Isaiah's parable came as a stinging rebuke, one that continued to ache for many generations after the Babylonians had trampled the Hebrews so cruelly.

> Let me sing now for my well-beloved
> A song of my beloved concerning His vineyard.
> My well-beloved had a vineyard on a fertile hill.
> He dug it all around, removed its stones,
> And planted it with the choicest vine
> And He built a tower in the middle of it
> And also hewed out a wine vat in it;
> Then He expected it to produce good grapes,
> But it produced only worthless ones.
>
> "And now, O inhabitants of Jerusalem and men of Judah,
> Judge between Me and My vineyard.

"What more was there to do for My vineyard that I have not done
    in it?
Why, when I expected it to produce good grapes did it produce
    worthless ones?
"So now let Me tell you what I am going to do to My vineyard:
I will remove its hedge and it will be consumed;
I will break down its wall and it will become trampled ground.
"I will lay it waste;
It will not be pruned or hoed,
But briars and thorns will come up.
I will also charge the clouds to rain no rain on it."

For the vineyard of the LORD of hosts is the house of Israel
And the men of Judah His delightful plant.
Thus He looked for justice, but behold, bloodshed;
For righteousness, but behold, a cry of distress.

Isaiah 5:1–7

Before Jesus concluded His first sentence, disciples and conspirators alike
sat in rapt attention.

"There was a landowner who planted a vineyard and put a wall around
it and dug a wine press in it, and built a tower, and rented it out to vine-
growers and went on a journey. When the harvest time approached, he
sent his slaves to the vine-growers to receive his produce. The vine-growers took his slaves and beat one, and killed another, and stoned a third.
Again he sent another group of slaves larger than the first; and they did
the same thing to them. But afterward he sent his son to them, saying,
'They will respect my son.' But when the vine-growers saw the son, they
said among themselves, 'This is the heir; come, let us kill him and seize
his inheritance.' They took him, and threw him out of the vineyard and
killed him. Therefore when the owner of the vineyard comes, what will
he do to those vine-growers?"

Matthew 21:33–40

The high priest's officials and the Pharisees began to squirm when someone from the crowd answered, "He will bring those wretches to a wretched end, and will rent out the vineyard to other vine-growers who will pay him the proceeds at the proper seasons" (Matthew 21:41).

THE TRUE VINE

Each year, the Hebrew people celebrated Passover with a weeklong festival— the combined observance of the Passover Feast and the Feast of Unleavened Bread. For nearly two thousand years, they paused annually to commemorate their ancestors' liberation from Egypt and God's planting them in the Promised Land. Jesus gathered His disciples in a specially prepared room for what He knew to be His last time with them before His death. At this final meal celebrating God's faithfulness to Israel, He would summarize His teaching, prepare His disciples to carry on His ministry, and give the familiar rituals of the Passover celebration a new significance.

As the ministry of Jesus had progressed, His disciples matured and His message changed accordingly. To the general public, He called, "Come to Me." To those who came, He invited, "Follow Me." And to those who followed, He urged, "Abide in Me." He crafted His message in the Upper Room for believers, those who had accepted Him as their Messiah and the embodiment of God, though it would be some time before they completely understood the implications of this truth.

After reiterating His earlier prediction that He would be beaten and murdered by the religious leaders in Jerusalem, Jesus returned to an earlier theme to illustrate how His relationship with the disciples would continue nonetheless. "I am the true vine, and My Father is the vinedresser" (John 15:1).

Compare this vineyard parable to the others and you will see a dramatic recasting of the images. In this version, Jesus took the place of Israel, claiming to be the authentic, healthy vine the nation had failed to become. The kingdom of God was its king.

The purpose of Jesus' parable is to teach believers how to live as citizens of the new kingdom by applying a concept He termed *abiding*. The reason

God planted the vine in the Promised Land—the reason anyone plants a vine—was to produce fruit. Tragically, though, Israel failed. Likewise, many Christians fail to abide and, therefore, fail to bear anything. The British pastor Andrew Murray lamented,

> It is to be feared that there are many earnest followers of Jesus from whom the meaning of [*abiding*] is very much hidden. While trusting in their Savior for pardon and for help and seeking to some extent to obey Him, they have hardly realized to what closeness of union, to what intimacy of fellowship He invited them when He said, "Abide in Me." This is not only an unspeakable loss to themselves, but the church and the world suffer in what they lose.[1]

Typically, Christians assume that the production of fruit is their responsibility, something they must do in gratitude for what Christ has done for them. They try to be good and cheerful and righteous and generous and faithful—every quality that defines Jesus. They work hard only to eventually fail, pick themselves up, promise to do better, and try again . . . only to fail again. As they begin to realize they cannot possibly meet their self-imposed standard of goodness, they either lower the standard or distract themselves with activities that create the illusion of success. That may very well describe your relationship with God.

Lewis Sperry Chafer, the founder of Dallas Theological Seminary, wrote, "Much of our Christian life is nothing more than a cheap anesthetic to deaden the pain of an empty life."[2] A. W. Tozer put it another way: "May not the inadequacy of much of our spiritual experience be traced back to our habit of skipping through the corridor of the kingdom like children in the marketplace, always chattering about everything, but learning the true value of nothing."[3]

Those words describe the spiritual state of Israel at the time of Jesus. But lest we allow ourselves to sit in condemnation, we must acknowledge that this indictment of Israel bears our name as well. The kind of life God has called us to live is not merely difficult, but it's absolutely impossible—at least as we have tried to live it. Fortunately, Jesus offered a better way.

THE LIFE OF A GOOD-FOR-SOMETHING

The parable involves three principle figures: the vine (Jesus, "I am"), the vinedresser ("My Father"), and the branches (His followers).

> "Every branch in Me that does not bear fruit, He takes away; and every branch that bears fruit, He prunes it so that it may bear more fruit."
>
> John 15:2

The expression "in Me" represents what theologians call positional truth. Paul the apostle often described Christians as those who are "in Christ." This expression figuratively describes a person's relationship with Christ such that God treats the person as He would Jesus.

Think of it this way. If you were to drive to the front gate of the White House in Washington, D.C., you would eventually have to turn around. The guards will not let you in. If, however, the president sent his official car to pick you up and drive you to the gate, you will receive the same treatment he does. By virtue of your placement in the president's car, the guard will give you the same treatment due the president. He will press a button and the gate will open before the driver even has a chance to tap the brakes.

Being "in Christ" puts the person in right relationship with the Father. Paul says, "There is now no condemnation for those who are in Christ Jesus" (Romans 8:1). The believer is regarded as having the same righteous standing as Jesus. With the believer's eternal destiny secure, Jesus turned from the issue of position—"in Me"—to that of production. The purpose of a branch is no different than that of the vine: to produce fruit. Jesus said, "Every branch in Me that does not bear fruit, He takes away."

Many versions of the Bible translate a key Greek term in this verse as "takes away," "removes," or even "cuts off," but its primary definition is "to lift from the ground."[4] The word can and often does mean "to lift with a view to carrying, to carry off or put away."[5] In keeping with the metaphor, Jesus most likely referred to the vinedresser's practice of lifting a sagging branch and tying it to the trellis—a procedure called "training." The vinedresser also carefully prunes the branches to encourage healthy growth.

Interpreting a parable demands we appreciate the richness of the story's imagery without seeing more than the author intended. Stare at anything long enough, and it will bear the imprint of your imagination. So we must restrain ourselves from seeing more than what the parable says. Jesus did not identify what the fruit represents. Some have suggested that the fruit of a believer is another believer—in other words, a person has chosen to place his or her faith in Jesus Christ as a result of a believer's influence. This may be what Jesus had in mind, but "fruit" may also refer to another noteworthy product.

The apostle Paul used the image of fruit to describe the character qualities that mark a healthy, mature believer. He listed a number of Christlike qualities in his letter to the Galatians. "The fruit of the Spirit is love, joy, peace, patience, kindness, goodness, faithfulness, gentleness, self-control; against such things there is no law" (Galatians 5:22–23).

Nevertheless, we don't know specifically what Jesus meant by fruit. In biblical imagery, fruit provides unmistakable proof of identity. For instance, an untrained eye will have difficulty telling the difference between an apple tree and a pear tree. But if its branches hang heavy with pears, no one can mistake the tree's identity. Furthermore, a full harvest of fruit is an unmistakable sign of health. Even a novice in horticulture knows that lots of lush, delicious fruit can come only from a strong, vibrant plant.

> "Abide in Me, and I in you. As the branch cannot bear fruit of itself
> unless it abides in the vine, so neither can you unless you abide in Me.
> I am the vine, you are the branches; he who abides in Me and I in him,
> he bears much fruit, for apart from Me you can do nothing."
>
> John 15:4–5

Note that Jesus never commanded believers to produce fruit. Fruit is the *purpose* of the branch, but it is not the *responsibility* of the branch. The branch cannot produce anything on its own. However, if it remains attached to the vine, it will receive life-sustaining sap, nourishment, strength, everything it needs. If it remains connected to the vine, it will inevitably hang heavy with grapes.

The focus of a Christian's activity is not to work hard enough to make fruit, but to keep his connection to Jesus Christ clean and strong. One way to do that is to absorb the teaching of God's Word, the sixty-six books of the Bible. Read God's Word . . . think about it, apply it, talk about it with others, ask questions, commit sections of it to memory. Strength and productivity come from staying connected. However, according to Jesus, failing to remain connected to the vine leads to tragic consequences.

> "If anyone does not abide in Me, he is thrown away as a branch and dries up; and they gather them, and cast them into the fire and they are burned."
>
> John 15:6

The interpretation of John 15:6 is a topic of considerable debate among believers. Some have suggested that the one who "does not abide in Me" is a believer who has failed to be faithful and has lost his or her salvation. But Jesus said that no one can be saved and then unsaved (John 10:27–29). Others propose that the one who "does not abide" was never a genuine believer—such as those who reject Jesus entirely or those who merely profess to believe but don't. But the context of Jesus' entire illustration is focused on and limited to believers. We know this because John 15:2 speaks of every branch "in Me," which presumes a relationship exists, and because 15:3 specifies Jesus' audience as those who are "already clean."

Jesus perhaps thought of the Old Testament prophet Ezekiel's analogy.

> Then the word of the LORD came to me, saying, "Son of man, how is the wood of the vine better than any wood of a branch which is among the trees of the forest? Can wood be taken from it to make anything, or can men take a peg from it on which to hang any vessel? If it has been put into the fire for fuel, and the fire has consumed both of its ends and its middle part has been charred, is it then useful for anything? Behold, while it is intact, it is not made into anything.

How much less, when the fire has consumed it and it is charred, can it still be made into anything!

Ezekiel 15:1–5

The point is simply this: vinedressers toss disconnected branches aside because they are dead. Dried up branches are good for nothing. Bible commentator Warren Wiersbe puts it well:

> It is unwise to build a theological doctrine on a parable or allegory. Jesus was teaching one main truth—the fruitful life of the believer—and we must not press the details too much. Just as an unfruitful branch is useless, so an unfruitful believer is useless; and both must be dealt with. It is a tragic thing for a once-fruitful believer to backslide and lose his privilege of fellowship and service.[6]

Someone who fails to abide is someone trying to transform his or her own character in order to produce Christlike qualities without maintaining a connection to Christ. And that's futile; it never works. In fact, it's a perfect plan for drying up and withering away. Jesus, drawing upon Ezekiel's analogy, calls such a life good for nothing. Not only does trying to produce good character on our own lead to futility, it often produces the very opposite of what we desire.

The apostle Paul took the image of fire a step further. Picturing the deeds of a Christian as construction material for a house, he imagined how the building might survive a fire.

> For no one can lay any foundation other than what is being laid, which is Jesus Christ. If anyone builds on the foundation with gold, silver, precious stones, wood, hay, or straw, each builder's work will be plainly seen, for the Day will make it clear, because it will be revealed by fire. And the fire will test what kind of work each has done. If what someone has built survives, he will receive a reward. If someone's work is burned up, he will suffer loss. He himself will be saved, but only as through fire.

1 Corinthians 3:11–15 NET

Living a life apart from complete dependence upon Christ is like building a house with dry, cracking wood and then stuffing the walls with straw for insulation. One spark and the whole thing will go up in flash. The homeowner escapes the flames, but he has nothing to show for his efforts.

As Jesus continued His parable of the vine, He chose to focus on the positive.

> "If you abide in Me, and My words abide in you, ask whatever you wish, and it will be done for you. My Father is glorified by this, that you bear much fruit, and so prove to be My disciples."
>
> John 15:7–8

As the believer abides—that is, remains vitally connected to Jesus Christ—he or she begins to bear the fruit of Christlike qualities. The believer is transformed from the inside out. His or her mind dwells on the kinds of thoughts that God thinks. The believer's heart begins to beat in perfect rhythm with the Father's, so that his or her desires reflect those of God. When that occurs, we see at least four other results.

First, *prayers are answered.* That doesn't mean God will become our personal genie. The promise is conditional. If we are connected to the vine and we are becoming more and more like Jesus, our prayers will not be selfish, but the kind of requests *He* would make. And Jesus received everything He asked because He and the Father were completely and consistently aligned in their thinking.

Second, *God is glorified.* As we model the character of Jesus, obeying His commands in the same way He obeyed those of the Father, the triune God receives all the credit. He delights to see us reflecting His character, and He looks for opportunities to dote on His children in response.

Third, *love is stimulated.* Note the absence of struggle or exertion. As we abide in Christ, the character qualities that honor the Lord begin to emerge, like grapes naturally growing from a healthy, well-connected branch. Because God is love (1 John 4:8), others will notice this divine quality develop within us.

Fourth, *joy will overflow.* Joy doesn't refer to superficial happiness or fleeting cheerfulness. Joy is a deeply felt contentment that transcends difficult circumstances and derives maximum enjoyment from every good experience. It isn't only about laughter, but abiding in Christ inspires laughter like you've never experienced before. Deep, contented joy comes from a place of complete security and confidence—even in the midst of trial. As the saying goes, "Joy is the flag that flies over the castle of our hearts, announcing that the King is in residence."

THE NEW VINEYARD

Many centuries before the arrival of Jesus Christ in Jerusalem, God planted a vineyard in the Promised Land. But the branches of that vineyard withered and wasted and failed to produce good fruit. Israel, like each one of us could testify, failed to please God.

Jesus came to do what neither Israel nor we can do. Now, He is the vineyard, and He will be faithful to bear fruit. And He invites us to attach ourselves to Him, like a branch abiding in a vine, so that we can become a part of this great fruit-bearing enterprise. This is not referring to salvation. By the time of His last evening with His disciples, the issue of salvation had been settled. This is a matter of living abundantly and producing a bumper crop of Christlike qualities in our character.

If your eternal destiny has been sealed by your belief in Christ, the crucial question for you is how you will live now. Will you try to become good and righteous on your own . . . and become good for nothing? Or will you abide in Christ . . . and allow Him to produce good within you?

That evening as Jesus broke the unleavened bread and called it His body, and as He poured the ceremonial wine and called it His blood, He invited His disciples to eat and drink. He used this—yet another symbol—to teach His followers that life must come from Him.

Even as I sat to write this book, I found the principle of "abiding" at work. Not long after I began the first chapter, I was met with an unusually heavy season of stress. Several significant events in my personal life, my ministry at church, even my radio ministry—each of which was life altering in its own right—converged to upset just about everything in my world. I honestly had no idea how I would complete this manuscript with everything else coming apart. But my daughter Charissa made an interesting and helpful observation: "What better time could there be to write a book about Jesus than when you have no choice but to rely upon Him?"

She was right. The research had been done. I had outlined everything I needed to express. However, the process of getting the right words onto the page was another matter. It's difficult enough when I'm feeling fit and my mind is free of distracting stresses, but the challenges I faced made the task humanly impossible. I found the more effort I put into the book, the slower the process went. Only as I confessed my utter inability to complete the task and as I submitted myself to God's sovereign design did the words come. If I neglected my regular time in Scripture and in prayer for the sake of getting a few more pages complete, the work was unusable and I had to begin again. In fact, as I look back on every writing project I've ever completed, the same was true. I just didn't realize it until this project made the principle of abiding a matter of survival.

Now, how much more foolish can a minister be than to try to write a book about Jesus Christ without spending time getting to know Him personally? Why, that's about as foolish as a dried-up twig trying to grow a grape!

Part Three

The Substitute

Chapter Eleven

The Gathering Storm

Y ou probably know where this narrative leads. Before the story is over, Jesus will be crucified and, at least for a time, His disciples will be completely disillusioned, wondering, *Where did it all go wrong?* They would likely trace the unraveling of their messianic hopes to a particular day in Capernaum, when Jesus began to winnow the multitudes of His followers.

Jesus, on the other hand, never regarded His path to the cross as anything but the successful unfolding of a plan. He had said early in His ministry, "Do not think that I came to bring peace on the earth; I did not come to bring peace, but a sword" (Matthew 10:34). The sword of which He spoke is the sharpest of all implements of conflict: truth. And those who hold it will find themselves hunted by evil.

After feeding the five thousand men and their families in the hill country of Galilee, Jesus rendezvoused with His disciples on the waves of the nearby sea and then sailed to Capernaum. Meanwhile, the multitudes frantically tried to trace His steps and finally deduced that He must have accompanied the disciples back to the hometown of Peter, Andrew, James, and John.

They arrived to find Jesus teaching in the synagogue. They then confronted Him with the suspicion that He had deliberately eluded them, but Jesus returned their objection with an indictment.

> I tell you the solemn truth, you are looking for me not because you saw miraculous signs, but because you ate all the loaves of bread you wanted. Do not work for the food that disappears, but for the food that remains to eternal life—the food which the Son of Man will give to you.
>
> John 6:26–27 NET

To the Jews gathered around Jesus in the synagogue, the rebuke echoed the voice of Moses, who had challenged the wandering generation of Israelites:

> Remember the whole way by which he has brought you these forty years through the desert so that he might, by humbling you, test you to see if you have it within you to keep his commandments or not. So he humbled you by making you hungry and then feeding you with unfamiliar manna. He did this to teach you that humankind cannot live by bread alone, but also by everything that comes from the LORD's mouth.
>
> Deuteronomy 8:2–3 NET

In the wilderness, God's covenant people struggled with a choice between feeding their bellies and nourishing their souls. God provided manna—a breadlike food that fell to the ground during the night—to sustain the wandering Israelites and to teach them how to value His Word more than physical fulfillment. Similarly, Jesus provided more than enough food for the five-thousand-plus followers on the hill. Throughout His ministry, He promised, "Above all pursue his kingdom and righteousness, and all these things [your physical needs] will be given to you as well" (Matthew 6:33 NET).

Teachers usually know when a student has traded ignorance for a willful blindness to the truth. No amount of education or persuasion will turn them. The majority of the followers gathered around Jesus in the synagogue wanted a king who would merely provide political security and physical abundance. They wanted a Messiah to rid them of Rome, not a Savior to rescue them from sin. They wanted to know how to please God, not because they feared Him or loved Him but because happy gods bless people and angry ones do mean things. "What must we do to accomplish the deeds God requires?" (John 6:28 NET), they had asked.

The question was pivotal—not only to the eternal destiny of the people who asked, but to the future of the Messiah. He had come to die on behalf of those who trusted Him, to save them from their sin and from the just penalty of God's wrath. However, He should have died at the hands of Israel's enemies—the adversaries of God's kingdom—not His own kinsmen.

But the battle line between good and evil doesn't run along borders or around races or even across thresholds. The cosmic battle between good and evil divides heart from heart without discrimination, for each person chooses his or her side. Oddly, it is not a choice between truth and untruth—God would never require a darkened mind to make such a choice. That would be crueler than requiring a paralytic to drag himself to a pool in a race for healing. We choose by how we respond to the Redeemer, who holds out something we innately know to be missing within. Those who push it away do so knowingly. At some point in every life, ignorance ceases to be the issue, and we either choose to heed the voice resonating in the hollows of our soul or we opt for willful disobedience.

That's why Jesus said, "Do not think that I have come to bring peace to the earth. I have not come to bring peace but a sword. For I have come to set a man against his father, a daughter against her mother, and a daughter-in-law against her mother-in-law, and a man's enemies will be the members of his household" (Matthew 10:34–36 NET). Obviously God wants families together, but, unfortunately, the truth of Jesus Christ is a divider. On most issues, there are many shades of gray, but not this one. And the whole world—right down to the individual households—has been partitioned into realms, that of light and darkness.

What must we do to accomplish the deeds God requires? Jesus said,

"This is the deed God requires—to believe in the one whom he sent" (John 6:29 NET). With the arrival of Jesus Christ, the kingdom of God ceased to be one defined by geography, but one established in the hearts of those who choose to believe.

At one point in His ministry, perhaps on that very day in Capernaum, Jesus began to teach primarily by way of parable. When asked why by the Twelve, He replied, "For this reason I speak to them in parables: Although they see they do not see, and although they hear they do not hear nor do they understand" (Matthew 13:13 NET). Parables of Jesus allow the observer to see what his or her heart chooses to see, which is determined by how he or she responds to Jesus.

With that decision made, Jesus then offered a fate-sealing parable—a crack that would become a chasm.

> Then Jesus told them, "I tell you the solemn truth, it is not Moses who has given you the bread from heaven, but my Father is giving you the true bread from heaven. For the bread of God is the one who comes down from heaven and gives life to the world. . . . I am the bread of life. The one who comes to me will never go hungry, and the one who believes in me will never be thirsty."
>
> John 6:32–33, 35 NET

Some believed, many grumbled. Jesus continued,

> "Your ancestors ate the manna in the wilderness, and they died. This is the bread that has come down from heaven, so that a person may eat from it and not die. I am the living bread that came down from heaven. If anyone eats from this bread he will live forever. The bread that I will give for the life of the world is my flesh."
>
> John 6:49–51 NET

This, of course, was Jesus' prediction that He would sacrifice Himself to provide eternal life for anyone who would receive it. But the fault line between the true believers and His eventual conspirators grew wider.

Then the Jews who were hostile to Jesus began to argue with one another, "How can this man give us his flesh to eat?" Jesus said to them, "I tell you the solemn truth, unless you eat the flesh of the Son of Man and drink his blood, you have no life in yourselves. The one who eats my flesh and drinks my blood has eternal life, and I will raise him up on the last day. For my flesh is true food, and my blood is true drink. The one who eats my flesh and drinks my blood resides in me, and I in him. Just as the living Father sent me, and I live because of the Father, so the one who consumes me will live because of me. This is the bread that came down from heaven; it is not like the bread your ancestors ate, but then later died. The one who eats this bread will live forever."

John 6:52–58 NET

Nothing would be the same after that. If Jesus had been running for political office, His campaign manager would have resigned. That day in Capernaum, Jesus divided His core constituency and alienated the majority. The political experts among the Twelve put their heads in their hands as they saw their future in Israel's new government go up in smoke. But Jesus didn't come to win the approval of people or to swing the majority of a disenfranchised voter base to embrace His platform and sweep Him into a position of power in Jerusalem. He came to speak "the solemn truth." And let's face it; the truth is rarely popular. In fact, it usually offends the majority.

Speaking of that, it was at this time many left Jesus. He was not the Messiah they were looking for. Jesus turned to the Twelve and asked, "You don't want to go away too, do you?" (John 6:67 NET). Peter said, in effect, "Lord, we don't exactly understand everything You just said, but You're our only hope. We have nowhere else to turn. We've chosen You, and that's that."

These were the sweetest, most authentic words a disciple could have spoken.

Jesus responded by clarifying a subtle point and revealing a chilling insight. "Didn't I choose you, the twelve, and yet one of you is the devil?" (v. 70 NET). The cosmic battle between good and evil divides heart from heart and, on that day, a subtle crack—barely a sliver—formed within one of their number.

BLIND GUIDES

The division between Jesus and the Pharisees had never been anything less than a canyon. He came to speak truth; they desired control. And one thing will always be true of controllers: what they cannot control, they destroy.

While Jesus was still ministering in Galilee, an envoy of Pharisees traveled from Jerusalem to meet with Jesus on a matter of grave concern to them. They likely felt it was a mission of mercy in which they would redeem a wayward rabbi. Of course, people who seek control don't see the world in terms of conformity with truth or untruth, but in terms of agreement with them.

> "Why do Your disciples break the tradition of the elders? For they do not wash their hands when they eat bread."
>
> Matthew 15:2

Their opening statement contains the first clue that something was terribly wrong. Emissaries of the Jewish religious capital made a four-day journey to complain that the disciples of Jesus didn't wash up before dinner. To us, that's trivial; but to the Pharisee, the issue of ceremonial hand cleansing epitomized everything a faithful Jew should value, including purity and distinction from the world at large.

Alfred Edersheim captured the tedium of the Pharisees' rite very well:

> Water jars were kept ready to be used before every meal. The minimum amount of water to be used was a quarter of a log, defined as enough to fill one and a half egg-shells. The water was first poured on both hands, with fingers pointing upward, and must run through the arm as far as the wrist. It must drop off from the wrist, for the water was now itself unclean, having touched the unclean hands, and, if it ran down the fingers again, it would render them unclean. The process was repeated with the hands held in the opposite direction, with the fingers pointing down; and then finally each hand was cleansed

by being rubbed with the fist of the other. A very strict Jew would do all this, not only before a meal, but also between each of the courses of the meal.[1]

Many centuries before this confrontation, the Jewish people were conquered by the Babylonians and carried off to serve the empire in Babylon. With their temple destroyed and their homeland colonized by other cultures, the Jews looked to the law of God to sustain their national identity and to maintain their distinctiveness as God's specially chosen people. And to help them apply the Law to everyday life in their new, unfamiliar home, teachers of the Jewish Scriptures wrote very careful instructions for the people to follow. However, what began as a practical aid for conscientious Jews became a sacred tradition that took on a life of its own.

This body of strict traditions eventually supplanted the very Law it was intended to uphold. And by the time of Jesus, failure to observe this tradition was regarded as disobedience to the law of God. Furthermore, this man-made religiosity became the means by which the Pharisees maintained the illusion of moral superiority. Ironically, their religious zeal put them at odds with God. Not only were they motivated by lust for power, but their traditions very often violated the very Law they supposedly cherished.

> [Jesus] answered them, "And why do you disobey the commandment of God because of your tradition? For God said, 'Honor your father and mother' and 'Whoever insults his father or mother must be put to death.' But you say, 'If someone tells his father or mother, "Whatever help you would have received from me is given to God," he does not need to honor his father.' You have nullified the word of God on account of your tradition. Hypocrites! Isaiah prophesied correctly about you when he said,
>
> 'This people honors me with their lips,
> but their heart is far from me,
> and they worship me in vain,
> teaching as doctrines the commandments of men.'"
>
> Matthew 15:3–9 NET

The sword of truth has but one target: the heart. And when the heart of a hypocrite is pierced, it bleeds resentment . . . ultimately, hatred. Jesus concluded His rebuke with a clarification. "Listen and understand. What defiles a person is not what goes into the mouth; it is what comes out of the mouth that defiles a person" (Matthew 15:10–11 NET).

After the Pharisees turned for Jerusalem, His hand-wringing disciples approached Him with an observation I'm certain they thought would be helpful. "Do you know that when the Pharisees heard this saying they were offended?" The Twelve understood the ramifications; they feared more than political fallout over the clash. The Pharisees had successfully established themselves as the epitome of Jewishness in the collective Jewish mind. To offend the Pharisees was to stand against an institution more than four hundred years old.

In 167 BC, the Seleucid conqueror Antiochus Epiphanes invaded Israel and forced pagan worship upon the Jews. But in the town of Modi'in, a righteous priest took up the sword and sparked what later became known as the Maccabean Revolt. Hanukkah, the Feast of Lights, celebrates the victory won as a result of this one priest's refusal to compromise his Jewish purity. This was the heritage claimed by the Pharisees. Their "traditions" were the cornerstone upon which they sought to rebuild the nation.

The disciples understood the stakes. To reject this cornerstone was to risk being crushed by it.

Jesus knew this as well.

"WOE TO YOU"

The triumphal entry of Jesus to the capital of the Hebrews marked a change in His relationship to the Holy City. He no longer visited as a worshiper; He claimed it as King. His subjects had strewn His path to the city with cut palm branches and their own cloaks, shouting "Hosanna!" which means, "Save us!"

While the people cheered, Jesus wept.

"If you had only known on this day, even you, the things that make for peace! But now they are hidden from your eyes. For the days will come upon you when your enemies will build an embankment against you and surround you and close in on you from every side. They will demolish you—you and your children within your walls—and they will not leave within you one stone on top of another, because you did not recognize the time of your visitation from God."

Luke 19:42–44 NET

Jesus' first official act came shortly after arriving in the temple. On several occasions, He had spoken against the corruption taking place in the outer courts, an institution known then as the Annas Bazaar, but that was before assuming office.

The Maccabean Revolt began with a priest and the resulting government came under the leadership of his sons. So, by AD 6, the office of high priest had become a royal post, for all intents and purposes. Also by that time, Israel had ceded most of its independence to Rome in exchange for protection. Quirinius, the Rome-appointed governor of Syria, selected a wily young aristocrat named Annas to rule as Israel's priest-king. But within a few years, the political winds had shifted and a new procurator favored someone else. He deposed Annas, but, by then, Annas had established himself as the patriarch of what could only be described as a Jewish crime family, not unlike an ancient mafia.

Annas retreated from public view but continued to control every Jewish political office in Jerusalem, including that of high priest. After his removal from office, no fewer than five sons and a grandson succeeded him, and at the time of Jesus, his son-in-law, Caiaphas, ran the temple.

The Annas Bazaar kept money flowing into the family's pockets and funded their corrupt hold on power. The chief priests refused to accept any currency except shekels minted in Israel. Money changers within the temple precincts gladly exchanged any currency for Jewish shekels at an inflated rate and then pocketed the difference. Furthermore, the law of Moses stated that any animal offered to God had to be flawless; only the best would do. So the men running the temple would inspect the animals brought for sacrifice, ostensibly to verify that the offerings were worthy. However, this was nothing more than a ruse. They arbitrarily rejected animals so that they could offer a suitable replacement in exchange . . . plus a fee. Ironically, the "suitable" animal offered for exchange had, only moments before, been the unsuitable sacrifice of a previous worshiper!

> Jesus entered the temple area and drove out all those who were selling and buying in the temple courts, and turned over the tables of the money changers and the chairs of those selling doves. And he said to them, "It is written, 'My house will be called a house of prayer,' but you are turning it into a den of robbers!"
>
> Matthew 21:12–13 NET

The Sadducees—the skirmishing collection of rivals and pawns of Annas—found in Jesus a common enemy. None of them appreciated His shutting down their money machine. Consequently, "the chief priests and the experts in the law and the prominent leaders among the people were seeking to assassinate him, but they could not find a way to do it, for all the people hung on his words" (Luke 19:47–48 NET).

After cleansing the temple courts of the Sadducees' corruption, Jesus called the Pharisees' hypocrisy into account.

> "The scribes and the Pharisees have seated themselves in the chair of Moses; therefore all that they tell you, do and observe, but do not do according to their deeds; for they say things and do not do them. They tie up heavy burdens and lay them on men's shoulders, but they themselves are unwilling to move them with so much as a finger. But they do all their deeds to be noticed by men; for they broaden their phylacteries and lengthen the tassels of their garments. They love the place of honor at banquets and the chief seats in the synagogues, and respectful greetings in the market places, and being called Rabbi by men."
>
> Matthew 23:2–7

Just before the Israelites entered the Promised Land, Moses challenged them to make the Word of God a prominent motivation for everything they did. It was to permeate every aspect of their lives. One customary response to this challenge took the form of a phylactery, a black leather box containing strips of parchment on which key verses of Scripture had been carefully penned by hand. Many conscientious Jews tied them to their forehead and left arm.

Ironically, this dedication had become largely symbolic, and the Pharisees ordered their phylacteries extra large so everyone would know how much they revered God's Word. But God didn't provide Scripture just to have it sit on someone's forehead or strapped to his or her arms. He wanted His people to revere it, to take it in, to animate their choices, and shape their decisions.

Another custom of the Jews began during the wilderness wanderings. God instructed Moses,

> "Speak to the sons of Israel, and tell them that they shall make for themselves tassels on the corners of their garments throughout their generations, and that they shall put on the tassel of each corner a cord of blue. It shall be a tassel for you to look at and remember all the commandments of the LORD, so as to do them and not follow after your own heart and your own eyes."
>
> Numbers 15:38–39

The Pharisees made their token tassels extra long to show how seriously they took the law of Moses and to emphasize their identity as sons of the covenant. But their show-off dedication had become nothing more than a means to inflate their pride.

The Pharisees anticipated the arrival of a conquering Messiah. Their tradition said He would come suddenly to His temple. Indeed, He had arrived, but not as they had expected. Jesus forcefully handed down what could very well be the sharpest rebuke recorded in Scripture. Eight times He uttered "woe," an exclamation used to express deep, anguished sorrow over something grievous. Seven times He called them "scribes and Pharisees, hypocrites." Five times He called them "blind." And in this stinging indictment, Jesus spelled out a detailed catalog of sins that had been plainly evident for years but had gone unchecked for fear of retribution. But no more. The true

Messiah had come to take His stand for truth in the place where truth was being trampled.

The gleaming white marble walls of the temple resonated with Jesus' voice as He closed His case against the Pharisees, pronouncing severe judgment.

> "Woe to you, scribes and Pharisees, hypocrites! For you build the tombs of the prophets and adorn the monuments of the righteous, and say, 'If we had been living in the days of our fathers, we would not have been partners with them in shedding the blood of the prophets.' So you testify against yourselves, that you are sons of those who murdered the prophets. Fill up, then, the measure of the guilt of your fathers. You serpents, you brood of vipers, how will you escape the sentence of hell?
>
> "Therefore, behold, I am sending you prophets and wise men and scribes; some of them you will kill and crucify, and some of them you will scourge in your synagogues, and persecute from city to city, so that upon you may fall the guilt of all the righteous blood shed on earth, from the blood of righteous Abel to the blood of Zechariah, the son of Berechiah, whom you murdered between the temple and the altar. Truly I say to you, all these things will come upon this generation."
>
> Matthew 23:29–36

The Pharisees and Sadducees would have seized Jesus on the spot were it not for the thousands who openly supported Him. For the next several weeks He traveled freely around the city and taught regularly in the temple, protected from assassination by His immense popularity. His enemies would have to catch Him alone and unaware, but for that they would need help. They needed someone on the inside.

ENDURING LESSONS FOR TRUTH TELLERS

Few weapons against evil can rival the sword of truth. Though readily available to anyone brave enough to hold it, few will. And it's little wonder. The privilege of wielding so powerful a tool comes at great cost—misunderstandings, false accusations, broken relationships, loneliness, frustration. Furthermore, standing for what's right frequently involves terrifying bouts with self-doubt and even self-recrimination. Sometimes the choice to take truth by the handle results in glorious victory, but more often the counterstrike of evil comes with startling ferocity and lasting devastation.

For those who are called to grip the sword of truth, I offer four lessons from the example of Jesus.

First, *knowing your mission will help you stay focused on the goal.* Jesus clearly understood the reason for His coming to earth and never allowed popularity, success, opposition, threats, or even dissention within His ranks to distract Him. He remained steadfastly focused on that mission, though not without due care for those around Him. He worked hard to make the truth plain. He often repeated the invitation to embrace the truth. But He never allowed the failure of others to pull Him off course.

Second, *encountering evil requires confrontation.* Few people enjoy confrontation, but standing for the truth against evil will inevitably require it. And sometimes what must be said will be difficult to say as well as difficult for others to hear. Only rarely—perhaps once in a lifetime—will confrontation require the kind of severe rebuke Jesus brought against the Pharisees. The greater the evil, the stronger must be the confrontation. In general, I advise kindness unless a kind approach is irresponsible, but never kindness at the expense of plain talk.

Be prepared to state the truth plainly.

Third, *boldness in the course of a noble fight is worth the risk.* Standing for truth requires boldness. Some will be offended by it, so expect to be criticized for style when the opposition can find no fault with content. Furthermore, boldness may require strong action to accompany strong speech. You may have to quit a job, end a relationship, confront a powerful opponent, cope with a fear, deal with threats, perhaps even face certain defeat. Don't back down. If you stand on truth, you'll only regret your timidity later, but you'll never regret being bold.

Fourth, *truth telling offers no guarantee of victory.* We live in a world that does not operate according to God's rules. The present world system punishes good deeds and rewards those who choose evil. In the words of James Russell Lowell, "Truth forever on the scaffold; wrong forever on the throne."[2] And, unfortunately, truth tellers often find themselves on the receiving end of the most outrageous abuse imaginable. So be realistic. Take courage. Your stand on truth will not likely be vindicated anytime soon or even in your lifetime. To finish Lowell's line: "Yet that scaffold sways the future, and, behind the dim unknown, standeth God within the shadow, keeping watch above his own."[3]

A two-fisted grip on the sword of truth, while sacrificial, does offer great reward. Truth grants freedom from guilt and shame. Truth breeds contentment, instills confidence, stimulates creativity, fosters intimacy, encourages honesty, inspires courage, and sets people free. But, most importantly, it puts us on God's side of the issue. We have His promise that He will amply reward any sacrifice that truth demands, if not in this life, then certainly the next.

Chapter Twelve

Betrayed and Arrested

K eep your eye on that one," the neighbors said. "He'll be quite the man of God someday." The people of Kerioth, a city in southern Judea, believed Judas would represent them well in the struggle for independence. He was born and raised in the rugged territory where mighty King David learned to become Israel's greatest shepherd. His father, Simon Iscariot, had earned fame as a freedom fighter under the previous regime. Even the name Judas bristled with rugged heroism. As one commentator notes, "Judah, or Judas, was the name of one of the twelve sons of Jacob in the Old Testament, and the brilliant uprising for independence in 164 BC was led by a man named Judas. This Judas Maccabaeus was looked upon by all Jews as a sort of George Washington."[1]

Judas Iscariot received his surname from his father, and it could have referred to the place of his upbringing. In Aramaic, *Ish-keriot* meant "man of Kerioth." However, Acts 21:38 refers to *sicarios* as a radical freedom fighter called a "dagger bearer," a member of a Jewish sect that thought nothing of assassinating Romans or anyone else collaborating with Rome. Whether or not Judas had been one of these extremists, his heritage suggests that he was looking for a Messiah who would secure freedom for Israel again.

As a son of the tribe of Judah, raised in the heart of Judea, and bearing the honored name Judas—could there have been a more loyal Jew in all of Israel?

Many would have seen Jesus' selection of the Twelve as curious. He didn't scour the temple for the best and the brightest of the scholars. He ignored the teeming schools of Pharisees who devoted their entire lives to winning God's favor. Instead, He chose James and John, who bore the nickname "sons of thunder," perhaps because of their bombastic tempers. He chose timid Andrew and brash Peter. He invited the Roman collaborator Levi to join Him and then called him Matthew, which means "gift of God." He picked cynical Nathaniel and Thomas, known for their questions and doubts. He hand-selected working-class men who did little to conceal their flaws, and all eleven of them from Galilee as far as we know. Judas was the only selection that would have made sense to onlookers in his day—this fine, strong-hearted Zealot from Kerioth of Judea.

Judas received the same training, the same benefit of close association with the Son of God, even the same empowerment to heal the sick and condemn the agents of Satan who had taken control of certain men and women. He eventually inspired enough trust to hold and administer the group's treasury (John 13:29). But something was different down deep inside. Something occurred within the upstanding disciple that sent him down a very different path from the others. No one knows exactly when it happened, although Jesus offered a clue.

After the five thousand men and their families filled their bellies on the abundance Jesus had multiplied in the hill country, they wondered how they might bring down the present government and install Jesus as their king. When Judas heard this, his heart probably skipped a beat. *This is it! They've accepted their future king! The end of Rome will be the beginning of the new kingdom!* But "Jesus, perceiving that they were intending to come and take Him by force to make Him king, withdrew again to the mountain by Himself alone" (John 6:15).

This must have confused Judas as he tramped down to the Sea of Galilee with the other disciples and boarded the boat as his master had instructed. Judas was alone with his secret thoughts. The magic hour for Jesus' ascension to the throne had slipped by. Then, as Jesus sat to teach in Capernaum, He deliberately winnowed His true disciples from those who were merely hungry for power or physical abundance. Many of them saw His feeding the multitude as a sign that He would fill the breadbaskets of every home in Israel, but Jesus clarified His teaching for those willing to hear:

> "For My flesh is true food, and My blood is true drink. He who eats My flesh and drinks My blood abides in Me, and I in him. As the living Father sent Me, and I live because of the Father, so he who eats Me, he also will live because of Me. This is the bread which came down out of heaven; not as the fathers ate and died; he who eats this bread will live forever."
>
> John 6:55–58

Those who were unwilling to see that true abundance comes through "abiding" began to grumble, "This is a difficult statement; who can listen to it?" (John 6:60). Jesus turned to the Twelve and called for them to decide between remaining with Him and departing with the others. The resulting exchange suggests that something shifted within Judas.

> So Jesus said to the twelve, "You do not want to go away also, do you?" Simon Peter answered Him, "Lord, to whom shall we go? You have words of eternal life. We have believed and have come to know that You are the Holy One of God." Jesus answered them, "Did I Myself not choose you, the twelve, and yet one of you is a devil?" Now He meant Judas the son of Simon Iscariot, for he, one of the twelve, was going to betray Him.
>
> John 6:67–71

Something prompted John, writing some sixty years later, to single out Judas. It must have stung when the beloved disciple, decades later, reflected on the one who betrayed his Master. This would have been an ideal time for Judas to voice his concerns. Jesus created the ideal opportunity for Judas to say, *Help me, Lord. I'm the one. I've lost confidence in You and the seeds of resentment have germinated. I am afraid of where this will lead. Save me.* But he didn't. He remained silent and sullen as Peter spoke for the group and affirmed their loyalty.

THE DEADLY DOUBLE LIFE

Sometime after Jesus had raised Lazarus from the dead, He and His disciples traveled to Jerusalem in anticipation of the Jewish feasts of Passover and Unleavened Bread. And rather than lodge in the city, they chose to visit their friend Lazarus and his sisters, Martha and Mary. One evening, they reclined at the banquet table of a man in Bethany. Mark calls him "Simon the leper" (14:3) and Luke identifies him as a Pharisee (7:39). Lazarus attended as a guest while Martha helped serve, but Mary had not been invited in any capacity. Apparently, the Pharisee who would have been shunned in the temple as "unclean" did not approve of Mary because of her sin-stained past.

As Jesus enjoyed the meal and engaged Simon and his Pharisaical friends in debate, Mary slipped into the house unnoticed. She carried with her an alabaster jar of expensive perfume, which she used to anoint Jesus' head. Then something deep within her took over. Enormous gratitude for salvation from sin? Overwhelming grief for the ordeal He was about to suffer? She knelt over His feet, suddenly broke the alabaster jar, and emptied the perfume on Jesus' feet in a lavish gesture of worship. As she drenched His feet with her tears and dried them with her hair, the aroma filled the room and brought everything to a standstill.

Simon silently protested, "If this man were a prophet he would know who and what sort of person this woman is who is touching him, that she is a sinner" (Luke 7:39 NET). But Judas objected for another reason.

> "Why was this perfume not sold for three hundred denarii [three hundred day's wages] and given to poor people?" Now he said this, not because he was concerned about the poor, but because he was a thief, and as he had the money box, he used to pilfer what was put into it.
>
> John 12:5–6

Again, John could write of that so many years later. The truth could now be told. Judas, the trusted treasurer, had been embezzling the group's funds for some time. The secret thief couldn't bear the thought of nearly one year's salary disappearing through the cracks in the stone floor.

Secret sin has a way of warping the mind and twisting one's values grotesquely out of shape. Embezzlers rarely steal very much at first. Then, as the pilfering becomes habitual, and then ritualized, they must rationalize their sin in order to maintain some sense of dignity. Meanwhile, the cycle of compulsion and shame drives a wedge between their private thoughts and a carefully crafted public image, which they eventually accept as their true selves. When caught in their sin, embezzlers are almost always indignant, convinced that no one can see the true self they once chose to ignore and had long ago forgotten.

Of course, the same is true of all sin, not just embezzling. The gaping chasm between a public persona and a private self—what may be called a double life—always begins as a tiny crack, a decision to conceal sin. Sin abhors the light of truth; it demands secrecy of the sinner. And the only remedy is unguarded, genuine confession. Not merely to a minister, though it can be a good start, but to the person most harmed by the offense.

Judas had been cultivating a double life for months or quite possibly years. His charming religious facade kept a seething resentment safely concealed from the other disciples. No one suspected his secret sin or even thought to conduct an audit of the ministry funds. Even his warped values appeared pious to his companions. When he lashed out at Mary's "waste," he somehow managed to pull the other disciples into the denunciation. Before long, the majority of the house stood in condemnation of Mary for one reason or another.

Jesus wasn't fooled. He saw the truth and quickly took command of the situation. He first addressed the hypocrisy of Simon with a parable, and then turned to give the Twelve a severe dressing down for their shortsighted response to Mary's spontaneous and extravagant worship. Even though Jesus rebuked the disciples as a group, Judas felt the sting of Jesus' words more keenly, not only because he led the chorus of critics but because of his pride.

When you encounter a proud person, beware; you face grave danger. Pride is but a paper-thin, glossy veneer disguising layers of private shame. And some people polish theirs to a mirror finish so that any criticism will be safely reflected onto others. Anyone who successfully penetrates this gleaming barrier and glimpses the underlying truth finds himself the bearer of a deadly secret. Then the arrogant person feels compelled to destroy anyone who knows the shameful truth he or she has labored so diligently to conceal and ignore.

Soon after the banquet, perhaps even before midnight, the resentment of Judas eroded into bitterness and, by dawn, had turned to murder.

> Then one of the twelve, named Judas Iscariot, went to the chief priests and said, "What are you willing to give me to betray Him to you?" And they weighed out thirty pieces of silver to him. From then on he began looking for a good opportunity to betray Jesus.
>
> Matthew 26:14–16

The Gospel of Luke describes the betrayal in even more chilling terms.

> The chief priests and the scribes were seeking how they might put [Jesus] to death; for they were afraid of the people. And Satan entered into Judas who was called Iscariot, belonging to the number of the twelve. And he went away and discussed with the chief priests and officers how he might betray Him to them. They were glad and agreed to give him money. So he consented, and began seeking a good opportunity to betray Him to them apart from the crowd.
>
> Luke 22:2–6

I don't pretend to know the full meaning of Luke's description, "Satan entered into Judas," but several facts are clear. This involved more than the mere influence of evil; it was personal. Of the twelve disciples, Satan chose the one who nurtured secret sin and cultivated a double life. Clearly, as the gap grows between one's public and private self, Satan finds greater freedom to work. Judas created a doorway and Satan invisibly slipped in.

Several commentators describe the relationship between Judas and Satan similarly:

Frederick Godet: "[Satan] entered into him so as to take entire possession of his will."[2]

A.T. Robertson: "Judas evidently opened the door of his heart and let Satan in. Then Satan took charge and he became a devil as Jesus said."[3]

John Calvin: "Luke means that he was at that time wholly given up to Satan, so that, like a desperate man, he violently sought [Jesus'] destruction. He is said to enter into the reprobate, when he takes possession of all their senses, overthrows the fear of God, extinguishes the light of reason, and destroys every feeling of shame."[4]

Darrell Bock, my colleague at Dallas Theological Seminary, has written perhaps the finest scholarly work on the Gospel of Luke currently available. Of Judas's resolute defection to the side of evil, Bock writes,

> Judas does not act alone. Deception has infiltrated the camp. The passage does not explain how this happened or what may have led to it. What is important is that the subsequent events occur because Satan has his way with Judas. No matter what the devil promises, Satan's entry into one's life is destructive. For when Satan enters a life, he leads the person in sinister directions.[5]

Beware the temptation to dismiss Satan as a remnant of more superstitious times. His primary weapon is deception, and he'd like nothing more than to have everyone think he's merely the figment of medieval imagination or the product of Hollywood hype. The scaly, horned monster you see flickering across the screen is the product of an animator's imagination, not reality. Like sin itself, Satan appeals to the senses. He originated and perfected the art of disguising evil as good.

No one can say for certain what Judas knew at the moment he became Satan's tool. He undoubtedly thought his desire to free Israel from the tyranny of Rome justified almost any means necessary. Even the thought of betraying a faithful friend didn't weigh on his conscience.

A FINAL OFFERING OF PEACE

Passover was just around the corner. The paschal meal marked the beginning of the eight-day celebration, which always occurred on the fourteenth day of the first month in the Jewish lunar calendar. But preparations always began well in advance. For weeks, Jews from all over Israel and across the empire ascended to the Holy City to find lodging and to prepare for the most significant meal of the year.

As Jesus had instructed, the disciples selected a sacrificial lamb and then located a secluded private room on the second floor of someone's home. In keeping with Jewish law, they began purging the room of any trace of leaven (yeast) two full days before Passover, which, on this particular year, began at sundown on Thursday. By midday all work came to an end as a representative of each family carried his lamb to the temple. At about 3 p.m., a Levite blew the ram's horn, worshipers filled the temple court, and the massive gates closed behind the men. Each worshiper then killed his own lamb, skinned it, and drained its blood into a basin.

While this sounds brutal to the twenty-first-century reader who buys packaged meat from the grocery store, this was how any meal involving meat began in the first century. On Passover, however, the lamb bore special significance and was killed in the temple to consecrate it as a substitute. The blood was drained into a basin held by a priest who then splashed it against the base of the altar to signify atonement for sin. The fat and kidneys were surrendered for burning on the altar as a part of the "peace offering," which signified the friendship between God and the worshiper.

After the sacrifice was complete, each household representative slung the paschal lamb over his shoulder, took it home, and roasted the meat in preparation for dinner. In keeping with the instructions given for the first Passover in Egypt, the disciples smeared some of the blood on the doorposts and lintel of the main entrance and prepared the other elements of the ritual meal: bitter herbs, unleavened bread, and wine.

Thursday evening, just before sundown, the Master and His disciples arrived in their festive, white tunics. As they entered the room, a servant should have been available to help them loosen their sandals and rinse their feet. But they were alone. The disciples chattered and laughed as each lay down on a cushion and propped himself on one elbow near the table. Only two of them knew this would be their last meal together: Jesus and His betrayer.

After Jesus settled into the honored place reserved for Him at the head of the table, He lit a ceremonial lamp to signify the end of work and the beginning of celebration. He filled a cup of wine, the first of four ceremonial cups for the evening, and held it up. He gave thanks to the Father for His faithfulness to Israel and then dedicated the evening to remembering the Exodus. As each man drained his cup and then reached for a bowl of water for the first ceremonial washing of hands, Jesus stood up, removed His outer tunic, and wrapped a towel around His waist. After retrieving the pitcher and basin from the servant's station, He assumed a servant's position at one disciple's feet, rinsed them clean, dried them with the towel, and then silently moved to the next. As He knelt before Peter, the brash disciple pulled them away and said, "Never shall You wash my feet!"

Jesus replied, "The one who has bathed needs only to wash his feet, but is completely clean. And you disciples are clean, but not every one of you." (For Jesus knew the one who was going to betray him. For this reason he said, "Not every one of you is clean.")

So when Jesus had washed their feet and put his outer clothing back on, he took his place at the table again and said to them, "Do you understand what I have done for you? You call me 'Teacher' and 'Lord,' and do so correctly, for that is what I am. If I then, your Lord and Teacher, have washed your feet, you too ought to wash one another's feet. For I have given you an example—you should do just as I have done for you. I tell you the solemn truth, the slave is not greater than his master, nor is the one who is sent as a messenger greater than the one who sent him. If you understand these things, you will be blessed if you do them.

"What I am saying does not refer to all of you. I know the ones I have chosen. But this is to fulfill the [prophetic] scripture, 'The one who eats my bread has turned against me.'"

John 13:10–18 NET

The disciples sat and blinked in confused silence as Jesus continued to teach. But after a few moments, they witnessed that grief had overtaken Him.

"Truly, truly, I say to you, that one of you will betray Me."

John 13:21

The disciples burst into animated conversation, debating the meaning of the words and speculating which of them He meant. During the commotion, Peter gestured to John, who reclined next to Jesus and mouthed, "Ask Him who it is." Jesus replied, "The one for whom I shall dip the morsel and give it to him" (John 13:26). And with that, He took a piece of vegetable, dipped it in a bowl of saltwater representing the tears shed by Israel during their slavery in Egypt, and deliberately placed it in the mouth of Judas.

Judas smiled as he received the traditional gesture of friendship and, as he chewed, Jesus said loud enough for everyone to hear, "What you do, do quickly." The morsel slid down the bitter disciple's throat. The spirit of Satan took full control as he rose to complete his despicable mission. He slipped out of the room into the darkness of night. Few took notice as Judas left the room and Jesus returned to His place to begin a series of lessons on love, abiding, fellowship, the future coming of God's Holy Spirit, and how His own sacrificial death will establish a new kingdom covenant.

While they were eating, Jesus took bread, and after giving thanks he broke it, gave it to his disciples, and said, "Take, eat, this is my body." And after taking the cup and giving thanks, he gave it to them, saying, "Drink from it, all of you, for this is my blood, the blood of the covenant, that is poured out for many for the forgiveness of sins. I tell you, from now on I will not drink of this fruit of the vine until that day when I drink it new with you in my Father's kingdom."

Matthew 26:26–29 NET

The prospect of that kingdom launched the disciples into yet another debate as to who was most qualified to fill which official posts once Jesus became king. Jesus squelched the argument with the prediction that He would be arrested, tortured, and executed . . . alone. Simon Peter protested, "Even though all may fall away because of You, I will never fall away" (Matthew 26:33), clearly implying he loved Jesus more than any of the other disciples. Jesus refused to let that statement go by without a reply.

> "Simon, Simon, behold, Satan has demanded permission to sift you like wheat; but I have prayed for you, that your faith may not fail; and you, when once you have turned again, strengthen your brothers." But he said to Him, "Lord, with You I am ready to go both to prison and to death!" And He said, "I say to you, Peter, the rooster will not crow today until you have denied three times that you know Me."
>
> Luke 22:31–34

Sometime they had left the Upper Room and made their way to a familiar retreat, a private garden called Gethsemane on the Mount of Olives, just across the Kidron Valley from Jerusalem. Soon after passing through the entrance of the little garden, Jesus asked His disciples to pray for Him while He sought comfort from His Father. He asked Peter, James, and John to follow Him a little farther and said, "My soul is deeply grieved, to the point of death; remain here and keep watch with Me" (Matthew 26:38). Then He disappeared into the darkness.

THE VIOLENT KISS

In another part of town, a few of the more prominent religious leaders left their own Passover meals to meet with Judas and plan the arrest of Jesus. Fear of His immense popularity kept them from acting before, but the time was perfect. Because it was a holiday, hopefully everyone would be preoccupied. Judas knew where Jesus would be alone and unprotected by throngs of followers. It was night, so they could overwhelm the Twelve and seize Jesus before anyone could react.

The chief priests and Pharisees assembled a small contingent of temple guards, but Caiaphas and the Sadducees weren't satisfied. To be certain nothing

would go wrong, they petitioned the procurator for a cohort of Roman sol-
diers, six hundred heavily armed men of war! When the troops were assembled,
Judas revealed where they would find his rabbi and proposed a plan of attack.
"Whomever I kiss, He is the one; seize Him and lead Him away under guard"
(Mark 14:44).

Meanwhile, Jesus wrestled with temptation. The terror of His coming
ordeal gripped Him mercilessly. His blood dripped like sweat through the
pores of His skin. As He stumbled through the darkness at Gethsemane,
occasionally staggering and falling, thoughts kept returning to challenge
His resolve. Why should He have to suffer on behalf of humanity? No
moral imperative required God to sacrifice His Son. He would be no less
holy or righteous if He allowed the race of sin-sick humans to suffer the
just consequences of their own rebellion. Nothing compelled Jesus to
complete the mission—nothing, that is, except love for the people He had
made and obedience to His Father.

"My Father, if it is possible, let this cup pass from Me; yet not as I will,
but as You will" (Matthew 26:39). But no sooner would Jesus submit to
the plan of the Father than the temptation would seize Him again. No
fewer than three distinct times would He have to submit. Each temptation
was met with the same resolve: "Not as I will, but as You will."

Jesus periodically emerged from the dark recesses of the garden to find
His disciples sleeping instead of praying. "Are you still sleeping and resting? Behold, the hour is at hand and the Son of Man is being betrayed into
the hands of sinners. Get up, let us be going; behold, the one who betrays
Me is at hand!" (Matthew 26:45–46). Indeed, while Jesus prayed and the
men dozed, a small army directed by Judas surrounded the garden and
closed around it like a noose.

Just then, Judas emerged out of the shadows alone. "Hail, Rabbi!" He
bowed to his Master and began smothering Jesus' hands and cheeks with
nervous, enthusiastic kisses. Incredulous, Jesus responded, "Judas, are you
betraying the Son of Man with a kiss?" (Luke 22:48). "Friend, do what
you have come for" (Matthew 26:50). But Judas stood silent and motionless. He had done his part. Finally, Jesus moved away and called into the
darkness, "Whom do you seek?"

"Jesus the Nazarene," a voice shouted back.

"I am He."

The glimmer of torches emerged from the darkness and cautiously weaved their way through the trees as the disciples instinctively formed a circle around Jesus. Peter quietly drew a short sword from its sheath and hid it in the folds of his tunic. Eventually, the light of a hundred or more flames flooded the clearing and glinted off a forest of swords and spears.

Jesus searched the faces in the crowd for a commanding officer. "Whom do you seek?"

The captain of the temple guard stepped forward. "Jesus the Nazarene."

"I told you that I am He; so if you seek Me, let these go their way."

The captain motioned and three men moved toward Jesus with a set of chains. Suddenly, Peter flung his sword high above his head, lunged toward the lead soldier, and brought it down hard, aiming for the center of his head. The blade glanced off the side of his helmet and lopped off his exposed right ear. Peter drew back for another lunge when Jesus shouted, "Stop! No more of this" (Luke 22:51). "Put the sword into the sheath; the cup which the Father has given Me, shall I not drink it?" (John 18:11).

Jesus tenderly reached for the injured soldier, who stood clutching the side of his head, and gently pulled his hand away. As He repositioned the dangling mass of flesh, He said to no one in particular, "Have you come out with swords and clubs as you would against a robber? While I was with you daily in the temple, you did not lay hands on Me; but this hour and the power of darkness are yours" (Luke 22:52–53).

Once the man's ear had been restored, Jesus held out His arms and allowed a soldier to place irons on His wrists and ankles. By the time the soldiers led Jesus down the side of the mountain toward Jerusalem, most of the disciples had scattered and fled into the night. No one was quite sure what had happened to Judas.

The trials of Jesus before the religious leaders proved that He was condemned even before His arrest, which, for some reason, came as a surprise to Judas. Overcome with remorse, he returned to his fellow conspirators and said, "I have sinned by betraying innocent blood," to which they responded, "What is that to us? See to that yourself!" (Matthew 27:4). Judas tried to return the money, but the chief priests refused to accept the thirty silver coins they had paid.

Judas went straight from the court to stand outside the sanctuary, where only priests could enter, and flung his blood money through the door. The bag landed on the floor of the holy place with a loud thump. The traitor, now unable to live with his sin yet unwilling to repent of it, went out, found a remote tree growing over a cliff, and that very night hanged himself from it.

In death, Judas failed to make the necessary connection between remorse and repentance, just as he had in life. The years he spent with Jesus had taught him nothing. His tragic choice to end his life rather than confess his sin and seek forgiveness merely consummated the hypocritical double life he had been cultivating for months. In the end, Judas died as he had lived, entangled in a secret love affair with sin.

LESSONS FOR THE JUDAS IN ALL OF US

Judas will forever be remembered as the most heinous traitor of all time. However, we are foolish to think that his story cannot become ours. Despite all the advantages he enjoyed as a close associate of Jesus, the promising young disciple became a Satan-possessed monster. And if we think we could never become something so despicable, we have failed to heed the warning of Scripture. Secret sin is an indiscriminant killer, and those who think they are immune are the most vulnerable of all.

Four timely principles worth our consideration emerge from the tragic example of Judas.

First, *association with godliness is no guarantee that we will become godly.* Joining a healthy church and cultivating relationships with spiritually mature people should be a priority. We need healthy influences. However, associating with mature believers will not nourish the soul any more than merely sitting at a table in a restaurant will nourish the body. To grow wise and to develop spiritually, we must personally take in what Jesus has offered. For that to occur, we must submit to the truth we receive through His Word. Otherwise, we deceive ourselves and become our own worst enemy. A quaint, old English couplet says it all:

Still, as of old,
Man by himself is priced;
For thirty pieces Judas sold
Himself, not Christ.[6]

Second, *moral corruption in secret is deadlier than visible moral corruption.* There is no cancer deadlier than one that goes undetected. The same is true of sin. Keeping our sinful nature carefully concealed keeps us from applying the remedy Jesus provided through the gift of salvation. One of His disciples later wrote, "If we confess our sins, He is faithful and righteous to forgive us our sins and to cleanse us of all unrighteousness" (1 John 1:9). Failure to confess and receive forgiveness forces us to cope with the deadly effects of sin in ways that are sure to cause more damage later. In the case of Judas, it consumed him.

Third, *Satan and his demons are looking for any opportunity to work against the Lord.* Several passages of Scripture teach that the person who bears unresolved sin is an ideal vessel by which the Devil can attack the people and plans of God (Genesis 4:6–7; Ephesians 4:25–27; 5:15–16; 1 Peter 5:6–8). At first, the person appears to be immune, but when Satan has done all the damage he can do, he allows the vessel to be consumed by the sin it carried.

Fourth, *no sorrow can compare to the remorse of one who discovers too late that he's misunderstood Jesus and spurned His love.* Satan's primary tool is deception, which he uses to twist unresolved sin and selfish motivation to serve his purposes. And once he's finished using someone, he cruelly unmasks the truth to reveal the consequences of his or her foolish choices. The flood of shame, humiliation, regret, self-condemnation, and hopelessness can be overwhelming.

Jesus, on the other hand, said (and continues to say), "If you continue in My word, then you are truly disciples of Mine; and you will know the truth, and the truth will make you free" (John 8:31–32).

Let me ask . . . where are you in all of this?

Chapter Thirteen

Analysis of a Courtroom Fiasco

From the moment Jesus came into the world until the day He left it, everyone who encountered Him struggled to answer the simple question, "Who is this man?"

Angels sang and shepherds worshiped and wise men prostrated themselves, and while Mary "treasured these things," she nevertheless could only "ponder them" (Luke 2:19). Jesus healed the sick and raised the dead, yet His own kinsmen from Nazareth rejected Him (Luke 4:28–30). Even John the Baptizer, the forerunner of the Christ, began to doubt as a result of Herod's persecution (Matthew 11:2–3). His own disciples—the twelve men He had chosen to train and equip to carry on the ministry—failed to see the significance of His miracles and only partially heard His repeated predictions concerning the meaning and purpose of His death. One of them not only failed to recognize the true identity of Jesus, but he betrayed Him into the hands of evil men. And when the religious leaders bound the Son of God in chains and led Him away, the other disciples ran and hid.

The religious leaders in Jerusalem struggled with Jesus' identity at first but came to understand the significance of His ministry more fully than anyone.

They understood the significance of the prophecies (Matthew 2:4–6); some recognized His power as divine (John 3:1–2); others acknowledged His message as coming from God (Luke 20:21). Theirs was not a crisis of insight; they understood but deliberately chose to reject Him as their Messiah. The leaders resented His public and relentless criticism of their religiosity. They jealously clung to their political power and popular influence. They refused to relinquish their own pursuit of abundance for the kind God intended to bring through His King and His kingdom, so they plotted the murder of anyone who dared lay claim to the throne.

Jesus was too popular to assassinate. One word from the disciples might have ignited the powder keg of popular resentment that lay beneath Jerusalem. And the leaders dared not turn Him into a martyr for fear of making Him even more influential in death than in life. So they hatched a plan to discredit Him as a blaspheming kook and have Him publicly executed in the most shameful manner possible.

They needed to do everything out of the public eye, but that proved difficult. Jesus stopped traveling in public except when protected by the adoration of the multitudes. And no one except His closest companions knew where He would be most vulnerable to attack. So, when Judas approached them with his scheme, they quickly struck a bargain. They signed on to a nighttime arrest of Jesus in exchange for thirty silver coins—roughly four months' wages for an unskilled worker or the redemption price of a common slave.

From the first moment of His arrest, Jesus conducted Himself with utmost dignity yet never backed away from speaking the truth with gentle candor. "Have you come out with swords and clubs as you would against a robber? While I was with you daily in the temple, you did not lay hands on Me; but this hour and the power of darkness are yours" (Luke 22:52–53). Of course, they all knew what they had chosen to do was wrong or they would have done it by day and in full view of the multitudes. Nevertheless, Jesus understood His mission and that truth has its consequences. He never wavered. Looking at Peter, He said, "The cup which the Father has given Me, shall I not drink it?" (John 18:11).

THE MOCK TRIALS OF JESUS

The nighttime capture at Gethsemane initiated a series of six trials; three before the Jewish religious authorities and three before the civil authorities of Rome. As we shall see, all were illegal. And unlike most trials, these did not make the pursuit of truth their primary object.

First-century Israelites were, above all, a law-conscious people, and they maintained a strict procedure for hearing civil and criminal cases. A Jewish document called the Mishnah, compiled around AD 200, records the oral traditions handed down from one generation to another over several centuries. A portion of this document describes the guidelines that governed the Jewish ruling council, called the Sanhedrin, which heard cases, rendered judgment, and passed sentence on the guilty. This document very likely describes the traditions that governed the Sanhedrin during the time of Jesus. The Gospel accounts of Jesus' arrest and trials demonstrate that most if not all the rules of jurisprudence were blatantly ignored.

Here are eighteen specific laws governing cases like that of Jesus.[1]

- No trials were to occur during the night hours before the morning sacrifice (Mishnah: *Sanhedrin* 4:1).
- Trials were not to occur on the eve of a Sabbath or during festivals (Mishnah: *Sanhedrin* 4:1).
- All trials were to be public; secret trials were forbidden (Mishnah: *Sanhedrin* 1:6).
- All trials were to be held in the Hall of Judgment in the temple area (Mishnah: *Sanhedrin* 11:2).
- Capital cases required a minimum of twenty-three judges (Mishnah: *Sanhedrin* 4:1).
- An accused person could not testify against himself (Mishnah: *Sanhedrin* 3:3–4).
- Someone was required to speak on behalf of the accused (Mishnah: *Sanhedrin* 3:3–4).
- Conviction required the testimony of two or three witnesses to be in perfect alignment (Deuteronomy 17:6–7; 19:15–20).

The Trials of Jesus

Trial	Officiating Authority	Scripture	Accusations	Legality	Type	Result
1	Annas, former High Priest from AD 6–15	John 18:12–23	No specific charges were brought.	Illegal: No jurisdiction, Held at night, No charges, No witnesses, Abused during trial	Jewish and Religious	Jesus was found "guilty" of irreverance and sent to Caiaphas.
2	Caiaphas, High Priest from AD 18–36, and the Sanhedrin	Matthew 26:57–68, Mark 14:53–65, John 18:24	Jesus claimed to be the Messiah, the Son of God, which they deemed blasphemy.	Illegal: Held at night, False witnesses, No formal charge, Abused during trial	Jewish and Religious	Jesus was declared "guilty" of blasphemy and held for sentencing until morning.
3	The Sanhedrin	Mark 15:1, Luke 22:66–71	As a continuation of the earlier trial before the Sanhedrin, the charges remained the same.	Illegal: Accusation changed, No witnesses, Improper vote	Jewish and Religious	Jesus was sentenced to be turned over to Romans for execution.
4	Pontius Pilate, Governor of Judea from AD 26–36	Matthew 27:11–14, Mark 15:2–5, Luke 23:1–7, John 18:28–38	Jesus was charged with treason and sedition against Rome.	Illegal: Found "not guilty," yet kept in custody, No defense representation, Abused during trial	Roman and Civil	Jesus was declared "not guilty" and passed off on Herod Antipas to find a loophole.
5	Herod Antipas, Governor of Galilee from 4 BC–AD 39	Luke 23:8–12	No specific charges were brought. Jesus was questioned at length by Herod.	Illegal: No jurisdiction, No specific charges, Abused during trial	Roman and Civil	Jesus was mistreated, mocked, falsely accused, and returned to Pilate without a decision made.
6	Pontius Pilate	Matthew 27:15–26, Mark 15:6–15, Luke 23:13–25, John 18:39–19:16	As a continuation of the earlier trial before Pilate, the charges remained the same.	Illegal: Declared "not guilty," yet condemned	Roman and Civil	Jesus was declared "not guilty" but sentenced to be crucified to mollify the angry mob. Simultaneously, a man guilty of murder, treason, and sedition was released.

- Witnesses for the prosecution were to be examined and cross-examined extensively (Mishnah: *Sanhedrin* 4:1).
- Capital cases were to follow a strict order, beginning with arguments by the defense, then arguments for conviction (Mishnah: *Sanhedrin* 4:1).
- All Sanhedrin judges could argue for acquittal, but not all could argue for conviction (Mishnah: *Sanhedrin* 4:1).
- The high priest should not participate in the questioning (Mishnah: *Sanhedrin* 3:6).
- Each witness in a capital case was to be examined individually, not in the presence of other witnesses (Mishnah: *Sanhedrin* 3:6).
- The testimony of two witnesses found to be in contradiction rendered both invalid (Mishnah: *Sanhedrin* 5:2).
- Voting for conviction and sentencing in a capital case was to be conducted individually, beginning with the youngest, so younger members would not be influenced by the voting of the elder members (Mishnah: *Sanhedrin* 4:2).
- Verdicts in capital cases were to be handed down only during daylight hours (Mishnah: *Sanhedrin* 4:1).
- The members of the Sanhedrin were to meet in pairs all night, discuss the case, and reconvene for the purpose of confirming the final verdict and imposing sentence (Mishnah: *Sanhedrin* 4:1).
- Sentencing in a capital case was not to occur until the following day (Mishnah: *Sanhedrin* 4:1).

THE FIRST TRIAL (JOHN 18:12–23)

Once the commander of the temple guard had Jesus bound, he and the small army led Him down the Mount of Olives, across the Kidron Valley, into Jerusalem, and straight to the home of Annas. Though the old patriarch no longer ruled as high priest, he remained the head of a vast empire of organized corruption in Jerusalem. "He and his family were proverbial for their rapacity and greed."[2]

When Jesus cleansed the temple of what He called "robbers," several religious authorities demanded to know, "By what authority are You doing these things, and who gave You this authority?" (Matthew 21:23). Understandably, they could not imagine one man challenging the Annas crime family. This was why Jesus wasn't taken to jail or to the Jewish council or to the duly appointed high priest or even to the Roman procurator. He stood alone before the godfather of Jerusalem.

Though the disciples had all fled, two returned to learn the fate of their Master. Peter and John followed the cohort at a distance and learned where they took Jesus. Because John knew Annas, he managed to find his way into the courtyard and then the great hall where Jesus would be arraigned. Peter, on the other hand, lurked in the shadows, taking great care to remain anonymous. So when the outer gates to the courtyard closed, he found himself locked out.

John instructed the gatekeeper to admit Peter and then returned to the trial. As Peter slipped through the gate, the girl asked, "You're not one of this man's disciples too, are you?" (John 18:17 NET). "I am not," Peter lied as he crossed the courtyard to join a group of citizens and soldiers around a fire.

The soldiers positioned Jesus before an empty chair in the great hall of Annas's house and then stood a few paces away on either side. After a short pause, Annas entered, fully dressed, even though it was a little after midnight. He took his seat and arranged his robes before raising his eyes to find Jesus looking straight into them.

> The high priest then questioned Jesus about His disciples, and about His teaching. Jesus answered him, "I have spoken openly to the world; I always taught in synagogues and in the temple, where all the Jews come together; and I spoke nothing in secret. Why do you question Me? Question those who have heard what I spoke to them; they know what I said."
>
> John 18:19–21

At first glance, Jesus appears to offer a curt response. In reality, He merely objected to no fewer than a half-dozen points of order in the proceedings. The trial took place at night, during the week of Passover, behind closed doors, and away from the temple. If Annas were going to pretend he had jurisdiction and presume to play the role of high priest, he was not to participate in questioning, and the answers he sought would have compelled the accused to testify against himself. Furthermore, as Jesus pointed out, witnesses should have been easy to find, but none had been summoned.

> When He had said this, one of the officers standing nearby struck Jesus, saying, "Is that the way You answer the high priest?" Jesus answered him, "If I have spoken wrongly, testify of the wrong; but if rightly, why do you strike Me?"
>
> John 18:22–23

Jesus again pointed to the fact that no one had testified against Him and that He wasn't guilty of anything more than allowing Annas to make a fool of himself. Clearly, the object of the trial was not to discover truth or render a just verdict, therefore Jesus refused to cooperate with the mockery they were making of Jewish law. Without another word, "Annas sent Him bound to Caiaphas" (John 18:24).

THE SECOND TRIAL
(MATTHEW 26:57–68; MARK 14:53–65; LUKE 22:63–65; JOHN 18:24)

The odd collection of household servants and temple soldiers had barely settled around the fire when the doors to the house suddenly opened. A detail of soldiers led Jesus across the courtyard as the servant-girl ran ahead of them to open the outer gates. The procession marched toward the temple and the home of Caiaphas, who had assembled a majority of the Sanhedrin.

The Sanhedrin was the supreme governing body of Israel, insofar as Rome allowed Jewish autonomy. This council of seventy elder statesmen and religious experts acted much like a modern Supreme Court and Parliament combined. They created laws and other rules of conduct. They managed the day-to-day operation of the temple. They also ruled on civil cases, minor criminal cases, and charges of religious misconduct. The council occasionally heard capital cases, but Rome retained exclusive right to carry out a death sentence. No one could be put to death for any crime unless convicted by a Roman official and only for a crime against the empire.

Because Jesus presented such a serious challenge to the authority of the Sanhedrin, Caiaphas had little trouble convening the council in the wee hours of the morning. While Annas questioned Jesus, most if not all of the seventy members filled a large upper chamber in the high priest's palace. They presumably met for the purpose of hearing a case against Jesus, but His destiny had been decided long before He arrived.

Again, the council failed to abide by its own jurisprudence. The trial was held in secret, at night, and in the high priest's palace instead of the council's meeting hall. Furthermore, no advocate for the accused had been provided.

Most likely because John came from a wealthy family, he was allowed to attend the second trial and would have gained entrance for Peter as well. But Peter preferred to keep his identity a secret. As the soldiers and a larger collection of servants sought refuge from the chilly night air around a fire, Peter avoided making eye contact and spoke as little as possible. However, one of the servants had apparently spoken to the gatekeeper at the home of Annas and had whispered the news to the others. Eventually, someone put the question to him directly.

> As Peter was below in the courtyard, one of the servant-girls of the high priest came, and seeing Peter warming himself, she looked at him and said, "You also were with Jesus the Nazarene." But he denied it, saying, "I neither know nor understand what you are talking about." And he went out onto the [vestibule leading from the gateway].
>
> Mark 14:66–68

Meanwhile, the Sanhedrin pressed their case against Jesus, which was itself a violation of the council's own rules. According to their law, the role of the Sanhedrin was to presume innocence and even argue for acquittal until accusers and corroborating witnesses left them no alternative than to convict the defendant. Witnesses were to be questioned individually and if their stories conflicted, both testimonies were to be thrown out. The high priest was to preside over the trial, facilitate debate among the seventy members, and was forbidden to question the accused. And no defendant was ever required to testify against himself. Nevertheless . . .

> The chief priests and the whole Council kept trying to obtain testimony against Jesus to put Him to death, and they were not finding any. For many were giving false testimony against Him, but their testimony was not consistent. Some stood up and began to give false testimony against Him, saying, "We heard Him say, 'I will destroy this temple made with hands, and in three days I will build another made without hands.'" Not even in this respect was their testimony consistent.
>
> Mark 14:55–59

The testimony was a half-truth and deliberately twisted the context of a lesson Jesus had given in the temple. After one of His many confrontations with Annas's racketeering operation, the Sadducees challenged Jesus, asking, "What sign do You show us as your authority for doing these things?" (John 2:18). In other words, "We operate under the authority of the high priest. Whom do you represent?" Jesus answered the question with a prediction— one by which He claimed both authority and superiority over the temple.

> Jesus answered them, "Destroy this temple, and in three days I will raise it up." The Jews then said, "It took forty-six years to build this temple, and will You raise it up in three days?" But He was speaking of the temple of His body.
>
> John 2:19–21

The witnesses also attached an epithet to the words of Jesus, intending to make Him guilty of blasphemy. The Hebrew phrase "made with hands" was a common reference to anything constructed for the purpose of idolatry. Jesus didn't use it in His lesson. Nevertheless, the irony of their false testimony struck a nerve with the council.

If Jesus had indeed disparaged the temple, the council would have had plenty of reason to censure Him. But it was not enough to stone Him under Jewish law and nowhere near enough to convince a Roman official that killing Him would serve the interests of the empire. Caiaphas and his minions needed more. If, on the other hand, Jesus claimed to be the Messiah, the Christ, the rightful King of Israel, they could portray Him as a threat to the wobbly political balance they and the procurator struggled to maintain.

> The high priest stood up and came forward and questioned Jesus, saying, "Do You not answer? What is it that these men are testifying against You?" But He kept silent and did not answer. Again the high priest was questioning Him, and saying to Him, "Are You the Christ, the Son of the Blessed One?" And Jesus said, "I am; and you shall see the Son of Man sitting at the right hand of Power, and coming with the clouds of heaven." Tearing his clothes, the high priest said, "What further need do we have of witnesses? You have heard the blasphemy; how does it seem to you?" And they all condemned Him to be deserving of death.
>
> Mark 14:60–64

Jesus not only affirmed the charge of Caiaphas, but He also quoted Psalm 110:1 and Daniel 7:13 to drive His messianic claim deep into the hearts of the corrupt religious leaders. If they were to convict Him of a crime, it would be the crime of being their Savior.

A casual observer might have been impressed by the religious zeal of Caiaphas, who "tore his robes and said, 'He has blasphemed!'" (Matthew 26:65). In reality, though, he and Annas wanted Jesus dead for two other reasons. First, Jesus dared to defy the high priest's sovereign control over the temple. Second, and more importantly, Jesus was bad for business.

To maintain at least the appearance of propriety, the council disbanded. According to their strict rules, the members were to withhold judgment until morning. In the meantime, they were to meet in pairs, share a sparse meal, and discuss the case exhaustively in preparation for a final ruling the following day. Instead, they took the time to vent their anger, one by one. The scene got ugly.

Then they spat in His face and beat Him with their fists; and others slapped Him, and said, "Prophesy to us, You Christ; who is the one who hit You?"

Matthew 26:67–68

The doors to Caiaphas's palace flung open, and the murmuring dignitaries spilled out into the courtyard. John emerged in time to find Peter embroiled in a debate with the crowd of servants and soldiers.

"Certainly this man also was with Him, for he is a Galilean too," the servants claimed (Luke 22:59).

Peter insisted, "I do not know what you are talking about" (Luke 22:60).

"Surely you too are one of them; for even the way you talk gives you away" (Matthew 26:73).

Peter began to swear oaths and call down divine curses upon himself if he were lying. "I do not know the man!" (Matthew 26:74).

Just then, the second call of a rooster drew Peter's attention to the east. The blue-grey seam that separates the black of night from the glow of dawn was just beginning to show along the horizon. And with the light of day came the realization that Peter had not only abandoned his Lord, but he had sought the camaraderie of those who desired to see Him dead. As the guards pushed Jesus outside, the commotion at the door drew Peter's attention and his eyes immediately locked onto those of his Master. Then a memory washed over him and rinsed him clean of any pride or confidence in his own faithfulness. The verbal flashback drove a sharp stake of shame into his heart:

"Simon, Simon, behold, Satan has demanded permission to sift you like wheat; but I have prayed for you, that your faith may not fail; and you, when once you have turned again, strengthen your brothers." But [Peter] said to Him, "Lord, with You I am ready to go both to prison and to death!" And He said, "I say to you, Peter, the rooster will not crow today until you have denied three times that you know Me."

Luke 22:31–34

197

Feeling the utter humiliation of his boast, "Even though all may fall away, yet I will not" (Mark 14:29), Peter fled the courtyard and wept bitterly for days.

THE THIRD TRIAL
(MATTHEW 27:1–2; MARK 15:1; LUKE 22:66-71)

By the time the Sanhedrin had adjourned for the night, the sun was rising on the next day, and they had found their charge: treason against Rome. They feared Jesus' popularity, supposing that a word from Him would spark a rebellion and bring the wrath of Rome down on all of them. More than three years prior to the trials, Caiaphas had inadvertently spoken a prophecy that he, himself, would fulfill.

> The chief priests and the Pharisees convened a council, and were saying, "What are we doing? For this man is performing many signs. "If we let Him go on like this, all men will believe in Him, and the Romans will come and take away both our place and our nation." But one of them, Caiaphas, who was high priest that year, said to them, "You know nothing at all, nor do you take into account that it is expedient for you that one man die for the people, and that the whole nation not perish."
>
> John 11:47–50

With the specific charge determined and the verdict already decided, the high priest summoned the council to the official place of judgment, a semicircular hall at the east end of the Royal Portico of the temple. The place was designed to resemble a threshing floor. In ancient times, the place where farmers separated wheat from chaff became the forum where all matters of justice were aired before the entire community.

Finally in the light of day, and finally in the proper venue, and finally before the eyes of the public, the third trial began. Still, the religious leaders violated their own rules. The arbiters of justice were also the accusers. No one advocated for the accused. The trial took place during the Feast of Unleavened Bread, part of the Passover festival. And they compelled the accused to testify against Himself. The purpose of the trial was merely show. The council quickly played out before the public what they had already rehearsed in private.

> When day came, the council of the elders of the people gathered together, both the chief priests and the experts in the law. Then they led Jesus away to their council and said, "If you are the Christ, tell us." But he said to them, "If I tell you, you will not believe, and if I ask you, you will not answer. But from now on the Son of Man will be seated at the right hand of the power of God." So they all said, "Are you the Son of God, then?" He answered them, "You say that I am."
>
> Luke 22:66–70 NET

Each time Jesus parted His lips to answer, He called attention to the impropriety of the proceedings without denying His claim to be the Messiah. He agreed to their assessment that He claimed the right of kingship, but He would not accept the implications they attached to the charge. Insurrection had never been a part of His plan.

Because truth had never been their object, the council closed the case against Jesus.

> Then they said, "Why do we need further testimony? We have heard it ourselves from his own lips!"
>
> Luke 22:71 NET

By the end of the third trial, after fishing for a suitable charge that would both convince the Roman governor and mollify the agitated Hebrew masses, the religious leaders had what they felt they needed. Jesus claimed to be the Christ, whom Jews widely regarded as their hope of expelling their Roman oppressors. Certainly, the empire would want to rid itself of a potential revolutionary; and if Jesus were executed, the people would reject Him as just another false Messiah. It was an ideal solution that brought together an unlikely alliance of Pharisees (mostly scribes and lay teachers), Sadducees (aristocratic chief priests), and Zealots (underground revolutionaries).

ENCOURAGEMENT THROUGH SUFFERING

Our historical perspective allows us to see with clarity what many in Jesus' day could not see. But He understood better than anyone that the trials were a ruse, nothing other than the machinations of corrupt men jealously guarding their power. And to make matters worse, they draped their outrageous behavior in the august robes of religious purity. How pathetic they must have appeared through the eyes of deity.

The religious authorities successfully cast Jesus in the role of villain and accepted the applause—even the admiration—of an unwary public. They successfully covered their tracks so that no one saw their impropriety, their lust for power, and their shameful conspiracy to destroy an innocent individual. Nor did the Hebrew people see the astounding blessings they were forfeiting by killing their Messiah. No one will ever know how God's plan would have unfolded if they had embraced Him.

Very few situations in life are more frustrating than suffering injustice alone and unnoticed. Feelings of outrage demand justice. Bitterness demands revenge. Hopelessness begs heaven for relief. Loneliness screams to be heard as a watching world stands aloof. During those dark, painful, lonely times, the silence from heaven can be deafening.

If this is presently your experience, rest assured, you are not alone. The Lord does see your suffering, and He will not allow it to go unanswered. He will see justice done, though perhaps not at the time or in the manner you would prefer. Nevertheless, the agony you suffer, though it feels overwhelming, will not go to waste. If you allow it, this experience can be the means by which God brings you His greatest blessings. George Matheson expressed this well in his book *Thoughts for Life's Journey*:

> My soul, reject not the place of thy prostration! It has ever been thy robbing-room for royalty. Ask the great ones of the past what has been the spot of their prosperity; they will say, "It was the cold ground on which I once was lying." Ask Abraham; he will point you to the sacrifice on Moriah. Ask Joseph; he will direct you to his dungeon. Ask Moses; he will date his fortune from his danger

in the Nile. Ask Ruth; she will bid you build her monument in the field of her toil. Ask David; he will tell you that his songs came from the night. Ask Job; and he will remind you that God answered him out of the whirlwind. Ask Peter; he will extol his submersion in the sea. Ask John; he will give the palm to Patmos. Ask Paul; he will attribute his inspiration to the light which struck him blind. Ask one more—the Son of Man. Ask Him whence has come His rule over the world. He will answer, "From the cold ground on which I was lying—the Gethsemane ground; I received My sceptre there." Thou too, my soul, shalt be garlanded by Gethsemane. The cup thou fain wouldst pass from thee will be thy coronet in the sweet by-and-by. The hour of thy loneliness will crown thee. The day of thy depression will regale thee. It is thy *desert* that will break forth into singing; it is the trees of thy silent *forest* that will clap their hands. . . .

The voice of God to thine evening will be this, "Thy treasure is hid in the ground where thou wert lying."[3]

The apostle Peter stood at a distance watching his Master endure the greatest injustice ever suffered. No one was ever more innocent than Jesus. Few were ever more hypocritical and corrupt than Annas and Caiaphas. Perhaps reflecting on how Jesus conducted Himself during that awful time, Peter later wrote to persecuted Christians, "What credit is there if, when you sin and are harshly treated, you endure it with patience? But if when you do what is right and suffer for it you patiently endure it, this finds favor with God" (1 Peter 2:20).

What are the messages in that to us twenty centuries later? Stop trying to be heard. Stop hoping for vindication. Speak the truth, in love and without apology, to whoever will listen. Expect to suffer for doing so. Then quietly and calmly submit yourself to the sovereign will of God.

Jesus accepted that He would not receive justice from men. He knew that the world was then—as it is now—dominated by sin and governed by fallen people. So He did not look to the courts for justice or to the approval of people for affirmation. He instead submitted Himself to the will of the Father. He spoke the truth and refused to allow anger or bitterness to distract anyone from seeing it—should anyone truly desire to see. Throughout the ordeal, He entrusted Himself to the One who will ultimately and inevitably judge every soul righteously. What a magnificent model to follow!

Chapter Fourteen

The Last Trials and Torture of Jesus

In AD 26, Emperor Tiberius retired to the resort island of Capri. From there, he would run his empire through Lucius Sejanus, whom he left in Rome to administer all the practical matters of government. Sejanus had worked hard to earn the assignment. He had taken a small regiment of the imperial bodyguard and transformed them into the Praetorian Guard, a powerful and influential arm of the Roman government. Furthermore, he deftly disposed of anyone who might challenge his rise to power, including the emperor's own son, Drusus.

Soon after becoming the de facto leader of Rome, Sejanus granted his friend, Pontius Pilate, a post that had become one of the most coveted in the empire: procurator of Judea. It came with great risks yet great political rewards for the one who did the job well. Sejanus needed someone strong, a man he could trust to bring stability to this crucial, volatile region.

The historian Philo of Alexandria described Pilate as "a man of a very inflexible disposition, and very merciless as well as very obstinate."[1] Pilate's disposition had served him well in previous assignments, but it nearly destroyed his career soon after assuming command in Judea. He, like most Romans, failed to appreciate the unique challenges that came with governing Jews. Not long after his arrival, he sent a clear message to Jerusalem that a new prefect was in town and that he would not be the pushover others had been. He sent an army from his headquarters in Caesarea to spend the winter in Jerusalem, ordering them to bear Caesar's image on their shields and display it in the public squares, just as they had everywhere else in the empire. Other procurators had honored Jewish law by avoiding the display of any "graven image" (Deuteronomy 4:15–18).

When the leaders in Jerusalem traveled en masse to Caesarea to stage a protest, Pilate found himself in an unenviable quandary. To remove the images would not only show weakness, but it might insult Caesar, who was to be worshiped like a god. Yet keeping peace was his primary responsibility, and the Jewish leaders wouldn't go home. Josephus described how the confrontation ended.

> On the sixth day [of the protest] he ordered his soldiers to have their weapons [hidden], while he came and sat upon his judgment seat, which seat was so prepared in the open place of the city, that it concealed the army that lay ready to oppress them: and when the Jews petitioned him again, he gave a signal to the soldiers to encompass them round, and threatened that their punishment should be no less than immediate death, unless they would leave off disturbing him, and go their ways home. But they threw themselves upon the ground, and laid their necks bare, and said they would take their death very willingly, rather than the wisdom of their laws should be transgressed; upon which Pilate was deeply affected with their firm resolution to keep their laws inviolable, and presently commanded the images to be carried back from Jerusalem to Cesarea.[2]

Another standoff, similar to this one, ended with a Jewish bloodbath, and within days a letter was on its way to Capri asking for Pilate's removal. By that time, Tiberius had discovered that Sejanus was responsible for his son's death and promptly executed him. With the citizens of Rome dragging the body of Sejanus around the streets in celebration, Pilate suddenly found himself without a friend in the world.

THE FOURTH TRIAL
(MATTHEW 27:11–14; MARK 15:2–5; LUKE 23:1–7; JOHN 18:28–38)

With the Jewish Passover celebration in full swing and Jerusalem packed with nearly ten times its normal population, Pilate took up residence in the Praetorium to ensure law and order. Nevertheless, he was surprised to hear the Jews clamoring for an audience during the feast. Their concern for ritual purity wouldn't allow them to enter the Roman building, so he had to meet them in the courtyard, which had nearly filled to capacity. Seventy-plus Jewish elders, dressed in their finest regalia, stood in a semicircle around a chained prisoner. The swelling and dried blood on the man's face and the angry crowd behind the elders let the procurator know he should take the early morning audience seriously.

> "What accusation do you bring against this Man?" They answered and said to him, "If this Man were not an evildoer, we would not have delivered Him to you." So Pilate said to them, "Take Him yourselves, and judge Him according to your law." The Jews said to him, "We are not permitted to put anyone to death."
>
> John 18:29–31

The original charges of heresy or blasphemy were religious concerns, and the Romans were remarkably flexible when it came to religions. They had hundreds of gods, unlike the obstinate Jews who insisted there was only one. But unless local beliefs stopped the flow of money into Roman coffers or local squabbles threatened stability in the region, procurators generally chose to remain aloof.

The Jewish leaders recognized that Rome cared only about Rome, so they would have to present Pilate with charges that portrayed Jesus a threat to the state.

> And they began to accuse Him, saying, "We found this man misleading our nation and forbidding to pay taxes to Caesar, and saying that He Himself is Christ, a King."
>
> Luke 23:2

Therefore Pilate entered again into the Praetorium, and summoned Jesus and said to Him, "Are You the King of the Jews?" Jesus answered, "Are you saying this on your own initiative, or did others tell you about Me?" Pilate answered, "I am not a Jew, am I? Your own nation and the chief priests delivered You to me; what have You done?" Jesus answered, "My kingdom is not of this world. If My kingdom were of this world, then My servants would be fighting so that I would not be handed over to the Jews; but as it is, My kingdom is not of this realm." Therefore Pilate said to Him, "So You are a king?" Jesus answered, "You say correctly that I am a king. For this I have been born, and for this I have come into the world, to testify to the truth. Everyone who is of the truth hears My voice." Pilate said to Him, "What is truth?"

John 18:33–38

Truth. Let's face it; the Roman world was not much different from ours today. Pilate didn't rise to his place of power and prominence by following truth wherever it led. And when truth becomes the servant of expediency, success no longer becomes a matter of seeking the light and walking in it, but discovering which shadows will offer the best protection from having to live honestly. Choosing between truth and expediency is how one chooses which kingdom he or she will serve.

Jesus presented Pilate with a choice—the same choice He offers us: compromise what you know to be truth and preserve your place in the kingdom of Tiberius, or walk in the light of truth and receive unseen rewards in God's kingdom. Apparently, the bruises around Jesus' eyes didn't make the latter option especially attractive.

And when [Pilate] had said this, he went out again to the Jews and said to them, "I find no guilt in Him."

John 18:38

Pilate probably wondered how these conundrums always seemed to find him despite his best effort to remain neutral. With Sejanus dead, he would not likely survive another controversy. Yet there stood before him a man clearly not guilty of any crime against Rome and a riotous crowd insisting He was a serious threat to Tiberius. They had appealed to Rome many times and always seemed to gain the upper hand. And the last letter he received from Tiberius made it clear he had better respect the Jews' religious sensibilities or suffer the end of his career.

> But they kept on insisting, saying, "He stirs up the people, teaching
> all over Judea, starting from Galilee even as far as this place."
>
> Luke 23:5

As Pilate sat reeling in yet another impossible political quandary, a single word rose above the clamor to offer him hope: *Galilee.* Jesus was from Galilee!

Not far away from the Praetorium, Herod Antipas, the tetrarch of Galilee, had taken up residence for the Passover celebration. The Jewish aristocracy recognized him as a leader. The jurisdiction was his. It was a perfect way to pawn the problem off on someone else.

THE FIFTH TRIAL (LUKE 23:8–12)

Herod Antipas was the son of Herod the Great and had inherited many of his qualities, among them a great love of building and an especially cruel disposition. Despite an impressive list of buildings and cities to his credit—including a capital city named for Tiberius—Antipas was a caricature of Roman debauchery. His rule consisted mostly of self-indulgence and frivolous parties. For example, he drove his current wife away and then consummated an affair with his brother's wife, Herodias, by marrying her. His actions not only violated a marriage treaty but flouted Jewish law, drawing criticism from John the Baptizer. Then, at one of Herod's parties, "the daughter of Herodias danced before them and pleased Herod, so much that he promised with an oath to give her whatever she asked" (Matthew 14:6–7). She asked for the Baptizer's head on a platter, which Herod promptly delivered.

Antipas cleverly balanced his Roman ties with the appearance of loyalty to his people. During several of the controversies with Pilate, he had advocated for the Jewish leaders and had successfully brought the wrath of Tiberius to bear. This made him an important potential ally for Pilate, who needed a powerful friend. Pilate knew that Herod "had wanted to see [Jesus] for a long time because he had been hearing about Him and was hoping to see some sign performed by Him" (Luke 23:8). So, in a gesture not unlike a good-natured practical joke, he sent "the King of the Jews" to Herod for judgment.

> [Herod] questioned Him at some length; but [Jesus] answered him nothing. And the chief priests and the scribes were standing there, accusing Him vehemently.
>
> Luke 23:9–10

If Antipas wanted a show, he was disappointed. Jesus recognized a basic fact of life: words are wasted on people who have no desire for truth. Earlier He referred to this as "throwing pearls before swine" (Matthew 7:6). Jesus' enemies hurled accusations while Herod cajoled Him for a display of miracles, but He remained silent. Eventually, Herod and his court grew tired of the game and sent Jesus back to Pilate. While he refused to take the problem off Pilate's hands, Herod acknowledged the procurator's joke by returning Jesus draped in a royal robe from his own collection.

As a result of the laugh the two men shared, Pilate gained the ally he so desperately needed. Nevertheless, Jesus remained his problem.

THE SIXTH TRIAL
(MATTHEW 27:15–26; MARK 15:6–15;
LUKE 23:13–25; JOHN 18:39–19:16)

In a cell not far from the Praetorium judgment seat, a man waited for execution. One can only wonder how he came to be known as Barabbas. His name was nonsensical, meaning "son of a father." Perhaps it was an alias, a clever "John Doe" he had adopted to protect his family when he joined a band of thugs and eventually became their leader. By the time he was caught, he had become a notorious killer, the kind of criminal Romans delighted to execute using the most agonizing means possible. He was soon to be crucified.

Men like Barabbas gave the Roman procurators and the religious leaders a rare opportunity to find common ground. Until brigands were caught, their activities caused the Romans grief, much to the delight of every Jew. However, these rogue insurrectionists were equally contemptuous of the Sadducees, who cooperated with Rome. Consequently, the arrest of an insurrectionist became an opportunity for Jewish leaders to feign support for the Roman occupation.

This gave Pilate an idea. A custom of his predecessors had been to release one prisoner in honor of the Jewish festival. If he forced them to choose between an innocent man and one proven guilty of numerous crimes against Rome, certainly they wouldn't support a genuine enemy of the state. Choosing to release a renowned insurrectionist would put them on the opposite side of the issue from Caesar. But Pilate underestimated their hatred for Jesus. When he made the offer for them to choose between the two, they shouted, to his surprise, "Not this Man, but Barabbas" (John 18:40).

Pilate's ploy not only failed to release him from the political web, but it entangled him further. Reluctant to pardon a notorious murderer, Pilate decided to scourge Jesus in order to spare Him the cross, hoping that "the halfway death" would satisfy the Jewish leaders' thirst for His blood.

Scourging involved the use of a *flagrum*, a whip with long, leather tails. The leather straps could be merely knotted or, if the *lictor*—a trained expert in the art of torture—wanted to inflict more damage, he could choose one with small, metal weights or even bits of sheep bone braided into the straps. "The iron balls would cause deep contusions, and the leather thongs and sheep bones would cut into the skin and subcutaneous tissues. Then as the flogging continued, the lacerations would tear into the underlying skeletal muscles and produce quivering ribbons of bleeding flesh."[3] According to one physician, the scourging typically resulted in "rib fractures and severe lung bruises and lacerations with bleeding into the chest cavity and partial or complete pneumothorax (collapse of the lung)."[4] The Romans were expert in the art of torture and knew exactly how to beat a man within an inch of his life. The procedure usually sent the victim into shock in less than five minutes and then took months to heal.

As the lictor chained Jesus' wrists to either side of a low wooden pillar, the entire cohort in the garrison filled the gallery to become a part of the humiliating spectacle. They jeered and hurled insults as the lictor chose his instrument, drew back, and snapped the weighted leather tails across Jesus' back. Jewish scourging limited the number of blows to thirty-nine and restricted the area to the back and shoulders, but Roman lictors were not given any rules. Back, legs, buttocks, chest, abdomen, face—no part of the body was off limits and the beating could continue as long as everyone was entertained. And if the victim passed out, the lictor waited until he was conscious again before resuming the sadistic torture.

According to physicians, most victims would have suffered the onset of shock within just a few minutes of continuous lashing, so it's very likely that the lictor delivered three or four blows at a time and then allowed others to taunt and humiliate Him. In the case of Jesus, the soldiers twisted together a crown of thorns and pressed it down on His head. I have a replica brought to me by a group of friends who had returned from Israel. The thorns are two to three inches long and slightly tapered to a needle-sharp point. To this day, it's dangerous to handle.

They followed the humiliating coronation with more beating. They threw an officer's cape over Jesus' flayed shoulders as a royal robe, thrust a measuring rod in His hands to be His scepter, and bowed before Him in mock reverence. "Hail, King of the Jews!" More beating followed. They paraded Him around the fortress courtyard and threw objects at Him from the gallery. Then they battered His head with the measuring rod and scourged Him yet further. Finally, they beat Him with their fists and shamelessly spewed their phlegm in His face before sending Him back to Pilate, bleeding, trembling from shock, barely able to stand by His own strength, and still wearing His dreadful crown of thorns.

Within an hour, Jesus had been returned to the Praetorium. After all that had been done to Him, the procurator felt sure the people would now be satisfied. He pushed Jesus, barely able to stand and utterly humiliated, onto the platform and said, proudly, "Behold, the Man!" But instead of cheering what he considered to be his very generous concession, the crowd began shouting, "Crucify, crucify!" The exasperated Pilate waved his hand, shrugged, and said, "Take Him yourselves and crucify Him, for I find no guilt in Him" (John 19:6). He then turned to go inside. But before he had taken more than a few steps, the leaders said something that stopped him cold. "We have a law, and by that law He ought to die because He made Himself out to be the Son of God" (John 19:7). Earlier, Pilate's wife had sent him a note: "Have nothing to do with that righteous Man; for last night I suffered greatly in a dream because of Him" (Matthew 27:19).

Romans were superstitious and remarkably inclusive when it came to appeasing a god—anyone's god. They generally took a better-safe-than-sorry approach to deities and paid attention to any omen that might suggest they were vulnerable. At the very least, Pilate took his wife's fear seriously and chose to question Jesus again.

> "Where are You from?" But Jesus gave him no answer. So Pilate said to Him, "You do not speak to me? Do You not know that I have authority to release You, and I have authority to crucify You?" Jesus answered, "You would have no authority over Me, unless it had been given you from above; for this reason he who delivered Me to you has the greater sin."
>
> John 19:9–11

The more Pilate tried to wriggle out of his predicament, the more entangled in the political web he became. Convinced Jesus was innocent, fearful of the bad omen from his wife, and by this time, aware of the cosmic dimensions of his decision, Pilate tried one last time to release Jesus. But the religious leaders played their trump card. "If you release this Man, you are no friend of Caesar; everyone who makes himself out to be a king opposes Caesar!" (John 19:12).

That did it. Pilate needed to hear nothing else. Every other time the religious leaders had appealed to Rome, the wrath of Tiberius shook his career to the core. The memory of Herod the Great losing his status as a "friend of Caesar" and his subsequent demotion doubtless haunted the ambitious politician. And with his friend Sejanus executed for treason, he surely wouldn't survive another controversy. Furthermore, his new friendship with Herod Antipas promised to turn everything around.

When Pilate heard these words he brought Jesus outside and sat down
on the judgment seat in the place called "The Stone Pavement." . . .
Pilate said to the Jewish leaders, "Look, here is your king!" Then they
shouted out, "Away with him! Away with him! Crucify him!" Pilate
asked, "Shall I crucify your king?" The high priests replied, "We have
no king except Caesar!"

John 19:13–15 NET

From the moment the leaders brought Jesus before Pilate, truth and power
fought for supremacy over Pilate's heart. But, in the end, he sacrificed truth on
the altar of his god. He stood up from his judgment seat, washed his hands in
front of the crowd, and said, "I am innocent of this Man's blood; see to that
yourselves" (Matthew 27:24). The leaders responded, "His blood shall be on
us and on our children!"

Within the hour, Jesus would take Barabbas's place on the cross.

REACTIONS

The trials of Jesus Christ are history. The sands of time have eroded the details.
The faces of the people have faded from memory. Their names have been
reduced to mere icons to which history and folklore have attached clichés.
But I challenge you to use your imagination and place yourself in their shoes
long enough to appreciate the intellectual, practical, and moral dilemmas they
faced. These people were not very different from you and me. And I find four
different perspectives in the case of *The State v. Jesus of Nazareth*, each one
represented by a primary figure in the historical accounts.

- *Pilate.* He was completely convinced by the truth, yet terrified to
  admit it or act upon it for fear of losing favor with certain people.
- *Herod.* He was so distracted by superficial pursuits that truth had
  long ago become irrelevant.
- *Pilate's wife.* She was so easily persuaded and carelessly undiscerning
  that truth and fiction commingled with ease.
- *The religious leaders.* They were willfully unconcerned with truth
  because it frustrated their personal agendas.

The trials of Jesus are over; nevertheless, every man and woman since that time has a seat in the jury box. And we, like Pilate, Herod, Pilate's wife, and the angry mob, must reach a verdict within our own hearts. Jesus has presented His case. He has been clear with His answers. Of the four categories, into which do you fall?

Some people today are like Pontius Pilate. They recognize the truth about Jesus Christ and even acknowledge it, but they refuse to yield themselves to that truth because it threatens to disrupt the plans they have for their own lives. They fear the rejection of people. They perhaps have a greater desire for power or money or comfort or a relationship or . . . the list is endless.

Some people are like Herod. They distract themselves from the most important issues in life with projects or parties or thrill-seeking. Belief in Jesus Christ is for fanatics and other people who take themselves too seriously. It's all a big joke. The truth about Christ is lost in the pursuit of the next good time.

Then people like Pilate's wife accept that Jesus' claims are authentic . . . along with every other passing philosophy or religious belief. They make the Bible, the cross, the church, even His name into treasured tokens of a sentimental faith or lucky charms to ward off guilt and other negative experiences. Theirs is a superficial, sentimental belief that fails to change them or transform their character.

Worst of all, many people reject Jesus Christ because He is not the messiah they have prescribed for themselves. They have a clear picture of the god they would like to worship—and even presume to worship—but have no desire for the God who actually exists and has revealed Himself.

Jesus said, "I have come into the world, to testify to the truth. Everyone who is of the truth hears My voice" (John 18:37). Pilate devalued the truth about the Son of God. Herod was too shallow and vain to see the truth. Pilate's wife accepted everything as truth and, therefore, failed to recognize it. And the angry mob ignored the truth as inconvenient.

So much for all of them. The question today turns to you: what have *you* done with the truth about the Son of God?

Chapter Fifteen

Delivered Up to Be Crucified

Some images are too difficult to see, yet too significant to ignore.

During my sixteen months on Okinawa with the Third Marine Division, my outfit visited a leprosarium on the north end of the island. As I greeted the people who had sequestered themselves for their own good and the good of their families—men and women whose bodies had been horribly disfigured by what doctors now call Hansen's disease—I wanted to look away. The suffering was almost more than I could handle. But to look away would be to dismiss the people, and we were there to help them forget their disease for a while.

I found that if I concentrated on their eyes, I could connect with the person whose body made him or her appear—and feel—less and less human. Once I encountered the humanity within, I could accept, and even embrace, their wasting, disfigured bodies as the most human of all.

I'm glad I didn't look away. As difficult as those images were to look upon, the people living in seclusion and obscurity on the north end of a tiny South Pacific island changed my life. The leprosarium has become, for me, a metaphor for the church. It's what keeps me in ministry when disfigured victims of depravity—still contaminated with the filth of sin—

fill the pews, and find their way into leadership, and presume to stand before others to teach . . . or even behind a pulpit to preach.

Sometimes the most horrific images can become the catalyst for our most significant life changes . . . only if we resist the urge to look away.

HANDED OVER

With Barabbas sitting in a cell beneath the Antonia Fortress, not five hundred yards from the Praetorium, Pilate clarified the issue for the religious leaders and their bloodthirsty minions, "Behold, I am bringing [Jesus] out to you so that you may know that I find no guilt in Him" (John 19:4). The rabble called again for the release of Barabbas and for the crucifixion of Jesus, saying, "If you release this Man [Jesus], you are no friend of Caesar" (John 19:12). Pilate symbolically washed guilt from his hands and gave them what they wanted.

The trials of Jesus came to a predictable end because they arrived at a foregone conclusion. Jesus was not the kind of Messiah the seditious rabble wanted. Jesus was not the puppet ruler the wealthy and powerful could control. Jesus was not the revolutionary threat Pilate hoped to condemn legitimately. The only matter these habitually contentious parties could agree upon was that the death of Jesus would solve their problems. "So [Pilate] handed Him over to them to be crucified" (John 19:16).

Throughout the centuries, mankind has devised hundreds of ways to kill a man, most of them designed to bring on death as slowly and as painfully as possible. But none of them rivaled crucifixion. The ancient orator Cicero described crucifixion as "the worst extreme of the tortures inflicted upon slaves."[1] Tacitus called it a "despicable death."

According to the Greek historian Herodotus, the Persians invented the practice after experimenting with other forms of slow death, including stoning, drowning, burning, boiling in oil, strangulation, and flaying. They eventually began executing people they considered particularly detestable by impaling them on stakes in order to keep them from defiling the ground, which their god, Ormuzd, had made sacred. Crucifixion later became a tool of Alexander the Great, the four generals who succeeded him, and finally the Carthaginians, from whom the Romans learned it.

The Greeks and early Romans reserved crucifixion for rebels, runaway slaves, deserting soldiers, and the worst form of criminals—people they considered lesser creatures—and abhorred the thought of allowing a civilized person to hang. Cicero wrote, "To bind a Roman citizen is a crime, to flog him is an abomination, to slay him is almost an act of murder: to crucify him is— what? There is no fitting word that can possibly describe so horrible a deed."[2] Crucifixion brought together four qualities the Romans prized most in an execution: unrelenting agony, protracted death, public spectacle, and utter humiliation. Therefore, it became "one of the strongest means of maintaining order and security. Governors imposed this servile punishment especially on freedom fighters who tried to break away from Roman rule."[3]

While the Romans didn't invent crucifixion, they transformed the technique into a macabre art. An *exactor mortis* was schooled in the finer points of death and led a team of soldiers called a *quaternion*. Their sole task was to make Roman execution a terrifying spectacle. And their experience gave them ample opportunity to experiment with different methods. "Josephus indicated that the soldiers would nail their victims in different positions either for their own amusement or out of rage, sadism, whimsy, or hatred."[4] Over time, they learned how to add various elements to the procedure and adjust them to achieve the desired effect. They could expertly control the amount of suffering, the cause of death, and even when the victim would die.

The victim typically endured a beating with the *flagrum* before execution, and the degree to which he was beaten usually determined how long he would survive on the cross. If the executioner wanted the victim to die very quickly, he would choose a scourge with jagged bits of sheep bone braided into the tails. On the other hand, a lighter scourging with simple leather straps could result in the person lasting for days on the cross and perhaps more than a week.

After the *lictor* completed his cruel task, the *exactor mortis* and the *quaternio* stripped the prisoner naked and forced him to carry the implement of his own demise to the place of execution. They hung a sign, called a *titulus*, around his neck. The *titulus* was nothing more than a crude board inscribed with the prisoner's name and a list of his crimes. It would eventually be attached to the cross above his head to let everyone know why he hung there to die.

Having placed the burden of death on his back and the *titulus* around his neck, the *quaternio* formed a square around the victim and began a long, slow march through the main parts of the city—a death march called, in later years, the Via Dolorosa, the "way of suffering." The purpose of the march was, of course, to enhance the public spectacle, which reinforced the warning to any other would-be criminals. While the United States still utilizes the death penalty, executions are carried out behind closed doors, away from the eyes of the general public. Not so under Rome. An execution was a deliberately public affair.

During the final trial, the *lictor* and his cohort had thrashed Jesus nearly to death. They sent Him back to the Praetorium bleeding, bruised, and trembling with shock. By the time Pilate handed Him over to the *exactor mortis*, Jesus would not have been able to carry His burden very far. He perhaps dragged it for some distance, but the soldiers became impatient and conscripted a man named Simon of Cyrene to carry it for Him.

The religious leaders objected to the *titulus* Pilate had prepared. Beneath the name "Jesus the Nazarene," Pilate wrote in Hebrew, Latin, and Greek the crime for which He was crucified: "The King of the Jews." The leaders wanted the sign changed to read, "Jesus the Nazarene called himself King of the Jews" for fear that someone might take the inscription literally. But Pilate felt he had compromised far enough. He wouldn't budge. "What I have written I have written" (John 19:22).

Jesus would not have carried the entire cross, which would have weighed more than two hundred fifty pounds. Even a man who had not been scourged would have trouble dragging—not to mention carrying— that much weight more than a hundred yards. The crossbeam, called the *patibulum*, "was placed across the nape of the victim's neck and balanced along both shoulders."[5] The vertical member, called the *stipes*, awaited the victim at the place of crucifixion, usually along a main road leading into the city. Once there, the *patibulum* would be attached to the top of the *stipes* by means of a mortise and tenon joint to form a giant capital "T."

If first-century Jerusalem looked anything like it does today, almost any route through the city would be a claustrophobic nightmare. The tight, winding alleys would have been packed with visitors for the Passover festival. And the uneven pavement of hand-laid stones would have made His steps uncertain as He stumbled under the weight of the wood beam on His shoulders. If He had fallen with His arms tied to the crossbeam, nothing would have kept His face from smashing into the stones.

LIFTED UP

When they reached a place the locals had nicknamed Golgotha, "Place of the Skull," they laid the *patibulum* on the ground and attached it to the top of the *stipes*. The victim was placed on top of the wood and attached to the cross with his arms outstretched and feet flat against the face of the *stipes*. Usually, the victim was tied in place, which doesn't sound particularly brutal until you consider that he took much longer to die than when nailed.

To better understand the effects of crucifixion on the body, Dr. Frederick Zugibe, a forensic pathologist, has made crucifixion a topic of scientific study for more than fifty years. His experiments include tying volunteers to a cross in order to observe their behavior and record their physiological response. He closely monitored their respiration, blood pressure, heart rate, circulation, and even the amount of oxygen in the blood. His findings have changed the way historians view crucifixion.

Most of Dr. Zugibe's test subjects experienced great discomfort within the first half hour. Their forearms went numb and they felt as if their shoulders were being pulled from their sockets. To relieve the pain and numbness in their arms, they instinctively pushed up with their legs. Then their legs would cramp, fatigue, and turn cold until they arched their backs. But this soon became too difficult to bear, so they returned to one of the other positions. Eventually, the volunteers had to keep their bodies in constant motion to cope with the pain in their arms, chest, back, and legs. Imagine doing this twenty-four hours a day, for days on end.

These experiments, together with a study of historical documents, revealed that death usually came by way of exposure, dehydration, starvation, or fatigue asphyxia. In the case of asphyxia, the victim's nonstop writhing finally left him too exhausted, dehydrated, and malnourished to pull in his next breath, which led to suffocation. If the executioner were especially sadistic, he would fit the cross with a *sedile*, a pointed saddle attached about halfway up the cross and between the victim's legs where he could periodically support his body. This cruel irony eased the prisoner's misery in order to extend his agony.

To hasten the end, the *exactor mortis* could suspend the victim using nails instead of rope, which caused death within hours instead of days. Whereas the victim suffered for a shorter time, the intensity of his agony can barely be imagined. Physicians have determined through a combination of means that the victim would have been nailed to the cross through the hand at the base of the palm and at an angle so that the nail exited the wrist. This not only supported the weight of the person, but it also caused him the greatest amount of pain.

The nail, driven through the palm of the hand close to the wrist, severely damaged the median nerve of the arm and forearm. Within a couple of hours, the victim experienced an affliction known as *causalgia*.

> This syndrome was commonly seen during the war years after the partial median nerve and other peripheral nerve injuries. The pain is exquisite and described as an unrelenting, peculiar burning or searing sensation that is so intense that even gentle contacts like clothing or air drafts cause utter torture. It may be aggravated by movement, jarring, noise, or emotion. The pain traverses the arm like lightning bolts. The patient becomes completely preoccupied with avoiding any contact and holding the limb a particular way. . . . Victims of causalgia frequently go into shock if the pain is not controlled.[6]

A victim nailed to a cross, like someone tied in place, also had to keep his body in constant motion to relieve the pain in his arms, chest, and legs, which only agitated the damaged nerves in the nail wounds. Later, as fatigue set in, breathing would have been difficult, requiring more and more effort. Jim Bishop combined science, historical information, and his imagination to describe what Jesus' experience must have been like.

His arms were now in a V position, and Jesus became conscious of two unendurable circumstances: the first was that the pain in his wrists was beyond bearing, and that muscle cramps knotted his forearms and upper arms and the pads of His shoulders; the second was that his pectoral muscles at the sides of his chest were momentarily paralyzed. This induced in him an involuntary panic; for he found that while he could draw air into his lungs, he was powerless to exhale.

At once, Jesus raised himself on his bleeding feet. As the weight of his body came down on the insteps, the single nail pressed hard against the top of the wound. Slowly, steadily, Jesus was forced to raise himself higher and higher until, for the moment, his head hid the sign which told of his crime. When his shoulders were on a level with his hands, breathing was rapid and easier. Like the other two, he fought the pain in his feet in order to breathe rapidly for a few moments. Then, unable to bear the pain below, which cramped legs and thighs and wrung moans from the strongest, he let his torso sag lower and lower, and His knees projected a little at a time until, with a deep sigh, he felt himself to be hanging by His wrists. And this process must have been repeated again and again.[7]

Unless the guards broke the legs of the victim, the primary causes of death for nailed victims were likely hypovolemic shock [excessive blood loss], traumatic shock, or cardiac and respiratory arrest.[8]

The soldiers took Jesus to Golgotha and initiated the gruesome ritual, which began with giving the victim a mild painkiller. This was no act of mercy. The process of nailing a person's limbs to a wooden beam is easier if he's drugged. Jesus refused the medicine, probably preferring to remain completely lucid during His ordeal.

They stripped Him completely naked—again to heighten the shame—and pushed His back down onto the cross. One soldier lay across His chest and another across His legs, while two others stretched out His arms and drove a five-inch long, three-eighths-inch square nail through each hand. They bent His knees, placed His feet flat against the *stipes*, and drove a nail through each foot. The soldiers then tilted the cross up and guided the base into a hole. The cross suddenly stood vertical and then fell to the bottom with a jarring thud. As they drove wedges between the beam and the sides of the hole to keep the cross firmly upright, Jesus offered a quiet prayer. "Father, forgive them; for they do not know what they are doing" (Luke 23:34). It was just another day at work for the soldiers, who barely knew anything was different. At the end of the day, shortly before dark, they would haul the bodies down and everything—the beams, the nails, and the hole—would be prepared to send another prisoner to an agonizing demise on another day.

Shortly after nine o'clock Friday morning, Jesus hung a few feet above the earth between two robbers—probably accomplices of Barabbas, who were surprised to see another man hanging on his cross. They had no doubt heard of Jesus and could guess what had happened by listening to the taunts of the religious leaders.

> Those passing by were hurling abuse at Him, wagging their heads, and saying, "Ha! You who are going to destroy the temple and rebuild it in three days, save Yourself, and come down from the cross!" In the same way the chief priests also, along with the scribes, were mocking Him among themselves and saying, "He saved others; He cannot save Himself. Let this Christ, the King of Israel, now come down from the cross, so that we may see and believe!"
>
> Mark 15:29–32

The brigands on either side of Jesus joined the others in taunting Him while the soldiers helped themselves to what few possessions the prisoners had. When they came to Jesus' clothing, they noticed that His tunic was unique in that it had been woven as one piece. Rather than ruin the garment, the men cast lots—rolled dice as it were—to determine who should keep it. Then, as the soldiers gambled and the religious leaders mocked, something changed within one of the robbers.

> One of the criminals who were hanged there was hurling abuse at Him, saying, "Are You not the Christ? Save Yourself and us!" But the other

answered, and rebuking him said, "Do you not even fear God, since you are under the same sentence of condemnation? And we indeed are suffering justly, for we are receiving what we deserve for our deeds; but this man has done nothing wrong." And he was saying, "Jesus, remember me when You come in Your kingdom!" And He said to him, "Truly I say to you, today you shall be with Me in Paradise."

Luke 23:39–43

The religious leaders continued their taunts, quoting Scripture as they watched their Messiah suffer. "He trusts in God; let God rescue Him now, if He delights in Him; for He said, 'I am the Son of God'" (Matthew 27:43).

At about noon, roughly three hours after the crucifixion began and when the sun should have been high overhead, an eerie darkness enveloped the entire region until three in the afternoon. As the darkness began to lift, Jesus drew a deep breath and shouted in Aramaic, His native tongue, "My God, My God, why have You forsaken me!" (Matthew 27:46). Those who only spoke Greek or Latin struggled to make sense of His words, but the chief priests and scribes understood completely. Jesus was quoting a psalm written by the prophet-king, David, centuries before crucifixion had been invented.

My God, my God, why have You forsaken me?
Far from my deliverance are the words of my groaning.
O my God, I cry by day, but You do not answer;
And by night, but I have no rest.
Yet You are holy,
O You who are enthroned upon the praises of Israel.
In You our fathers trusted;
They trusted and You delivered them.
To You they cried out and were delivered;
In You they trusted and were not disappointed.
But I am a worm and not a man,
A reproach of men and despised by the people.
All who see me sneer at me;
They separate with the lip, they wag the head, saying,

"Commit yourself to the LORD; let Him deliver him;
Let Him rescue him, because He delights in him."

For dogs have surrounded me;
A band of evildoers has encompassed me;
They pierced my hands and my feet.
I can count all my bones.
They look, they stare at me;
They divide my garments among them,
And for my clothing they cast lots.

But You, O LORD, be not far off;
O You my help, hasten to my assistance.

Psalm 22:1–8, 16–19

The taunts continued as blood seeped from Jesus' wounds and ran down the cross to mingle with the soil. When He called for something to drink, someone put a sponge on the end of a branch of hyssop, dipped it a jar of "sour wine," the drink "given with meals to soldiers and workers"[9] as an aid in reducing fever and giving refreshment. After drinking from the sponge, Jesus decided the work He came to do had been completed. He tilted His head back, pulled up one last time to draw a deep breath and cried, "*Tetelestai!*"

It was a Greek expression most everyone present would have understood. It was an accounting term. Archeologists have found papyrus tax receipts with "Tetelestai" written across them, meaning "paid in full." With Jesus' last breath on the cross, He declared the debt of sin canceled, completely satisfied. Nothing else required. Not good deeds. Not generous donations. Not penance or confession or baptism or . . . or . . . or . . . nothing. The penalty for sin is death, and we were all born hopelessly in debt. He paid our debt in full by giving His life so that we might live forever.

Having declared the debt of sin "paid in full," Jesus bowed His head. As He gave up His spirit, the ground rumbled beneath the centurion and his company of executioners, and a crack formed in the giant rock that formed the hill they stood upon. "The centurion, and those who were with him keeping guard over Jesus, when they saw the earthquake and the things that were happening, became very frightened." The seasoned officer of the crucifixion detail spontaneously declared, "Truly this was the Son of God!" (Matthew 27:54).

SUBSTITUTION

Imagine for a moment what all of that must have been like for Barabbas.

Jews throughout the Roman Empire had filled the city to capacity, which gave Pilate a rare opportunity to make a very public example of an insurrectionist and two accomplices. The thought of helping the Romans with anything kept Barabbas from drifting off to sleep the night before—that, and an overwhelming fear of the agony he was to endure on the cross. He sat rubbing his face in a dank cell down in the dregs of the Antonia Fortress when he heard the sounds of a riot coming from the Praetorium.

As the roar of angry, Jewish voices spilled over the palace wall and crashed against his cell door, droplets of words fell upon Barabbas. "Blasphemy! Sedition! No . . . friend . . . Caesar!"

When the clamor ebbed, Barabbas could hear the unmistakable voice of Pilate, but he couldn't make out the words. He surmised from the intonation of the procurator's voice that he asked a question of the crowd.

"Barabbas! Barabbas! The man, Barabbas!"

Another muffled question from Pilate gave way to the mob's unanimous shout, "Crucify Him, crucify Him!"

The blood of the insurrectionist ran cold. He had enjoyed the silent approval of the religious leaders and the open appreciation of the general population, most of whom delighted in the trouble he caused for their Roman oppressors. What had happened to suddenly incur their hatred?

Pilate spoke again, then even more violent than before, the crowd shouted. "Crucify, crucify, crucify, crucify, crucify! His blood shall be on us and our children!"

Barabbas sank into a corner, put his head in his hands, and waited for death to open his cell door. In less than thirty minutes, the foreboding sound of soldiers' feet echoed down the corridor and grew louder with every step. At last, the jangling of keys allowed sunlight to spill into the tiny, square room for the first time in many days.

"Barbaricus!" The deliberate distortion of his name meant "foreigner" in Latin, a well-placed jab in the man's Zionist ribs. "Get up. Time to haul your filthy carcass out of here!"

Barabbas stood up and held out his wrists for the guard to place them in irons. Instead, the soldier reached into the darkness, grabbed Barabbas by his grimy tunic, and pulled him sharply into the corridor. The light slammed his eyelids shut and sent pain shooting deep into his head. Another guard shoved him from behind and kept pushing him down the hallway toward the main exit from the dungeon. As the gate slammed shut behind him, he stood motionless, alone and alarmed in the blinding light of morning, peeking through his fingers, slowly allowing his eyes to adjust.

After several minutes, he realized that the voices around him belonged to passersby, and they were speaking Aramaic, not Latin or Greek. Barabbas quickly turned around to find no one behind him—or anywhere near him for that matter. He was free! After months in a cell barely big enough to lie down and stretch out, the expanse of the outside world felt disorienting and dangerous. He could go anywhere, but he found himself unable to move until friends arrived to lead him home.

For years, I have wondered how Barabbas reacted when he discovered how he gained his freedom. Recipients of organ transplants often want to know whose gift they received. Did Barabbas want to know who took his stripes from the lictor, who bore his cross through the streets and up the long climb to Golgotha, and who endured the agony he genuinely deserved? Did Barabbas understand that Jesus went willingly, not only for him but the whole world?

We are guilty of sin, each one of us. We have behaved in ways that dishonor our Maker. The commandments of the Old Testament reveal God's character and express the values that honor His creation and demonstrate our love for Him, but we have broken them. Wrongdoing demands a penalty, and that penalty is eternal separation from God in a place of torment. Justice cannot be set aside.

Nevertheless, the compassion of our Judge in heaven has delayed the gavel. God so loved the world that He gave His one and only Son, so that everyone who believes in Him will not suffer eternal death, but have eternal life. Jesus, though innocent, took the place of someone who deserved to pay the penalty of death for wrongdoing. He took the place of another on the cross. Yes, Barabbas went free, but the grace he received is merely an illustration of a greater, far more personal truth.

It was *your place* on the cross he took. Jesus died *for you.*

Try to imagine if Barabbas had said, "Freedom? No thanks. I'd rather suffer agony on the cross." Never! No one, if he or she fully understood the nature of crucifixion, would decline the offer of grace. So why do people refuse to accept the free gift of eternal life, purchased for them by the death of Jesus Christ in their place?

Have you refused His gift? If so, why?

Part Four

The King

Chapter Sixteen

Not to Worry . . . He Is Risen!

A
t about noon on Friday, the day Jesus was crucified, a sinister darkness blotted out the sun and smothered Jerusalem under a blanket of evil. His disciples had scattered during the trials, and all but one left Him to die alone. The one who sold his Messiah for the price of a common slave hanged himself and would not be discovered for several more days. The one who denied any association with his Messiah lay weeping uncontrollably in a hiding place, away from prying eyes and condemning words. The others—all except John—scurried away to cower in their own private corners of the darkness. Matthew's sentence is brief but eloquent: "Then all the disciples left Him and fled" (Matthew 26:56).

John remained near the cross as Jesus waged His lonely battle against evil, though even he didn't understand the significance of what he witnessed. He, like the other disciples, watched his dreams of a new kingdom slowly fade with each labored gasp of its king. It would have appeared to anyone seeing through eyes of flesh that the darkness, the devil, and death had defeated the Son of God once and for all.

I will admit to you that those three Ds lie at the root of almost every worry I suffer. I worry about *death*—in particular, the death of the people I love, for I dread the thought of life without them. And I worry over my own death, though not because I fear what will happen to me after I'm gone; I have complete confidence in the promises of my Savior. I just don't want to be there when it happens!

I worry about *darkness*, both literal and figurative. Some of my worst injuries—both literal and figurative—have been the result of tripping over what I could not see.

I also worry over what the *devil* is up to. And take it from a guy who's not given to superstition and who remains stubbornly skeptical when people talk about spooks and spirits: Satan is real, and he is relentless in his attacks on people of the light. Satan and his demons don't look anything like the depictions we see flickering across the screen in movies or on television. He subtly plays upon the fallibilities of good people to convince them that their darkest desires and most destructive activities are innocent, even righteous. His chief weapon is deception, and he uses it masterfully. That worries me often.

Demons, darkness, and death . . . all three worked diligently throughout the ministry of Jesus to bring about this long and anguishing day. They poisoned the heart of a man using his own secret sins to betray his faithful Master. They colluded with the guardians of religiosity in God's holy temple to destroy the man their own prophets had called "the Holy One of Israel." They wooed Pilate away from the truth he openly accepted and announced, offering in exchange promises of power in the kingdom of Tiberius. They blindfolded the seditious rabble with rage against the only man who could liberate them, not only from Rome, but from the very sin that kept them enslaved to godless masters.

What John and the other disciples didn't see—though Jesus had said it all along—was that the Messiah's death would strike at the very heart of evil. Nevertheless, appearances were deceiving. Even as the devil, darkness, and death suffered a mortal wound on Golgotha from which they will never recover, that unholy trinity danced in delight, thinking they had won the war, when in fact they had just met their Actium or Waterloo or D-day. The Puritan preacher John Owen insightfully called it "the death of death in the death of Jesus Christ."

THE DEATH OF HOPE

The long journey from Gethsemane to Golgotha took less than twenty-four hours and ended with Jesus giving up His spirit. Nightfall would bring with it the Jewish Sabbath, so the centurion would have to hasten the death of those who were still alive. According to Jewish law, no one was to remain hanging on the seventh day. Pilate had even more reason to honor their customs. The most common method for bringing a crucifixion to a sudden and dramatic end was to break the victim's legs. Not only did this make breathing more difficult, especially after many hours of physical trauma and fatigue, the violence literally drained the victim of any life that remained in him.

> A single closed femoral (thigh bone) fracture may result in the loss of 2 liters of blood, and up to 4 liters of blood may be lost with fractures of both femoral bones. . . . The marked hemorrhage from the breaking of the legs and the severe pain would deepen the level of hypovolemic and traumatic shock, with a consequent drop in blood pressure and rapid development of congestion in the lower extremities, resulting in unconsciousness, coma, and death.[1]

Having delivered crushing blows to the legs of the other two men, the soldiers saw that Jesus had already died. To be absolutely certain, one of them ran his spear through the side of Jesus and saw a mixture of blood and clear fluid pour out of His body (John wrote, "Immediately blood and water came out" [19:34]), an unmistakable sign of death.

Some skeptics have postulated that Jesus never really died but that He remained in a deep coma until He had been placed in the tomb. The so-called Swoon Theory is a desperate attempt to account for the resurrection of Jesus without accepting a supernatural explanation. But it makes less sense of the facts, not more.

People in ancient days were more intimately acquainted with death than we are. Most developed countries have professionals who work hard to make the process of losing a loved one as pleasant as possible. Once someone is pronounced dead by a physician, the family goes home after turning over the body to the mortician. He or she takes the corpse back to the funeral home, where every effort is made to give it the appearance of life. A dignified and respectful time of viewing is followed by a graveside service, during which the hole is concealed by an attractive device for lowering the casket. Even the dirt is concealed by green indoor-outdoor carpet. Other professionals then lower the casket and cover it with dirt after everyone has left the cemetery. The public is spared all the grim realities.

In much of the United States and Europe, the custom is cremation, in which no one even sees the body following death. So it would be safe to say that almost no one in our culture knows what it feels like to touch a corpse. Not so in the ancient world. Families and friends prepared their own loved ones for burial.

After the death of Jesus had been confirmed by the centurion's spear and reported to Pilate, two important members of the Jewish ruling council, Joseph of Arimathea and Nicodemus, requested His body. These formerly secret disciples, along with several women, would do the gruesome task of preparing His corpse for burial. Once the soldiers lowered the body of Jesus from the cross, His friends would have to flex and massage His arms in order to relieve rigor mortis, which kept the arms stuck in the V position after death. Then they would wash His body and anoint it with oil before wrapping it in a single linen cloth. A separate napkin tied under His chin kept His mouth from gaping open after the muscles began to loosen.

Next, they were to wrap His body from head to toe in long strips of linen, which had been soaked in a mixture of spiced resin. They would use seventy-five to one hundred pounds of heavily scented spices to offset the smell of decomposition. Then they would have laid Him on a shelf in a tomb excavated from the side of a limestone hill or mountain. After a year had passed and the body had completely decayed, they would have gathered His bones and placed them in a family ossuary—a bone box—along with those of His ancestors. Thus, He would have been "gathered unto His fathers."

As the sun sank below the horizon, the burial party found themselves pressed between two of God's commandments. They were to keep the Sabbath day sacred (which began at sundown), but Deuteronomy 21:22–23 required the body of someone who had been executed to be buried that same day. With night closing in, they had just enough time to hurriedly wrap His body in linen, apply at least some of the spices, and place Him inside the tomb. A team of men then rolled an enormous stone over the entrance in order to keep grave robbers out and foul odors in.

Whereas the followers of Jesus did their best to complete their tasks before sundown in honor of the Sabbath, the Sadducees and Pharisees were hard at work petitioning Pilate once again.

> "Sir, we remember that when He was still alive that deceiver said, 'After three days I am to rise again.' Therefore, give orders for the grave to be made secure until the third day, otherwise His disciples may come and steal Him away and say to the people, 'He has risen from the dead,' and the last deception will be worse than the first."
>
> Matthew 27:63–64

Pilate didn't care what people believed, and he didn't see how a fake resurrection should be of any concern to Rome. So he gave the religious leaders an official seal to place on the grave and suggested they post their own guard, which likely consisted of Roman soldiers paid through the temple treasury and temple guards assigned to supervise the gravesite details. Having sealed the tomb and posted a company of guards by the entrance, the chief priests, scribes, and Pharisees went to their respective homes to keep the law of the Sabbath. On Sunday morning, they would continue to observe the Feast of Unleavened Bread and prepare for the sacrifices of the closing convocation. Then, having silenced Jesus . . . it was business as usual.

Meanwhile, the followers of Jesus mourned alone and disillusioned, each one very likely wondering, *What now?*

DO NOT BE AFRAID

The first few hours of Sunday morning were nothing short of pandemonium, of which the four Gospels give account. Very often, when people tell the story of a chaotic event, they focus on the aspects of the story they consider important and may leave out other details. They also tend to compress some details into summary statements while drawing out every nuance of another. In this case, we have four witnesses to the event, which gives us much information. However, to see the whole picture, we have to correlate their accounts. John's record focuses on the experience of Mary Magdalene, while Matthew, Mark, and Luke tell us what happened to the other women (Luke 24:10).

The morning after the Sabbath—Sunday morning—the guards stood watch over their dead prisoner when, suddenly, the ground shook and a brilliant light flooded the garden.

> An angel of the Lord descending from heaven came and rolled away the stone and sat on it. His appearance was like lightning, and his clothes were white as snow. The guards were shaken and became like dead men because they were so afraid of him.
>
> Matthew 28:2–4 NET

Sometime later, Mary Magdalene, another Mary, Salome, Joanna, and some other women converged on the tomb of Jesus. Luke's account reveals that their purpose was to complete the burial process with the spiced resin they had prepared (Luke 24:1) and that they even wondered how they would remove the giant stone. As Mary Magdalene and the women approached the tomb, they saw that the giant stone had been tossed aside and the guards were lying unconscious nearby. According to the Gospel by John, Mary Magdalene immediately ran to tell Peter and John what she thought had happened. "They have taken away the Lord out of the tomb, and we do not know where they have laid Him" (John 20:2).

Place yourself in the sandals of these people for a moment. Imagine losing a very close friend or family member. Having buried him or her just a couple of days ago, you decide to place some flowers by the grave. You arrive in the early dawn hours to find that the dirt has been moved back from the grave, the coffin is lying open beside the hole, and the body is missing. Naturally, your first thought would be, *Someone has taken the body!*

While Mary Magdalene ran to tell Peter and John that someone had broken into the tomb, the other women moved in for a closer look.

> When they went in, they did not find the body of the Lord Jesus. While
> they were perplexed about this, suddenly two men stood beside them
> in dazzling attire. The women were terribly frightened and bowed their
> faces to the ground.
>
> Luke 24:3–5 NET

The grave was gaping open. The grave wrappings lay there, still together
and intact, but empty. The body was gone. The original Greek describes the
women as "without a way," meaning they were at a complete loss to explain
the mystery. They stood dumbstruck and staring for several moments, until
they realized that two angels appeared behind them. One sat on the stone
while the other stood nearby.

> "Why do you look for the living among the dead? He is not here,
> but has been raised! Remember how he told you, while he was still
> in Galilee, that the Son of Man must be delivered into the hands of
> sinful men, and be crucified, and on the third day rise again." Then
> the women remembered his words.
>
> Luke 24:5–8 NET

Place yourself in the story once again. As you're standing over the empty
coffin of your loved one, an angel gives you the news: "Your loved one has risen
from the dead!" You would probably want to tell the other mourning family
and friends as soon as possible. But, let's face it; you would probably sound like
you had lost your mind. You would likely reconsider telling anybody.

"[The women] went out and fled from the tomb, for trembling and
astonishment had gripped them; and they said nothing to anyone, for
they were afraid" (Mark 16:8). But then they encountered someone who
removed any doubt that might have lingered in their minds.

> Jesus met them, saying, "Greetings!" They came to him, held on to his
> feet and worshiped him. Then Jesus said to them, "Do not be afraid. Go
> and tell my brothers to go to Galilee. They will see me there."
>
> Matthew 28:9–10 NET

The women searched out the scattered disciples and told them one by one about the empty tomb, and the angels who appeared to them, and their encounter with the risen Jesus. "But these words appeared to them as nonsense, and they would not believe them" (Luke 24:11). The Greek word translated "nonsense" was a medical term to describe the feverish ramblings of delirium. The disciples dismissed their story as insane, exaggerated chatter.

While Mary the mother of James, Salome, Joanna, and the other women informed several of the disciples, Mary Magdalene located Peter and John. At first, they too dismissed her story as hyperemotionalism, but curiosity eventually got the better of them and they raced to the tomb.

> The two were running together, but the other disciple ran faster than Peter and reached the tomb first. He bent down and saw the strips of linen cloth lying there, but he did not go in. Then Simon Peter, who had been following him, arrived and went right into the tomb. He saw the strips of linen cloth lying there, and the face cloth, which had been around Jesus' head, not lying with the strips of linen cloth but rolled up in a place by itself.
>
> John 20:4–7 NET

As John wrote of his experience with Peter at the tomb, he used three distinct words to describe how the two men "saw." When John arrived, he stopped at the entrance of the tomb and looked inside. He used the Greek word *blepo*, which simply means to notice something without thinking about it. It describes a kind of observation that is accurate yet casual. A good example of this would be when a driver sees a red light at an intersection. He or she sees the light and then stops without giving it further thought. John saw the grave clothes and recognized them for what they were, but he didn't consider the implications.

Peter, on the other hand, ran straight into the tomb without stopping and "saw" the linen wrappings differently. John used *theoreo*, from which we derive the English word *theory*. Unlike John, Peter not only observed the grave clothes, but he studied them for clues and tried to comprehend what might have happened.

Why should the condition of the grave clothes excite Peter's amazement?

> There's a strong hint that the clothes were not folded as if Jesus had
> unwound them and then deposited them in two neat piles on the shelf.
> The word used to describe the napkin or head cloth does not connote
> a flat folded square like a table napkin, but a ball of cloth bearing the
> appearance of being rolled around an object that was no longer there.
> The wrappings were in position where the body had lain, and the head
> cloth was where the head had been, separated from the others by the dis-
> tance from the armpits to neck. The shape of the body was still apparent
> in them, but the flesh and bone had disappeared.[2]

The odd condition of the hollow linen wrappings still in the same shape
of a body did not suggest someone had quickly stolen the body. Something
else very strange had occurred.

Finally, John joined Peter inside the tomb, "and he saw and believed"
(John 20:8). In this instance, John used yet a third word, *eidon*, which
means to perceive with understanding. In other words, he saw the wrappings and he "got it." Everything fell into place. "The answer to the enigma
was that Jesus had risen, passing through the grave clothes, which He left
undisturbed as a silent proof that death could not hold Him, nor material
bonds restrain Him."[3] I like to think that John turned to Peter and whispered, "He's alive!"

After Peter and John left the tomb to tell their respective households
that Jesus had risen, Mary Magdalene had an extraordinary encounter of
her own. The angels who had greeted the other women appeared to her as
well (John 20:11–13). And as she left the garden, she saw the risen Jesus,
who gave her the same instructions He gave the others: *Go find My brothers and tell them.*

PROVE IT!

As Mary, Salome, Joanna, and the other women located the scattered followers of Jesus, and as word spread of His missing body, a multitude began

to assemble in an upper room—perhaps the same room in which Jesus had celebrated the Passover. The followers discussed everything that had been reported by the women and bandied theories as to what might have happened. Peter and John arrived followed by Mary Magdalene and, before long, almost everyone who had been a close follower of Jesus found his or her way to the customary place of meeting, hoping to hear some more news.

Then, with the doors shut tight for fear of persecution and the followers engaged in animated conversation, a familiar voice rose from the middle of the room.

> "Peace be with you." When [Jesus] had said this, he showed them his hands and his side. Then the disciples rejoiced when they saw the Lord. So Jesus said to them again, "Peace be with you. Just as the Father has sent me, I also send you." And after he said this, he breathed on them and said, "Receive the Holy Spirit. If you forgive anyone's sins, they are forgiven; if you retain anyone's sins, they are retained."
>
> John 20:19–23

When this occurred, Thomas, one of the Twelve, had not yet returned from Galilee. When he arrived, everyone he met told him the story of the empty tomb, and the bizarre way in which the grave clothes were left, and the dazzling appearance of angels, and their personal encounter with the risen Jesus. Nevertheless, Thomas wouldn't believe the reports. "Unless I see in His hands the imprint of the nails, and put my finger into the place of the nails, and put my hand into His side, I will not believe" (John 20:25).

Throughout the centuries since the disciple's classic demand for empirical evidence, expositors and preachers have assigned him the unfortunate title "Doubting Thomas." It's easy to criticize Thomas from the vantage point of history. I suspect Thomas was the harshest critic of all. But not everyone can be like the women, who heard the news and believed immediately. Not everyone is like Peter and John, who examined the evidence, compared it to the words of Jesus, arrived at the correct conclusions, and then quietly believed. Thomas did not have the good fortune to be present when Jesus presented Himself as tangible proof that He had fulfilled His promise to overcome death. Thomas undoubtedly wondered if wishful thinking had driven his friends to mass hysteria.

Let's not forget the mountain of empirical evidence Thomas had to overcome. He, like the other disciples, watched from a distance as Jesus staggered through the congested streets of Jerusalem toward Golgotha. He saw the blood oozing from the numerous wounds on Jesus' back and legs. He heard the crack of the mallet against the iron spikes that held Jesus to the cross. He cringed each time the anguished cry of his Teacher penetrated the darkness that had enveloped Jerusalem. He had heard His Master's lonely plea to heaven, "My God, My God, why have You forsaken Me?" He may have even seen the rigid remains of his Messiah lowered from the cross, wrapped like a mummy, and laid in a tomb. By Sunday morning, his disappointment fueled his flight from Jerusalem and toward the certainty and safety of his home in Galilee. For hours, Thomas grieved in solitude. His heart was broken. Disillusionment overwhelmed the man.

A few days later, rumors began to circulate. Synagogues and markets buzzed with stories of Jesus. How He was snatched in the middle of the night and hauled before the courts of the Sanhedrin and the procurator. How He was lifted up outside the camp of Jerusalem. How He was sacrificed on Passover and buried by sundown.

Thomas pretended not to notice the pointing fingers and sideways whispers ever since his return to normal life. He had determined to put the whole embarrassing matter of following a false messiah behind him. He had been duped, all in good faith, and would be wiser for the experience. He likely thought, *Be careful what you choose to believe. The more of your heart you give to something—or someone—the longer it will take to heal once it is eventually broken. I've learned my lesson!*

Despite his best effort to remain aloof and recover his dignity, Thomas could not ignore the latest rumor. *Jesus was alive!* A full eight days after the supposed resurrection, he found himself in Jerusalem again, surrounded by earnest followers of Jesus, pressing him with evidence they had experienced personally. But choosing to open his heart again felt like volunteering for a second scourging. Who in his right mind would do such a thing?

With the doors shut tighter than before and the followers of Jesus debating their next move, a familiar voice calmed the room. "Peace be with you." Again, Jesus stood in the middle of the room, only this time He came to see one person in particular. Not to scold or to chastise or to shame . . . but to heal. "Reach here with your finger, and see My hands; and reach here your hand and put it into My side; and do not be unbelieving, but believing" (John 20:27).

Thomas didn't move. He didn't even lift a finger. He didn't argue or resist. He had been given everything he needed and therefore responded as only a genuine follower of Jesus can respond. Thomas said, "My Lord and my God!"

Jesus replied, "Because you have seen Me, have you believed? Blessed are they who did not see, and yet believed" (John 20:28–29).

"PEACE BE WITH YOU"

The people who knew Jesus had the benefit of certain experiences we do not—most significantly, the tangible evidence of His resurrection and face-to-face encounters. Nevertheless, their responses that Sunday morning parallel the reactions I encounter every day as a modern-day bearer of this good news.

Some believed immediately. They were given the information, remembered what Jesus had predicted several times during His ministry, put all of the facts together, and accepted His resurrection as genuine.

Some believed with indirect evidence. They initially doubted the notion, but when they received further information, such as seeing an empty tomb and the peculiar way in which He left the grave clothes, they knew He had risen.

Some believed with direct evidence. They only believed that Jesus had risen after seeing Him with their own eyes.

The resurrection of Jesus Christ is a historical fact that carries far-reaching implications; far more significant than the mere novelty of a man reviving from the eternal quiet of death. Unlike any before Him, Jesus would never die again. The kind of life to which He has been raised surpasses the kind of life we continue to endure. These bodies get sick and suffer injury. Our present relationships are doomed to end, sooner or later, in betrayal, distance, or the inevitable demise of each person we know. Seasons of happiness must always yield to seasons of sorrow, though, thankfully, no sorrow remains forever. Demons, darkness, and death have been vanquished, yet they continue to lash out in desperate hatred against everything in God's creation.

But not to worry . . . Jesus is alive with a new kind of life that He longs to give any and all who will believe. As the late chaplain of the United States Senate Peter Marshall wrote,

> No tabloid will ever print the startling news that the mummified body of Jesus of Nazareth has been discovered in old Jerusalem.
>
> Christians have no carefully embalmed body enclosed in a glass case to worship.
>
> Thank God, we have an empty tomb.
>
> The glorious fact that the empty tomb proclaims to us is that life for us does not stop when death comes. *Death is not a wall, but a door.*[4]

Unfortunately, an open door may just as well be a locked prison gate for the one who refuses to cross the threshold. Not everyone responded to the evidence of Jesus' resurrection with belief. Remember the guards who felt the tremble of divine power and saw the bright flash of light?

> Some of the guard went into the city and told the chief priests everything that had happened. After they had assembled with the elders and formed a plan, they gave a large sum of money to the soldiers, telling them, "You are to say, 'His disciples came at night and stole his body while we were asleep.' If this matter is heard before the governor, we will satisfy him and keep you out of trouble." So they took the money and did as they were instructed. And this story is told among the Jews to this day.
>
> Matthew 28:11–15 NET

These are the men and women who keep me before the public in the pulpit and firm in my commitment to writing books. Though pardoned from the prison of sin, they steadfastly huddle in their cells with only doubt, fear, resentment, and worry to keep them company. God has placed within me a passionate desire to see them free. But all I can do is proclaim to them the good news. Are you in that company? Or, have you come to realize your need for a Savior and trusted your eternal soul to Him? Good for you! The devil, darkness, and death may swagger and boast, the pangs of life will sting for a while longer, but don't worry; the forces of evil are breathing their last. Not to worry . . . He's risen!

Chapter Seventeen

Encountering Jesus along Life's Road

Just days prior to the predawn raid on Gethsemane, Jesus mounted the foal of a donkey, a recognized symbol of peace and an unmistakable identification with the Messiah, and rode into Jerusalem to the cheering of thousands. Willing subjects of the King paved His path with their cloaks. Others cut palm branches, laid them along the stone pavement, and shouted, "Save us! Save us!"

He was their Messiah. He had promised abundant life. His followers fully expected He would become their king and that Israel would again be prosperous and free. But less than a week later, as the sun fell behind the horizon toward the end of an unforgettable week, the Son of God hung cold and lifeless on a Roman cross just outside the city walls.

His most faithful followers sat in dejected wonder as the sun set and the Sabbath began. In light of the prophecies, which Jesus had fulfilled, in light of the promises He made, and given the complete confidence they had placed in Him, nothing made sense. The people clearly wanted a righteous king, but as He lay dead, the chief priests were busy restocking the Annas Bazaar, and Israel's political leaders were seeking ways to exploit Pilate's newfound popularity. Not only had Jesus failed to improve Israel, but the nation's future seemed even bleaker than before. Discouragement and desperation reigned supreme.

Perhaps you can identify with the pain of Jesus' followers. Perhaps you have experienced the death of a dream or had the bridge to your ideal future crumble beneath your feet. Maybe you're suffering that difficult, disillusioning situation right now. If so, you have the opportunity to experience abundance like no other time in your life.

Does that surprise you? I mean, isn't spiritual enlightenment supposed to be enthralling? Isn't divine wisdom the result of an ecstatic encounter in which God's Spirit mystically touches ours? Many television and radio preachers make the spiritual life sound so exciting, like a miracle a day will drive all our problems away. Some talk of "victorious living" and "the good life" in which all our dreams will come true if we'll only choose to live by faith and claim God's best!

That's not abundant living. That's nothing more than a spiritualized spin on "the power of positive thinking." It's the same talk you'll hear from any motivational speaker in the country with the addition of a few Bible verses tossed in (usually out of context) to give it a sanctified shine.

Thanks to blockbuster movies, thrill rides, and Madison Avenue ad campaigns, we have come to expect that if life isn't "sensational," something must be wrong. We must be skinny and beautiful, pursue a career that's continually challenging and rewarding, become rich and famous, and enjoy a family life that's dynamic and fulfilling. If we're not careful, we can apply those expectations to our spiritual journey and fail to see the hand of God in the ordinary events of life. Even more tragic, we might fail to recognize His gentle teaching in the midst of life's most painful trials.

Many years ago, I was invited to speak at a small Bible college. The new president was fighting valiantly to help the school overcome its most recent troubles, and they were serious. I wanted to help however I could. He greeted me with overstated enthusiasm as I walked into the airport terminal. When I asked, "How are you today?" he replied loudly with a huge smile, "Fantastic!" I stuck out my hand and he shook it so hard my shoulder hurt.

"Well, that's good," I said. "How's the sch—"

"Outstanding! Just outstanding!"

I thought to myself, *OK, nothing's that good.* But I have to admit, his enthusiasm was infectious. He was exactly what motivators and leadership experts tell you to become. And while I wholeheartedly believe in choosing to approach every challenge with a great attitude, I don't mean that we should abandon authenticity and live in fantasyland.

A year later, I returned to speak and he met me again. Like the year before, everything was "Fantastic!" although the student body had dwindled noticeably and worry hung in the air like a haze. He was dreaming.

Sometime after my second trip and before my third, his world had come apart. The new president's wife had left him, his children were adrift, the school struggled financially, and enrollment had sunk to an all-time low. The place was on the verge of closing its doors. When I stepped into the now-familiar terminal, I didn't see him standing in his usual spot. He was sitting on a bench with his head down, clearly distracted until I walked up and stood right in front of him.

He looked up without a word. I took him by the shoulders, stood him up, and embraced him. "How are you?" I asked.

He hugged me in silence. Tears hung heavy from his eyelids as he said, "I'm growing and I'm learning. But I'm no longer fantastic." Pain had enrolled my friend in a very difficult curriculum that would earn him an advanced degree in reality and brokenness.

THE ROAD TO DISAPPOINTMENT

As the sun rose on Sunday morning and the Passover feast came to an end, two of Jesus' followers left for home, clearly disillusioned and resolving to leave their foolish dreams in Jerusalem forever. Even as rumors of resurrection circulated, the dejected pair began the seven-mile walk to the village of Emmaus.

> They were talking to each other about all the things that had happened. While they were talking and debating these things, Jesus himself approached and began to accompany them (but their eyes were kept

from recognizing him). Then he said to them, "What are these matters you are discussing so intently as you walk along?"

Luke 24:14–17 NET

Luke describes the disciples' conversation as bantering ideas back and forth with great emotion in a shared search for answers. When Jesus asked, "What are these matters you are discussing?" (24:17), Luke uses the term *antiballo*, which literally means "to throw back and forth." The disillusioned followers desperately wanted to know why their expectations of the Messiah had come to such a tragic end, and so they were exploring a number of theories.

Interestingly, the eyes of the two disciples were divinely prevented from recognizing Jesus. To them, He was just an ordinary man, a stranger out of the shadows joining them on their journey. As Luke recorded the story, he employed a clever narrative device called literary irony, in which the reader is aware of important facts that are hidden from the characters. (It makes for fascinating reading.) Note the delightful paradox we enjoy as one of the Emmaus-bound disciples responds to Jesus' question.

And they stood still, looking sad. Then one of them, named Cleopas, answered him, "Are you the only visitor to Jerusalem who doesn't know the things that have happened there in these days?"

Luke 24:17–18 NET

His question was laughable, given his audience. If anyone understood what had happened, it was Jesus! And if anyone was clueless, it was Cleopas! Nevertheless, Jesus encourages the disciples to talk, not to humiliate or chastise them, but for a very different purpose. He plays along with them by asking,

"What things?" "The things concerning Jesus the Nazarene," they replied, "a man who, with his powerful deeds and words, proved to be a prophet before God and all the people; and how our chief priests and rulers handed him over to be condemned to death, and crucified him. But we had hoped that he was the one who was going to redeem Israel."

Luke 24:19–21 NET

And with that statement, Cleopas revealed the source of his trouble. His noble expectations for a social, political, and economic Messiah had failed to materialize. His limited perspective would not allow him to embrace the Messiah's true agenda, of which economic prosperity and political liberation were only a tiny fraction. Cleopas's expectation yielded another tragic consequence.

> [Cleopas continued,] "Not only this, but it is now the third day since these things happened. Furthermore, some women of our group amazed us. They were at the tomb early this morning, and when they did not find his body, they came back and said they had seen a vision of angels, who said he was alive. Then some of those who were with us went to the tomb, and found it just as the women had said, but they did not see him."
>
> Luke 24:21–24

In the first century, Christian gatherings customarily read this and other writings aloud. So, when the audience heard Cleopas putting all the clues together without understanding their meaning, the tension must have become unbearable for the audience. I can imagine someone in the congregation finally reaching a breaking point and blurting out something like, "He's risen, you fool!"

Cleopas and his companion saw everything clearly in the sense that they had all the facts; nevertheless, they lacked the ability to see what should have been plainly visible. Three faulty perspectives coated their eyes like layers of dark film, shielding them from the truth and keeping them perpetually groping for answers in a despairing darkness. Jesus came to them to peel away the faulty perspectives one layer at a time until they could see clearly.

First, *their viewpoint lacked a spiritual dimension, leaving them with a merely human understanding of the events.* Take note of how Cleopas characterized the death of Jesus. Don't miss the lack of any divine involvement. He saw Jesus as "a prophet before God and all the people," but the chief priests and rulers "handed Him over" and "crucified Him."

Jesus, however, didn't see the events that way. In His trial before Pilate, He said, "You would have no authority over Me, unless it had been given you from above" (John 19:11). The disciple Peter would later declare to the same "chief priests and rulers,"

"Jesus the Nazarene, a man clearly attested to you by God with powerful deeds, wonders, and miraculous signs that God performed among you through him, just as you yourselves know—this man, *who was handed over by the predetermined plan and foreknowledge of God,* you executed by nailing him to a cross at the hands of Gentiles."

Acts 2:22–23 NET; emphasis added

Peter then added, "The things which God announced beforehand by the mouth of all the prophets, that His Christ would suffer, He has thus fulfilled" (Acts 3:18).

Shortly after this, the community of believers identified with the voluntary sacrifice of Jesus Christ. While enduring persecution, they praised God saying, "Indeed both Herod and Pontius Pilate, with the Gentiles and the people of Israel, assembled together in this city against your holy servant Jesus, *whom you anointed,* to do as much as *your power and your plan had decided beforehand* would happen" (Acts 4:27–28 NET; emphasis added).

Now, *that's* viewing the world from a divine perspective! They recognized that the people who thought they were playing such a significant role in history—people like Pontius Pilate, Annas, and Caiaphas—were nothing more than pieces of lint on the page of prophecy. While God is not the author of evil and He never prompts or condones sin, nothing occurs without His sovereign oversight. Others may choose to do evil deeds and God's people may suffer in the short term, but He will transform the evil intentions of evil people into opportunities for the enrichment of those in His care.

What happened to Cleopas's divine perspective? Before we start criticizing Cleopas and his partner, let's acknowledge a principle. When life is no longer "fantastic," when our expectations crumble and dreams fade, it's easy to slide into a funk. Circumstances become our taskmaster. People—especially those who took part in causing our pain—stand taller than God. Our vision becomes earthbound, horizontal. Our prayers seem to bounce off the ceiling, and God seems far removed from our pain. Let's face it; that's a natural response we're all guilty of choosing when our carefully constructed futures collapse under their own weight.

Let me point out that in the case of the two disillusioned disciples, God could not have been closer or more involved. But for reasons I'll point out later, He prevented their seeing Him. Still speaking as an anonymous stranger, Jesus peeled away the first layer.

> So he said to them, "You foolish people—how slow of heart to believe all that the prophets have spoken! Wasn't it necessary for the Christ to suffer these things and enter into his glory?" Then beginning with Moses and all the prophets, he interpreted to them the things written about himself in all the scriptures.
>
> Luke 24:25–27 NET

Peeling back the first layer, He then exposed the second. *Their own agenda determined their expectations.* Cleopas wistfully added, "We were hoping that it was He who was going to redeem Israel" (Luke 24:21).

As I stated earlier, the people of Israel made the mistake of thinking the Messiah would merely recapture the glory days of King David and victoriously lead Israel to become a Jewish world empire. Throughout His ministry, Jesus combated this limited perspective and tried to help people appreciate the much grander designs He had for the world. But as long as someone clings to his or her own agenda, he or she will remain blinded to the reality that God is in the process of creating.

God had a new covenant in mind. The new would build upon the old in order to provide His people much more than temporal power and material wealth. The King of Israel will indeed liberate the nation, and He will indeed rule the whole world. But not before liberating all people from the bondage of sin and not before recreating the world anew, all the way down to its atoms. It would be a new kind of kingdom, one in which material abundance would come as a result of having a right relationship with God, not in spite of being estranged from Him. After all, "Man does not live by bread alone, but by every word that comes from the mouth of God" (Matthew 4:4 NET).

Pause for a moment and consider a few questions: To what expectation are you clinging? What future have you determined for yourself? What perspective will you choose if your plans come unraveled or someone shatters your dreams?

We typically view circumstances, especially those involving loss, as difficult because reality does not fulfill our expectations. Moreover, the impression that God has abandoned us to our suffering only intensifies the pain of loss and the frustration of difficulties. The two followers on the road to Emmaus undoubtedly felt God-forsaken as they mourned the death of their dreams. Ironically, the very perspective that caused their pain kept them from seeing Jesus in their presence.

Let me encourage you to release your expectations. Hand them over to God, and open your hands to receive whatever He chooses to place in them. Here is a simple prayer that I recently discovered and have found to be of great help in recent days:

> Lord, I am willing
> To receive what You give;
> To lack what You withhold;
> To relinquish what You take;
> To suffer what You inflict;
> To be what You require.[1]

It was this mindset those two disciples lacked. Jesus helped them gain a divine, eternal perspective by teaching them from the Scriptures. Starting with the story of Genesis, applying the lyrics of the poets, and expositing the words of the prophets, He demonstrated how the sacrificial death of the Messiah was required to defeat evil. He very likely reminded them of the "Servant Songs" in the book of Isaiah, one of their favorite prophets. These songs feature a recurring figure called "the Servant of the Lord," who will bring justice to the world (Isaiah 42:1–4), lead His people into a right relationship with God (49:5), enlighten the nations and bring salvation to everyone (49:6), endure unjust humiliation (50:6), and bear the divine punishment others deserve (52:13–53:12).

The final song applauds the Servant for His sacrifice and extols His path to glory through His own humiliation. He is portrayed as a lamb led to an altar and slaughtered upon it as a sin offering. In the Hebrew temple, the brutal rite of animal sacrifice taught the worshiper that sin is costly and that "the wages of sin is death" (Romans 6:23). God established the practice as a means of giving His people grace. In the case of the Servant, unlike the Hebrew sacrifice in which *one* lamb was received by God as a token for *one* person's sin,

> He was pierced through for our transgressions,
> He was crushed for our iniquities;
> The chastening for our well-being fell upon Him,
> And by His scourging we are healed.
> All of us like sheep have gone astray,
> Each of us has turned to his own way;
> But the LORD has caused the iniquity of us all
> To fall on Him.
>
> Isaiah 53:5–6

As they approached the town of Emmaus, the two disciples found themselves so intrigued, they urged the stranger to stay the night in keeping with ancient Near Eastern rules of hospitality. Jesus accepted the offer, while maintaining His anonymity. The disciples were not yet ready. One final truth-obscuring layer remained on their eyes: *they failed to acknowledge the resurrection.*

They had heard the reports; they had all the facts. They simply refused to believe with their whole hearts. And their lack of belief affected everything. If these two disciples had believed that Jesus was alive, they would have behaved differently in at least two respects. First, they would have been walking *toward* Jerusalem, where Jesus was last seen, not away. Second, they would have accepted the trials, crucifixion, and burial of Jesus as the fulfillment of all He had promised, not as the end of their hopes.

As the afternoon sun drifted closer to the horizon, Jesus and the two followers prepared the evening meal and, no doubt, continued their discussion about the need for the Messiah to die. Of course, the death of Jesus begged an obvious question. "How, then, will the Messiah establish His kingdom and reign over it if He's dead?"

> When he had taken his place at the table with them, he took the bread, blessed and broke it, and gave it to them. At this point their eyes were opened and they recognized him. Then he vanished out of their sight.
>
> Luke 24:30–31 NET

The Greek phrase translated "their eyes were opened and they recognized Him" literally means "their eyes were *completely* opened and they came to *fully comprehend* Him." This was more than a passive, casual recognition of His features. They came to recognize Jesus in all His significance as the Messiah, the Suffering Servant, the Son of God, and their risen Lord!

Luke doesn't tell us why or how the breaking of bread opened their eyes. Maybe they saw the nail prints on His hands when He held up the bread to offer thanks. Perhaps they were present at the feeding of the five thousand men and their families in the wilderness and recognized the manner in which He broke the matzo. We can't be certain the final meal in the Upper Room on Passover didn't include more disciples than the inner Twelve. Maybe the sight of His sitting up and breaking the bread transported them back to that poignant moment when He said, "This is My body which is given for you; do this in remembrance of Me" (Luke 22:19). All we know for certain is that the scales fell from the eyes of the two disciples, and they saw everything clearly for the first time.

THE ROAD HOME

That's how it happens today. You're working your way through life, walking whatever path—school, work, home, ministry—and then something happens to upset the routine or, worse, something reduces your life to rubble. If God's presence seems far removed from you, be assured that He remains close by. However, you may have one or more faulty perspectives blocking the light from your eyes. Let me suggest three practical decisions that will help you cope with daily struggles as well as recover from life-altering circumstances.

First, *choose to view life through God's eyes.* This will not be easy because it doesn't come naturally to us. We cannot do this on our own. We have to allow God to elevate our vantage point. Start by reading His Word, the Bible. If you don't know where to begin, start at the front. I have found that reading truth from the Bible—even when it doesn't seem to have direct application to what I'm going through—gives my perspective a vertical dimension.

Pray and ask God to transform your thinking. Let Him do what you cannot. Ask Him to give you an eternal, divine perspective. Ask Him to replace your way of thinking with His. He delights to respond to prayer—invitations like that.

Second, *surrender your expectations.* Stop trying to change the universe to work the way you think it should. Grief is essentially the process of adjusting your mind to accept a radically new situation. The sooner you accept that you will not get your way, the sooner you'll heal. When you give up wishing things were different, you will start to change within. Let go of those resentments. Release your grip on what you want, no matter how good or right you think it is. Isn't it exhausting, anyway?

As you surrender your expectations, ask the Lord to show you *His* plan. Again, you can find it written in the sixty-six books of the Bible, our only reliable source of absolute truth. Pray. Ask Him to open your eyes to the future He desires, and determine to join Him in whatever He has chosen to do. Take your time with this. Transformation is a slow and sometimes tedious process.

Third, *acknowledge the resurrection of Jesus Christ and stake your future upon it.* A genuine belief in the fact of His resurrection will radically transform how you approach life. The death of Jesus conquered sin and overcame death's finality, but it's His resurrection that gives us life, hope, and reason to continue when everything appears hopeless. The risen Messiah offers us the same eternal, abundant life that He enjoys.

INSIGHT BEYOND SIGHT

Luke concludes this story with another bit of irony.

> When he had taken his place at the table with them, he took the bread, blessed and broke it, and gave it to them. At this point their eyes were opened and they recognized him. Then he vanished out of their sight.
>
> Luke 24:30–31 NET

A literal translation of that last statement would be, "he, invisible, became away from them," meaning that He suddenly vanished from their midst once their eyes were open. The disciples had been staring into the face of the risen Jesus, yet they were prevented from seeing Him. Why? Were they divinely prevented, or did their faulty expectations blind them to anything else? I believe both explanations are valid.

The Lord allowed their pain to continue until their own desires no longer held them captive. When they wearied of their pain, they willingly released their own expectation, the very thing that hurt them and kept them from seeing Jesus in their presence. To help them release their faulty perspective, Jesus offered them truth—a supernatural, divine perspective—which came from a careful review of the Scriptures.

As long as we hold onto our own desires and remain fixated on having our way, we will be unable to see God, even if He were to stand right before our eyes. God, in His patient, sometimes painful mercy, allows us to hold our desires as tightly as we wish until we tire of the pain and loosen our grip. Meanwhile, He holds before us a divine alternative, one that offers great abundance in exchange for the trinkets we clutch with desperate resolve.

Once the disciples' eyes were opened to the divine perspective, Jesus became invisible to their physical eyes. They had gained insight that transcended the need for sight. And their new, better-than-before, resurrected hope carried them back to Jerusalem to bear the good news to others.

They said to each other, "Didn't our hearts burn within us while he was speaking with us on the road, while he was explaining the scriptures to us?" So they got up that very hour and returned to Jerusalem. They found the eleven and those with them gathered together and saying, "The Lord has really risen, and has appeared to Simon!" Then they told what had happened on the road, and how they recognized him when he broke the bread.

Luke 24:32–35 NET

The self-made life is not an abundant life. It's bread made from stones. It is satisfaction that quickly dissipates and then leaves an even greater unsatisfied need. It tantalizes. It calls to the noblest desires of our nature, promising to resolve the difficulties that afflict us most and pledging to fulfill all the unmet needs that have left us chronically ill-equipped to overcome the challenges of life. Consequently, the fury and flurry of the fast lane—the dynamic yet vain pursuit of more money, greater security, and more fulfilling relationships—threatens to blind us to what matters most. Remember my friend? Remember when his world of "Fantastic!" went into a fast fade? Only then did he really begin to see what he had been missing. The pain of loss gave his inner eyes new lenses.

Jesus said, "Above all pursue his kingdom and righteousness, and all [your needs] will be given to you as well" (Matthew 6:33 NET). He also said at a time when His hunger had reached a depth it had never known, "Man does not live by bread alone, but by every word that comes from the mouth of God" (Matthew 4:4 NET), a direct quote from Scripture.

God has called His creation to find satisfaction in a personal relationship with Him, to stop trying to manage the world by conforming it to our expectations, and to allow Him to govern His creation. He continues to say through an ancient Hebrew worship song, "Be still and know that I am God!" Eugene Peterson paraphrases His command, "Step out of the traffic! Take a long, loving look at me, your High God, above politics, above everything" (Psalm 46:10 MSG).

Are you ready to do that? Aren't you weary of trying to get your way or trying to make life what *you* think it ought to be? Doesn't it make sense for you to turn your gaze from the trifling matters you consider so important to see what the risen Christ has to offer in exchange?

Jesus, the model human, is not only our Savior, but He's also our example. All of His dreams became reality because they perfectly aligned with the Father's will. However, let's not forget that He also suffered injustice, humiliation, prejudice, abandonment, agony, sorrow, and even death. His path to glory took Him down the Via Dolorosa, up to Golgotha, and into the grave.

If Jesus' life wasn't always "fantastic," neither is ours. "Fantastic" lies on the other side of our own resurrection. Until then, let's look for abundance in the ordinary events of life and especially during the trials. Let's invite Jesus into our homes, to sit at our tables, to break the bread of life, and, most of all, to open our eyes.

Chapter Eighteen

Listening to Jesus beside the Sea

Peter could always count on his passion. If he was anything, he was passionate. This ever-present, all-or-nothing hunger drove him to succeed at whatever he chose to pursue. When it came to running the family fishing business, he kept the boats in tip-top condition and hired the best deck hands in Galilee. And he was a hands-on proprietor. He loved hard work. He loved commanding the crews. Moreover, he shared a certain affinity with the Sea of Galilee, with its tempestuous, unpredictable nature. It frightened some men, like his brother, Andrew, but Peter found it irresistible. No other force in Galilee could match the intensity of Peter's passion—only the sea. And it taunted him.

Peter and his brother, Andrew, could not have been more different. Whereas Peter ruled the waves, Andrew loved the synagogue. As soon as Peter had the fishing fleet under control and appeared to be doing well, he encouraged Andrew to leave Galilee and to study in Jerusalem. While his brother sought learning, Peter hauled nets and counted his profits, although it wasn't about the money for him. It was just a way of keeping score in a friendly rivalry with John and James, the only men whose fiery temperaments rivaled his own.

Peter smiled as he remembered those earlier days. They were simpler times. But they felt decades removed from where he sat, which was in a small, dark room above the family home near Bethsaida in Galilee. The first flush of excitement had passed after the resurrection of Jesus, and His followers anxiously waited for further orders. He had instructed everyone to wait for Him in Galilee, which suited Peter just fine. The sea welcomed him. He could return home and figure out what to do with the rest of his life, maybe do some fishing again while the others formed the new government and planned the removal of Pilate and Herod Antipas.

More than a week had passed, and the silence was beginning to bother Peter. Jesus had been very warm toward him during their two previous encounters and never mentioned the issue most on Peter's mind. He wished Jesus would say something; it sat on the top of his head like a pan of hot coals. He felt certain Jesus was biding His time and would eventually let him down easy. He played out the conversation several times in his head. *Look, Peter, I think we both know you're not cut out for leadership in the new kingdom. I appreciate the passion with which you throw yourself wholeheartedly into whatever you put your mind to. But it's too unpredictable. I need someone like John, who has learned to tame his impulsiveness and can keep an even keel. I need someone I can count on. You're a splendid fisherman. Why don't you return to the nets and stick with what you know?*

The disappointment and the disgrace were almost more than he could bear. Others talked of the coming days and imagined what positions they would occupy, but he could barely gather the strength to leave his room. How had it come to this? Where did it all go wrong?

"FOLLOW ME"

Peter remembered the first time he laid eyes on Jesus and how he came by his nickname. Andrew had been a disciple of John the Baptizer for a number of months and then sent word home that the Messiah would be appearing soon. The family was understandably skeptical, but Andrew was not easily fooled. If anyone could spot a fake, it was him. So when Peter traveled to Jerusalem to celebrate one of Israel's many feasts, he took Andrew seriously when he said, "We have found the Messiah" (John 1:41). He followed his brother with more than idle interest to a modest home just outside the city and met the man who would change him forever.

Jesus greeted him with the customary embrace and a quick kiss on either cheek. But before removing His hands from Peter's shoulders, He shook him firmly and said, "Simon, son of Jonah, I think I'll call you Cephas [Peter, in Greek]. You're solid as a rock!" Peter took that as a great compliment from Jerusalem's newest and most dynamic rabbi.

After spending a few days with Jesus, Peter agreed with Andrew. "We have found the Messiah." He would have remained in Jerusalem to learn more from the remarkable man from Nazareth, but the fishing business would not tolerate his being gone too long. He returned home, resolving to obey the new king whenever the time came for Him to ascend the throne. He knew Andrew would keep him informed.

A few weeks later, Peter and his crew had completed a hard night's work on the sea and had pulled their boats close to the shore where James and John were cleaning their nets. Peter and the sons of Zebedee frequently pooled their resources, especially when times were tight. And, for some reason, the catches had been usually sparse lately.

A large congregation from nearby Capernaum sat on a gentle slope close to the water's edge, listening to the strong voice of a teacher. It was not an uncommon sight, although the crowd was much larger than Peter was used to seeing. But he barely took notice as he and his crew hauled their nets onto the shore and began the work of cleaning and mending and straightening. As the men bantered and chided one another to break the tedium, they failed to notice that the teacher's voice no longer echoed across the shore but stood nearby asking for a favor.

Peter recognized Him immediately. He was the Messiah. He wanted to use one of the boats as a speaking platform, which was a brilliant idea from an orator's point of view. The calm water and the indentation of the shoreline created a natural amphitheater with remarkably good acoustics. For the fishermen, however, this was a particularly annoying request after hauling empty nets all night long. Nevertheless, Peter patiently ordered his crew to roll up the nets, load them back onto the boat, and row a short distance from the shore.

Jesus concluded His lesson and dismissed the people, at which point Peter expected He would want to be let off on land. But the rabbi looked at Peter and said, "Put out into the deep water and let down your nets for a catch." Simon replied, "But Master, we worked hard all night and caught nothing, but I will do as You say and let down the nets" (Luke 5:4–5).

The haul of fish nearly sank his boat and that of James and John, who came alongside to help. For Peter, it was the first of many lessons. Good intentions and earnest effort are not enough. Only Jesus can make an otherwise futile life productive.

That very moment, Peter leaped after the Messiah's call: "Follow Me, and I will make you become fishers of men" (Mark 1:17). He didn't know where it led, what adventures it promised, or what dangers it entailed. People asked, but he didn't know. And he didn't care how foolish his neighbors thought him to be. He cast himself on the call of Jesus with wanton gusto, determined to ride it to the end.

"COME TO ME"

In the dark consolation of his upper room hideaway, Peter smiled at the bittersweet memory, and then winced. How often he had thrown himself into something with reckless abandon, only to appear and feel foolish later. Like the time he and the other disciples were straining against the oars in a terrible squall. Jesus had ordered them to go ahead of Him across the sea, but when they struggled to make progress their Master came to their rescue.

> At about four o'clock in the morning, Jesus came toward them walking on the water. They were scared out of their wits. "A ghost!" they said, crying out in terror.
>
> But Jesus was quick to comfort them. "Courage, it's me. Don't be afraid."
>
> Peter, suddenly bold, said, "Master, if it's really you, call me to come to you on the water."

He said, "Come ahead."

Jumping out of the boat, Peter walked on the water to Jesus. But when he looked down at the waves churning beneath his feet, he lost his nerve and started to sink. He cried, "Master, save me!"

Jesus didn't hesitate. He reached down and grabbed his hand. Then he said, "Faint-heart, what got into you?"

The two of them climbed into the boat, and the wind died down.

Matthew 14:25–32 MSG

"Faint-heart" indeed! He was a strong swimmer and had fallen into the drink more than once in his years on the sea. What *had* gotten into him? In a split second between steps, his mind flitted from complete confidence in Jesus, to the size of the waves lapping over his feet, to the fact that only he had the temerity to step out of the boat, and suddenly he was up to his neck.

The other disciples wouldn't soon let him forget that day! Or the day he received from Jesus a stunning affirmation and a withering rebuke within the same five minutes. On the outskirts of Caesarea Philippi, Jesus asked a simple question: "Who do people say that I am?" Some tossed out names like John the Baptizer, or the powerful Old Testament prophets, Elijah and Jeremiah. But when Jesus turned the question to His disciples, they suddenly fell silent.

"And how about you? Who do you say I am?"

Simon Peter said, "You're the Christ, the Messiah, the Son of the living God."

Jesus came back, "God bless you, Simon, son of Jonah! You didn't get that answer out of books or from teachers. My Father in heaven, God himself, let you in on this secret of who I really am. And now I'm going to tell you who you are, *really* are. You are Peter, a rock. This is the rock on which I will put together my church, a church so expansive with energy that not even the gates of hell will be able to keep it out.

"And that's not all. You will have complete and free access to

God's kingdom, keys to open any and every door: no more barriers between heaven and earth, earth and heaven. A yes on earth is yes in heaven. A no on earth is no in heaven."

Matthew 16:15–19 MSG

Peter felt pretty good at that point. He stood a little taller than the rest. He was to have immense authority in the new kingdom! And why not? Who was more committed than he? But his lofty place of honor didn't last long. Jesus revealed that His own path to glory ran along the Via Dolorosa.

"The Son of Man must suffer many things and be rejected by the elders, chief priests, and experts in the law, and be killed, and on the third day be raised."

Luke 9:22 NET

Peter didn't like the sound of that negative talk. That's no way to lead and inspire others. That's no way to enjoy the best life now. As the Rock, he felt it was his duty to advise their leader.

So Peter took him aside and began to rebuke him: "God forbid, Lord! This must not happen to you!" But he turned and said to Peter, "Get behind me, Satan! You are a stumbling block to me, because you are not setting your mind on God's interests, but on man's."

Matthew 16:22–23 NET

Then he learned the truth about leadership in the kingdom.

Jesus said to his disciples, "If anyone wants to become my follower, he must deny himself, take up his cross, and follow me. For whoever wants to save his life will lose it, but whoever loses his life for my sake will find it."

Matthew 16:24–25 NET

Peter remembered feeling rebuked yet emboldened to remain steadfast. He thought Jesus had changed the objective from conquest to martyrdom, and so he resolved to follow his Leader to the death.

"RETURN TO ME"

On the eve of Jesus' arrest, He encouraged His disciples to let love for one another become their distinguishing characteristic. Then, He prepared them for the difficult hours to follow. "This night you will all fall away because of me, for it is written: 'I will strike the shepherd, and the sheep of the flock will be scattered.' But after I am raised, I will go ahead of you into Galilee" (Matthew 26:31–32 NET). But Peter would hear none of it. "If they all fall away because of you, I will never fall away!" (Matthew 26:33 NET).

As Peter lay motionless in the dark quiet of his room in Bethsaida, he flinched at the audacity of his own words. To make matters worse, Jesus' tender warning remained indelibly etched on his conscience: "Simon, Simon, pay attention! Satan has demanded to have you all, to sift you like wheat, but I have prayed for you, Simon, that your faith may not fail. When you have turned back, strengthen your brothers" (Luke 22:31–32 NET).

To people of good conscience, there is no judge, jury, or executioner more severe than his or her own mind. Peter sat in a festering solitude for several days after returning to Bethsaida. Six of his closest friends among "the Twelve" had come to offer encouragement, but he had been inconsolable and refused to see anyone. Finally, Peter could stand his self-recriminations no longer. The sea beckoned . . . it was time to return to the familiar. He started out for the docks and, as he strode past his fellow disciples, he said over his shoulder, "I'm going fishing." His friends looked at each other and trailed after him.

The men rowed their boats into the deep, lowered their nets, and after a long night of labor, caught nothing. Row, toss, drag . . . nothing. Row, toss, drag . . .

Night gave way to the first glimmers of dawn, and the men made their way to a familiar spot on the shore, where they could groom the nets and let them dry for another day. A warm flicker of orange drew their attention as they rowed toward their customary landing. When they were still about a hundred yards out, a shadowy figure called out to them. "Children, you don't have any fish, do you?" (John 21:5).

Most fishermen will tell you that this is not a welcomed question after a long, futile night, and definitely not the most delicate way to ask it! The reply was probably a curt, "No!" But the men would have been respectful. The fact that he called them "boys" suggested he was a teacher or an elder in the community.

"Cast the net on the right-hand side of the boat and you will find catch!" (John 21:6).

Peter shot a quizzical look to John, who replied with a shrug. So they tossed the net overboard—on the right—ran the boat in a large circle, and then began to haul it in. At first, Peter thought the net had snagged something near the bottom. A sharp tug on the head rope tipped the boat and nearly pulled him in. But then it moved. The others fell in behind Peter and slowly lifted the seine to the surface to reveal a mass of shimmering movement and the sound of rushing water. Fish! Big fish! Lots of them!

Some other disciples manning the second boat rowed furiously to aid the first and made certain the fish didn't sink them. When the commotion settled for a moment, John remembered the day Jesus called them to become His disciples. He nudged Peter and said, "It's the Lord."

Peter grabbed his tunic from the deck, immediately plunged into the sea, and swam for shore. The prospect of seeing Jesus again caused him to forget the source of his disgrace, at least while he thrashed the water in his winsome race for land. Between strokes, he could hear the other disciples laughing at him. Fortunately, failure didn't rob the passionate disciple of his most endearing quality.

Peter slogged his way across the beach to find Jesus tending a charcoal fire. The smell of roasting fish reminded him of how hungry his long, futile night had made him. He dropped to his knees, grabbed a fish from the fire, peeled it, and started eating. The first morsels of food and the sight of Jesus brought strength to his body he hadn't felt in weeks, and the warm glow of the fire on his cheeks reminded him of how cold he had been. By the time he was warmed and filled, Jesus pointed to the struggling disciples, who had just reached the water's edge with the bulging net. "Bring some of the fish you have now caught" (John 21:10). Peter dashed to help his friends.

Having counted the fish—one hundred fifty-three—and laid them out along the shore, the disciples fell down by the glowing fire.

"KEEP FOLLOWING ME"

Campfires have a way of bringing calm to the people who take time to enjoy them. Mindless chatter usually gives way to thoughtful silence. And then when someone speaks, it's almost always something poignant or vulnerable or profound.

Peter felt content for the first time in nearly two weeks. Seven of his closest companions lay on their backs or sat facing the fire, their bellies full of broiled fish Jesus had provided and they had caught themselves. The scars on Jesus' hands no longer caused him heartache. The Messiah's agony was forever in the past; only glory for Jesus lay ahead. The nail prints were now meaningful, mute reminders of the priceless gift he and the other followers had been given.

Jesus broke the silence with a question. "Simon, son of John, do you love Me more than these?" (John 21:15).

The word for *love* used by John when he recorded the conversation was *agape*, which described a deliberate kind of love that is wrapped in emotion, but not fueled by it. *Agape* loves God first, loves neighbor as self, and loves enemies and friends alike. It forgives faults and finds its highest expression when it is least deserved. Far from impetuous, *agape* is a love that grows out of commitment.

The question stung. It grieved Peter deeply. It was one he had asked himself a thousand times since the night he stood around another campfire and denied knowing his Master, punctuated with curses. The added comparison, "more than these," resurfaced the pain of the past two weeks and placed it on his chest. And it felt like a boulder about to crush the life out of him. He looked at the other disciples, who kept their eyes fixed either on the stars or the glowing embers. "Yes, Lord; You know that I love You" (John 21:15).

As Peter spoke, John used a different word for love, *phileo*. It's a warm, heartfelt affection someone has for family and close friends. It was a favorite term among the Gentiles and certainly not one used carelessly or lightly. But

Peter understood the significance of Jesus' question. Affection was not the issue at hand. It was commitment.

Jesus replied, "Tend My lambs" (John 21:15).

The invitation came as a surprise to no one but Peter. He no longer felt qualified to be a "fisher of men," to say nothing of being a shepherd to Jesus' followers. After all, who was he to teach others about commitment? He had given his all for more than three years and he meant every word he spoke in the upper room, but when the crisis came, his passionate dedication to remain faithful ended in the same futility as the previous night's labor on the sea. He couldn't even catch fish without Jesus' help, to say nothing of leading people!

A few moments of silence suggested to Peter that the matter had been settled. The sheep needed a competent shepherd. But then Jesus asked, "Simon, son of John, do you love [*agape*] Me?"

"Yes, Lord; You know that I love [*phileo*] You."

"Shepherd My sheep" (John 21:16).

Again, *agape* . . . *phileo* . . . invitation . . . silence.

Peter's passion often kept him from seeing the truth about himself. As long as there was something external to fight, like the Sea of Galilee or a cohort of soldiers, his passion could pass for genuinely committed *agape* love. But with no storms to survive and no enemy to vanquish, having spent all his passion and having no pride to take its place in the void, Peter became painfully aware of how hollow he was—and had always been.

Peter's *phileo* reply fell short of what either man wanted, but it was honest. Fortunately, Jesus cares more about integrity than perfection.

> [Jesus] said to him the third time, "Simon, son of John, do you love [*phileo*] Me?"
>
> John 21:17

This time, *phileo*.

> Peter was grieved because He said to him the third time, "Do you love Me?" And he said to Him, "Lord, You know all things; You know that I love You."

Phileo.

Jesus said to him, "Tend My sheep" (John 21:17).

We tend to push others—and therefore ourselves—into certain molds. We have a mold for leaders. We want our leaders to be gregarious, thoughtful, experienced, wise, confident, visionary, and optimistic. We don't tend to tolerate failure, nor do we want leaders to put on airs. And so we erect a mental standard of perfection that no one can meet.

Peter had a mold. There by the campfire, still weary from his futile night of fishing, he held the broken pieces of his mold out to the Lord and said, in effect, "This is all I have." The repeated invitation of Jesus said in reply, "That's all I want."

After a long silence, Jesus stood up and motioned for Peter to join Him. What He had to say next was for Peter's ears only. Once they were several paces away from the others, Jesus offered a prediction that put the fallen disciple's passion—something Peter had come to loathe—into perspective, one that demonstrated God's sovereignty and affirmed His ability to transform weakness into strength.

> "I tell you the solemn truth, when you were young, you tied your clothes around you and went wherever you wanted, but when you are old, you will stretch out your hands, and others will tie you up and bring you where you do not want to go." (Now Jesus said this to indicate clearly by what kind of death Peter was going to glorify God.) After he said this, Jesus told Peter, "Follow me."
>
> John 21:18–19 NET

The passion that had propelled him through every challenge in life and had fueled his pursuit of greatness in the kingdom came from a place deep inside Peter. It appeared holy from the outside, but it served the most profane idol of all: self. And like all vain pursuits, Peter's led to despair.

As Peter listened to Jesus beside the sea, he came to terms with the void. Emptied of passion and repulsed by pride, he was ready to be filled. We know from later accounts that Peter endured prison and persecution with surprising—some would even say supernatural—resolve, and he was eventually martyred on a cross. But the transformation was not instantaneous. There was more to learn.

> Peter, turning around, saw the disciple whom Jesus loved [John] following them; the one who also had leaned back on His bosom at the supper and said, "Lord, who is the one who betrays You?" So Peter seeing him said to Jesus, "Lord, and what about this man?" Jesus said to him, "If I want him to remain until I come, what is that to you? You follow Me!"
>
> John 21:20–22

John was the first disciple to return to Jesus after fleeing and had remained with Jesus throughout the trials and crucifixion. He was the man Jesus entrusted with the care of His mother. John, of all the disciples, had been a picture of steadfast devotion.

The fallen human soul will not be emptied of pride for very long. And some habits die hard. Peter's first tentative steps on the sea of ministry promised to be sure-footed, but he faltered when he took his eyes off Jesus and turned them to comparison. "But Lord, what about John?" Jesus said to him, "If I want him to remain until I come, what is that to you? You follow Me!"

Jesus' final command is best translated, "You, Me keep on following!" Not John. Not any other great man. Not even your own lofty ambitions. "You, Me keep on following!" *Let your passion become a passionate pursuit of Me. And as you follow, the sheep will follow.*

FOLLOWING PETER'S PASSIONATE PURSUIT

Peter would have made a particularly good candidate for public office in our democratic, entrepreneurial, self-motivated culture. We admire the "self-made man." We cheer those who desire more power and wealth, those who inspire others with their infectious passion to conquer new territory or to overcome daunting challenges. Those are the people we love to follow.

Jesus looked for very different qualities in the men He chose to carry out His vision. He chose men with little formal education, though most would have learned to read and write in the synagogue. He chose men with obvious flaws, though none except Judas Iscariot was steadfastly dedicated to evil like the corrupt religious leaders. He chose men whose wills could not be easily bent, but could be or would be divinely compelled to follow. The eleven disciples were extraordinary people, yet for no other reason than their passionate pursuit of Christ and His calling.

You, too, have been called. The imperative, "You, Me keep on following," is not limited to Peter. Peter's destiny lay along a different path from John's. And your calling is unlike anyone else's. But the call remains the same: "Follow Me!"

Your calling will certainly affect others, yet it is yours alone to answer. Along with being unique, it is also costly and rewarding. It will likely lead you to places that frighten you now but will feel as natural as home when the time is right. The danger is real, but there is no safer place on earth than the path to which God has ordained for you. The place of greatest satisfaction is being in the nucleus of His will.

As you examine your unique calling, consider three important lessons from the call of Peter.

First, *when the Lord offers an opportunity to transform futility into fruitfulness, be open to change.* Be careful to avoid interpreting circumstances as indicators of God's will. Note that Jesus called Peter to leave his profession as a fisherman—a significant change in direction—*even after giving him a miraculously large catch.* The call will not be audible. Don't go looking for burning bushes or cloud formations. Your call will become clear as your mind is transformed by the reading of Scripture and the internal work of God's Spirit. The Lord never hides His will from us. In time, as you obey the call first to follow, your destiny will unfold before you. The difficulty will lie in keeping other concerns from diverting your attention.

Second, *when Jesus plans to move you in a new and challenging direction, expect a period of deep soul-searching.* Finding clarity can be a difficult challenge when distractions clamor for your attention. The days following the resurrection of Jesus were probably quiet ones for Peter, and he likely felt cast aside. Only when the time was right did Jesus confront His formerly impetuous disciple with a challenge. Peter's call came as the humiliation of his failure echoed in his head and his business associates prepared a huge haul of fish for the market. Circumstances would suggest that he would be a better fisherman than spiritual leader. For Peter, the defining issue was not passion, it was love. Don't miss that. Whom did he love, and would honoring that love be his first priority? Once those questions had been answered, his future became clear.

Third, *when the Lord makes it clear you're to follow Him in this new direction, focus fully on Him and refuse to be distracted by comparisons with others.* Even as Peter heard the call of Jesus for the fourth time, he could not resist a glance over his shoulder. Peter must have thought, *Who am I compared to Mr. Faithfulness?* But Jesus clarified the issue. John was responsible for John. Peter was responsible for Peter. And each had only one command to heed: "Follow Me."

If anyone had disqualified himself as the leader among the early Christians, it was certainly the one who denied his relationship with Jesus when the situation grew tense. Who would want an emotional, vacillating, impetuous firebrand to lead the people of God? Jesus did. After Peter came to recognize his own inadequacy, his utter inability to fulfill his destiny apart from obedience to his only true responsibility, he became a rock-solid leader. As his story unfolds in the book of Acts, we can clearly see that when Peter kept his eyes on Jesus and followed Him, others followed too. And they followed by the thousands.

Needed today: more Peters.

Chapter Nineteen

Challenged by Jesus on the Mountain

The angels must have wondered what He was thinking. The plan for God to become a man in the person of Jesus Christ had been ingenious. Only a human can represent humanity and bear the punishment they deserve, yet only God can overcome death. But to leave the responsibility of spreading the news in the hands of feeble, fickle humanity must have been baffling.

Joe Aldrich begins his book, *Life-Style Evangelism*, with an imaginative fable.

> The angel Gabriel approached [Jesus] and said, "Master, you must have suffered terribly for men down there."
>
> "I did," He said.
>
> "And," continued Gabriel, "do they know all about how you loved them and what you did for them?"
>
> "Oh, no," said Jesus, "not yet. Right now only a handful of people in Palestine know."
>
> Gabriel was perplexed. "Then what have you done," he asked, "to let everyone know about your love for them?"

Jesus said, "I've asked Peter, James, John, and a few more friends to tell other people about Me. Those who are told will in turn tell still other people about Me, and My story will be spread to the farthest reaches of the globe. Ultimately, all of mankind will have heard about My life and what I have done."

Gabriel frowned and looked rather skeptical. He knew well what poor stuff men were made of. "Yes," he said, "but what if Peter and James and John grow weary? What if the people who come after them forget? What if way down in the twentieth century, people just don't tell others about you? Haven't you made any other plans?"

And Jesus answered, "I haven't made any other plans. I'm counting on them."[1]

On dozens of occasions over a forty-day period after His resurrection, Jesus appeared to hundreds of His disciples scattered across Judea and Galilee. He walked with them, shared meals, taught lessons, and enjoyed their company. He took this time to restore, reassure, and rejuvenate His citizens after they had suffered the traumatic experience of seeing their king tortured and killed. Many, if not most, had considered the Messiah's cause lost to evil and needed to be rallied for the work that lay ahead. He would prepare His followers in two mountaintop meetings. At the first meeting in Galilee, Jesus gave them the plan (Matthew 28:16–20); at the second in Judea, He gave them His power (Acts 1:3–11).

THE EXTRAORDINARY PLAN

The mountain in Galilee has not been identified for us in the Gospel accounts. It could have been on the mountain where He commonly preached. It might have been the remote mountain top where Peter, James, and John saw Him momentarily shine with divine light. (Matthew 17:1–2). Or it may have been merely an elevated perspective from which the disciples could see a great distance. To stand at the top of Mount Tabor, for instance, is to see a vast expanse of flat land stretching out on all sides. Though less than two thousand feet above sea level at the summit, one feels like he or she can see the entire world.

It was on a high mountain that God originally took Abraham, the father of the Hebrews, and said, "To your descendants I will give this land" (Genesis 12:7). The followers of Jesus must have thought He was about to renew God's covenant and tell them the plan by which they would claim the Promised Land for the new kingdom. And, in a way, He would. He presented His plan for kingdom-building clearly and simply. Many call this divine directive the "Great Commission."

> "All authority in heaven and on earth has been given to me. Therefore go and make disciples of all nations, baptizing them in the name of the Father and the Son and the Holy Spirit, teaching them to obey everything I have commanded you. And remember, I am with you always, to the end of the age." (Matthew 28:18–20 NET)

The plan is to "make disciples of all nations."

The main verb in Jesus' directive to the disciples is "make disciples." Surprisingly, it isn't "go." It isn't "baptize." Nor is it even "teach." He included all of those verbs to give support to the main idea. The goal of the Great Commission is to tell people about the offer of salvation through the sacrifice of Jesus Christ, who bore their punishment for sin and offers them eternal life as a free gift. Furthermore, the followers are to remain with the new believers in order to mentor and encourage them, teaching them how to walk in obedience to their King.

The Greek word translated "go" in the Great Commission is a participle ("going"). Some preachers and teachers suggest that Jesus' command should be rendered, "while you are going, make disciples," implying that evangelism doesn't have to include anything beyond a natural part of our daily routine. However, this is not how a reader in the first century would have interpreted His command.

The phrase "go and make disciples" uses the participle in the same manner the angel did in warning Joseph, the husband of Mary: "Get up! Take the Child . . ." (Matthew 2:13). The angel did not say to Joseph, "While you are getting up, take the Child . . ." Herod's intention to kill the Christ Child demanded urgency. Likewise, the command of Jesus is both clear and urgent: "Go, make disciples." This command is not just for those in vocational Christian ministries—missionaries, evangelists, and preachers—but for all believers.

Note that Jesus included the rite of baptism as a part of disciple-making, which unfortunately has been the focus of controversy for centuries. Some teach that infants should be baptized for the same reason Jewish baby boys were circumcised, as a symbol of their participation in a covenant with God. Others say that baptism is merely a public testimony and an outward symbol of one's inner transformation. Others teach that baptism is a requirement of salvation or one of the means by which a person escapes the punishment of hell.

The Bible, however, clearly teaches that baptism is an act of obedience after a person has declared his or her trust in Jesus Christ. Baptism is an important step in a new believer's new life, not a requirement for salvation from sin. Believers are saved by grace, though faith in Jesus Christ, not the result of any good deeds . . . including baptism. Think of it this way: Salvation by faith alone in Christ alone because of grace alone.

Note also the scope of this mission. *All* authority . . . *all* nations . . . *all* that I commanded you . . . and I am with you *always*. This is a perpetual mission intended to extend His authority to all people, in all places, throughout all time. His goal is nothing short of a worldwide kingdom in which every person bends the knee to King Jesus. While Jesus was intense about the mission, He was nevertheless relaxed about the method.

He empowered His people for the task and He intended every ounce of that energy and creativity to be used in support of the mission. There are literally hundreds of effective ways people have devised to tell others about Jesus Christ. Evangelistic dinners, couple's gatherings, singles' meetings, home Bible studies, radio and television ministries, businessmen's and women's meetings, men's gatherings, women's gatherings, retreats, clubs, mayor's prayer breakfast, president's prayer breakfasts, Christian movies, videos, publishing, internet sites, camps, conferences, retreats, seminars, church-sponsored athletic gatherings, music ministries, arts and crafts, neighborhood teas, ministries to various specialized careers, free medical clinics, high school ministries, college campus discussion groups, ministry-sponsored debates, children's ministries, special needs ministries, divorce recovery, substance abuse programs, Christian schools . . . I could fill another page given enough time. And chances are, you have a great idea in mind that isn't on my list. My advice? What are you waiting for? Go! Make disciples!

The people who cannot answer the question, *Who is Jesus Christ?*, have a wide variety of needs, each one offering an opportunity for a believer to share the good news. A teenager in Littleton, Colorado has very different problems from a widow in New Orleans or a single mother in New York or a prisoner in Huntsville, Texas. One ministers to a family torn by grief very differently than one does an up-and-coming business person beginning a whole new way of life after a big promotion. Someone who earns a living in construction will respond differently than an artist or an athlete or a pilot or a salesman.

Fortunately, God made all varieties of people with a wide variety of interests and abilities. He has called people of every race and color who have been hurt by life in every manner imaginable. Even the scars of past abuse and injury can be the means of bringing healing to another. What wonderful opportunities to make disciples!

Jesus commanded His followers to go and to be relentless in their making disciples, but He left the methods in our hands. Let me encourage you to be creative, then follow through with enthusiasm.

HOLY POWER, ORDINARY PEOPLE

At a second mountaintop meeting—this one near Bethany in Judea—a multitude of Jesus' followers assembled with great anticipation. They hoped to hear a major announcement concerning the future kingdom. When Jesus came to them, they worshiped Him, and as part of their adoration they asked the question everyone wanted answered. "Lord, is it at this time You are restoring the kingdom to Israel?"

> Jesus replied, "You are not permitted to know the times or periods that the Father has set by his own authority. But you will receive power when the Holy Spirit has come upon you, and you will be

my witnesses in Jerusalem, and in all Judea and Samaria, and to the
farthest parts of the earth." (Acts 1:7–8 NET)

This announcement was nothing short of stunning for several reasons.
First, the idea of the citizens receiving power was upside-down thinking.
In our democratic, self-governing age, we have grown accustomed to the
idea that political and military power belong to the citizens, but in the first
century, only kings possessed power. Second, throughout most of human
history, no one *received* power; one rose to power by earning it or, more
commonly, took it at point of a spear or dagger. Third, the announcement
pointed to a very different kind of future than what the followers of Jesus
had anticipated. They never completely released their expectation of a
Hebrew renaissance, in which they would revive the kingdom and restore
the golden era of David and Solomon.

But one feature of Jesus' announcement overshadowed everything else.
It left the multitude standing in slack-jawed astonishment. "When the
Holy Spirit has come upon you . . ."

The Holy Spirit had always been a mysterious, almost "spooky" concept
in the Old Testament. When the Spirit of God interacted with someone, he
or she possessed godlike qualities or acted with an authority not his or her
own. Warriors gained superhuman strength and cunning. Prophets spoke
and wrote the mind of God. Sometimes, they demonstrated the power of
God to those who hated Him by controlling the weather, healing illnesses,
or calling down fire from heaven. Because of this, the activity of the Holy
Spirit became a sign of legitimate divine authority. Later in Israel's history,
the presence of the Holy Spirit would indicate who should sit upon the
throne of God's kingdom.

Israel's first king, Saul, looked like he was born for the role. He was
tall, handsome, intelligent, and sensitive to God's leading. But he eventually lost most of his attractive qualities, the most important being obedience. So God chose another to replace him; a shepherd from the remote
town of Bethlehem. The prophet, Samuel, traveled there under the direction of God to find the young man and pour ceremonial oil over his
head, thus making him "the anointed one of Israel." At that moment, "the

Spirit of the LORD came mightily upon David from that day forward" and "departed from Saul" (1 Samuel 16:13–14).

Saul refused to vacate the throne. His emotional stability eroded, resulting in his becoming increasingly insane, dedicating much of his army to hunting down David in order to kill him. For more than twelve years, Saul ruled as an illegitimate king while the rightful "anointed one," the man on whom "the Spirit of the Lord came mightily" lived in exile. Each citizen of God's kingdom embraced either the legitimate king or the usurper, though none did so blindly. The presence of the Holy Spirit identified each man clearly.

The evidence of the Holy Spirit had been obvious in the life of Jesus. So when He called His citizens together and promised that the Holy Spirit would come upon them as well, He was promising something of inestimable value. The same Power, who identified Him as the legitimate ruler of Israel, would be theirs as well. The presence of the Holy Spirit would identify them not only as legitimate citizens of the kingdom, but as co-regents with the King! Jesus told His subjects that they would be receiving the same powerful Presence that made prophets speak the mind of God and warriors wield unequaled skill and obscure shepherd boys employ God's delegated authority.

The announcement stunned everyone for another reason. The Messiah was delegating His divine power to very ordinary people. As the Apostle Paul later expressed it, "We have this treasure in clay jars, so that the extraordinary power belongs to God and does not come from us" (2 Corinthians 4:7).

The people who stood before Jesus on the mountaintop were not strangers, but close companions, all of them believers in His identity and His mission. They were not any more or less remarkable than the people we see shopping at the mall or filling the stands at a sporting event or going to work in a factory. They were farmers, fishermen, merchants, mothers, artisans, and laborers. Some held positions of authority; most did not. Many of them, though believers, had been weak in their faith. Matthew recorded that some at the first meeting "were doubtful," using a Greek idiom that meant, literally, "to be double-mouthed." Some of those to whom Jesus promised this power had been wavering.

Note also that He didn't fit them with halos or collars or crowns. He didn't issue uniforms or send them to special schools or bestow upon them titles, such as reverend, father, or pastor. I don't make that point to suggest that seminaries are not vital; I am the chancellor of one. And I don't suggest that churches shouldn't have pastors; I continue to serve as one. However, every believer was promised the same power equally and was called to become a part of His plan.

Let's face it; ninety percent of ministry is just showing up to serve. Once someone gets past the initial decision to participate, the Holy Spirit takes care of the rest.

THE ULTIMATE VICTORY

Jesus didn't limit the scope, yet He acknowledged that the plan would not be accomplished overnight. He empowered ordinary people to carry out an extraordinary plan and He foretold their success. He said, "You will be my witnesses in Jerusalem, and in all Judea and Samaria, and to the farthest parts of the earth" (Acts 1:8 NET) Note that the epicenter of evangelism was Jerusalem, the home of most of the disciples. They were to be witnesses for Christ first to their family, friends, neighbors, and coworkers. "Judea" referred to the area surrounding their home, in what we might call a county or state. "Samaria" indicated the neighboring region in which relations would be cross-cultural—telling others of different faiths and races about Jesus Christ. Finally, they were to carry the good news to all parts of the world.

His plan called for action, and how He expressed it predicted its success. He didn't say "you *might* be my witnesses," or "you *could* be my witnesses," or even "you *should* be my witnesses." He said "you *will* be my witnesses." He said this in reply to the question about the kingdom and when it would be established.

As Jews who knew well the words of the Old Testament prophets and who believed that God would keep all His promises, Jesus' disciples were naturally curious about the future of Israel. They were promised that the Messiah would someday take the throne of Israel (Psalm 2:6–7), defeat all its enemies (Psalm 110:1–2), establish a righteous regime (Isaiah 9:7; 11:4–5), lead the nation into unprecedented peace and prosperity, and even extend His rule to encompass the entire world (Psalm 2:8).

Inevitably, Jesus "will come in just the same way as [the disciples] watched Him go into heaven" (Acts 1:11) and seize the throne of Israel through the exercise of power. While God will indeed keep all His promises to Israel, He has established a period of grace between the first coming of the Messiah and the second, which is yet future. During this time, all of humanity—Jew and Gentile alike—are invited to approach the throne of King Jesus and become a part of His ever-enlarging ranks of disciples.

The followers of Jesus—from the day of His ascending to heaven until now—are invited to join Him in His great kingdom-building enterprise. While the work is ultimately His and He will be faithful to complete what He started, believers have been given a genuine stake in the success of His plan. He has no other strategy for the redemption of humanity. This is it.

While God certainly does not need the help of people to redeem the world from sin and evil, He has nevertheless chosen to include His followers in accomplishing the plan. The Old Testament prophets and the book of Revelation unambiguously point to the victory of good over evil. Sin and death will eventually succumb to the unstoppable power of Jesus Christ. Nothing will prevent the Kingdom of God from ruling the world. Therefore, the Great Commission is essentially an invitation to join God in this great enterprise that has no chance of failure. He does not need us, but He does want us.

> When David Livingston was asked what had sustained him in all the perils of his missionary work in Africa, he answered by quoting [the Great Commission]. When his wife died in Africa, he helped prepare her body for burial; he helped make the coffin and lower it into the grave. Then he opened his New Testament, read this text, and said to his African comrades, "These are the words of a gentleman of the strictest and most sacred honor and He will keep His word. Let us now get on with our task."[2]

Where is Jerusalem for you? For me, it's Frisco, Texas. That's home base, my community. Yours might be San Diego or Denver or Miami or New York. Home base for you may be Seattle or Chicago, Cleveland or Montreal, Raleigh or Richmond. It might be a large metropolitan area or a town of fewer than two thousand . . . or even two hundred people. If you are a believer in Jesus Christ, you have been called to join Him in making disciples, and wherever you are, that's where you begin. Think of it as your Jerusalem.

But you're not limited to Jerusalem. You've also been called to make disciples in Judea and Samaria. How can you become a witness to your region? Can you join with others who have established an effective ministry to your area? And what about cross-cultural ministry? In the first century, Samaria was the place Jews loved to hate, and—wouldn't you know it?—it lay right between Judea and Galilee. A loyal Jew traveling from one region to the other would never go through Samaria. They added no less than a full day to their journey by crossing over the Jordan River to go around the eastern border of Samaria, just to avoid dirtying their sandals with Samaritan soil.

Who in the area surrounding you speaks another language or has roots in another culture? Who in your area might be looked down upon or shunned as undesirable? How can you overcome your own fear, distrust, or discomfort to share the good news of Jesus Christ with them? Is there a homeless shelter nearby? A prison? An economically deprived part of town?

And let's not forget that the Lord has His eye on the whole world. He never set limits on how many people we can reach or how far we should go. Perhaps He is leading you to leave your comfort zone and experience disciple-making on a world scale. Mission agencies and other organizations exist for the very purpose of helping people move from where they live to places around the world where people have never heard the name, Jesus Christ.

You can participate in any one of three primary ways. First, you can pray for those who have given themselves to making disciples in other countries. Contact a missions organization or your local church, ask them for the names of some missionaries, and pray for them consistently. I can tell you from my own experience, those prayers help!

Second, you can give money to help pay for a missionary's expenses while serving overseas. Missions organizations make that a very easy and rewarding process, and churches often help keep you in contact with the missionaries they support through their congregation.

But the best and most rewarding way is to participate and go! Churches regularly provide opportunities to join with others to experience missions firsthand. Sometimes the trips last as little as a week. Others might devote an entire summer to cross-cultural ministry. Or, you might feel a divine prompting to become a fulltime disciple-maker overseas. Contact your church or a missions organization and start asking some serious questions. But I need to warn you. God has ways of redirecting those who get personally involved. So . . . stay open!

Whatever we do, we must not treat the Great Commission like it's the Great Suggestion. I started with a fable; I conclude with a story:

On a dangerous seacoast notorious for shipwrecks, there was a crude little lifesaving station. Actually, the station was merely a hut with only one rugged boat . . . but the few devoted members kept a constant watch over the turbulent sea. With little thought for themselves, they would go out day and night tirelessly searching for those in danger as well as the lost. Many, many lives were saved by this brave band of men who faithfully worked as a team in and out of the lifesaving station. By and by, it became a famous place.

Some of those who had been saved as well as others along the seacoast wanted to become associated with this little station. They were willing to give their time and energy and money in support of its objectives. New boats were purchased. New crews were trained. The station that was once obscure and crude and virtually insignificant began to grow. Some of its members were unhappy that the hut was so unattractive and poorly equipped. They felt a more comfortable place should be provided. Emergency cots were replaced with lovely furniture. Rough, hand-made equipment was discarded and sophisticated, classy systems were installed. The hut, of course, had to be torn down to make room for all the additional equipment, furniture, systems, and appointments. By its completion, the lifesaving station had become a popular gathering place, and its objectives had begun to shift. It was now used as a sort of clubhouse, an attractive building for public gatherings. Saving lives, feeding the hungry, strengthening the fearful, and calming the disturbed rarely occurred by now.

Fewer and fewer members were interested in braving the sea on lifesaving missions, so they hired professional lifeboat crews to do this work. The original goal of the station wasn't altogether forgotten, however. The lifesaving motifs still prevailed in the club's decorations. In fact, there was a liturgical lifeboat preserved in the *Room of Sweet Memories* with soft, indirect lighting, which helped hide the layer of dust upon the once-used vessel.

About this time a large ship was wrecked off the coast and the boat crews brought in loads of cold, wet, half-drowned, sick people. They were dirty, some terribly sick and lonely. Others were black and "different" from the majority of the club members. The beautiful new club suddenly became messy and cluttered. A special committee saw to it that a shower house was immediately built *outside* and *away from* the club so victims of shipwreck could be cleaned up *before* coming inside.

At the next meeting there were strong words and angry feelings, which resulted in a division among the members. Most of the people wanted to stop the club's lifesaving activities altogether and all involvements with shipwreck victims . . . ("It's too unpleasant, it's a hindrance to our social life, it's opening the door to folks who are not *our kind*). As you'd expect, some still insisted upon saving lives, that this was their primary objective—that their only reason for existence was ministering to *anyone* needing help regardless of their club's beauty or size or decorations. They were voted down and told if they wanted to save the lives of various kinds of people who were shipwrecked in those waters, they could begin their own lifesaving station down the coast! They did.

As years passed, the new station experienced the same old changes. It evolved into another club . . . and yet another lifesaving station was begun. History continued to repeat itself . . . and if you visit the coast today you'll find a large number of exclusive, impressive clubs along the shoreline owned and operated by slick professionals who have lost all involvement with the saving of lives.

Shipwrecks still occur in those waters, but now, most of the victims are not saved. Every day they drown at sea, and so few seem to care . . . so very few.[3]

Chapter Twenty

Watching for Jesus in the Air

Coming to the end of a biography is rarely a pleasant experience for me. For example, I read Doris Kearns Goodwin's excellent biography on Abraham Lincoln, *Team of Rivals*, and I discovered again why I had always admired this great American statesman. She expertly wove together the private letters and journals of Lincoln and the people he knew to tell his story. As she brushed away the dust from his portrait, her work revealed a highly intelligent, sensitive administrator and a leader with unparalleled conviction and resolve. I observed his impoverished childhood and his unrelenting desire to become something greater than his environment gave him a right to be. I learned to admire his personal integrity, his rigid political backbone, and his intuitive savvy yet utterly honest rise to power. I read with amazement how he cobbled together a remarkably strong government by choosing the men who had been his political rivals yet were clearly the most qualified men for their jobs. How Lincoln ran the government reflected the unvarnished character of the man, and because he was a man of undivided character, we remain a unified nation today.

As I read the final chapters of his life, a feeling of dread came over me.

I cringed as Booth slipped behind the president in Ford's Theatre and shot him in the head at point-blank range. As Lincoln lay comatose in the Petersen House, I found myself hoping beyond all reason that he would pull through and survive! And when he died nine hours later, I felt like I had lost a very dear friend.

I find biographies fun in the beginning, fascinating through the middle, and more often than not, depressing at the end. If the biography is complete, it always ends the same way: the hero dies! An epilogue ties up the loose ends and the book goes on the shelf to gather dust. Another great life has ended the way all of them do.

All except this one! This account of the greatest life of all is different. Not only does the subject continue to live, but a significant chapter in His story remains untold. The conclusion has been written in prophecy, but not yet in history.

Shortly after Jesus rode into Jerusalem to officially present Himself as the Messiah and to claim authority over the temple, the religious leaders rejected Him. As we have seen, His subsequent stand against the corruption of Annas and the chief priests then became a defining moment. Those who ruled over the house of God chose temporal power and wealth over the abundance of life Christ came to give them. And in so doing, they chose judgment over redemption. Jesus later sat on the western slope of the Mount of Olives and wept over the city.

> "O Jerusalem, Jerusalem, you who kill the prophets and stone those who are sent to you! How often I have longed to gather your children together as a hen gathers her chicks under her wings, but you would have none of it! Look, your house is left to you desolate! For I tell you, you will not see me from now until you say, 'Blessed is the one who comes in the name of the Lord!'"
>
> Matthew 23:37–39 NET

His lament prompted His disciples to ask about the fate of the city in the last days. Jesus used the opportunity to explain what would happen in the years to come and the centuries to follow. "Do you see all these things? I tell you the truth, not one stone will be left on another. All will be torn down!"

> His disciples . . . said, "Tell us, when will these things happen? And what will be the sign of your coming and of the end of the age?" Jesus answered them, "Watch out that no one misleads you. For many will come in my name, saying, 'I am the Christ,' and they will mislead many. You will hear of wars and rumors of wars. Make sure that you are not alarmed, for this must happen, but the end is still to come."
>
> Matthew 24:2–6 NET

> "Then the sign of the Son of Man will appear in heaven, and all the tribes of the earth will mourn. They will see the Son of Man arriving on the clouds of heaven with power and great glory. And he will send his angels with a loud trumpet blast, and they will gather his elect from the four winds, from one end of heaven to the other.
>
> "But as for that day and hour no one knows it—not even the angels in heaven—except the Father alone.
>
> "Therefore stay alert, because you do not know on what day your Lord will come."
>
> Matthew 24:30–31, 36, 42 NET

Little did anyone else know how soon His prediction would be fulfilled. In AD 39, the insane Roman emperor Caligula declared himself a god and ordered his image displayed in cities and temples throughout the empire, including the temple in Jerusalem. Then the procurator, Gessius Florus, took a great sum of money from the temple treasury. These two acts brought the Pharisees and the Sadducees into perfect alignment against Rome, which woke a sleeping giant in the Zealots and the Sicarii. By AD 66, Israel had risen up in rebellion and had won several military victories. They appeared to be on the verge of winning their independence.

Then, Vespasian became emperor and everything changed. He committed tens of thousands of soldiers to sweep down through Galilee and lay siege to Jerusalem. And in AD 70, the emperor's son, Titus, broke through the wall.

The fury with which the soldiers ravaged the city had been unprecedented. The Jewish historian Josephus described the aftermath.

> Now, as soon as the army had no more people to slay or to plunder, because there remained none to be objects of their fury (for they would not have spared any, had there remained any other such work to be done). Caesar gave orders that they should now demolish the entire city and temple, but should leave as many of the towers standing as were of the greatest eminency; that is, Phasaelus, and Hippicus, and Mariamne, and so much of the wall as enclosed the city on the west side. This wall was spared, in order to afford a camp for such as were to lie in garrison; as were the towers also spared, in order to demonstrate to posterity what kind of city it was, and how well fortified, which the Roman valor had subdued; but for all the rest of the wall, it was so thoroughly laid even with the ground by those that dug it up to the foundation, that there was left nothing to make those that came thither believe it had ever been inhabited.[1]

By this time, persecution by the religious leaders in Jerusalem had driven most of Jesus' followers away, many of them to the city of Antioch. The remaining disciples—those who had not been martyred—doubtlessly sat up and took notice. The first of many predictions had come to pass. More would follow. Wars and rumors of wars . . . tribulations . . . false Christs . . . and then on some future day—unknown to anyone but the Father—Jesus will return, first to gather His people, then to rule over the earth as King. He had promised on the eve of His death,

> "Do not let your heart be troubled; believe in God, believe also in Me. In My Father's house are many dwelling places; if it were not so, I would have told you; for I go to prepare a place for you. If I go and prepare a place for you, I will come again and receive you to Myself, that where I am, there you may be also."
>
> John 14:1–3

This simple four-word promise makes the biography of Jesus different from that of every other historical figure: "I will come again." He didn't say when, though many have tried to predict the date. However, the promise stands. He could come at any moment, and we should be ready when He does.

Naturally this prospect stirs the imagination, and many who haven't tried to calculate the date have used the enigmatic images of the book of Revelation to suit their own purposes. During the turbulent 1970s, many expositors stood in pulpits with the books of prophecy in one hand and the newspaper in the other and stirred a generation of believers into a frenzy. We must take seriously the command, "Stay alert!" but we must also keep it in proper perspective. Jesus intended us to be prepared, not jumpy.

A VIEW TO THE END

The first generation of believers lived in the eager expectation that Jesus would return and establish His kingdom in their lifetime. They had not been promised a date, but they had been told to be ready. Jesus could return at any time, and when He does, one fact is certain: it will be sudden. But as the years passed, false teachers began to play upon their doubts and questions began to undermine their trust.

What if I die before He returns? Will I miss out on the kingdom?

I'm suffering! When do I get to enjoy my promised abundance in the kingdom?

The kingdom promised justice. Will my tormenters be held accountable if they die before Jesus returns?

What about my deceased loved ones? Will I ever see them again?

To answer their questions, Paul the apostle set forth what he called a *musterion*, a mystery, providing information that God had not previously unveiled. In doing so, he addressed four important issues: death, destiny, resurrection, and Christ's return.

Death. In his letter to the Christians living in Corinth, Paul explained the lasting implications of Christ's resurrection. Eugene Peterson paraphrases his instruction well.

If all we get out of Christ is a little inspiration for a few short years, we're a pretty sorry lot. But the truth is that Christ *has* been raised up, the first in a long legacy of those who are going to leave the cemeteries.

There is a nice symmetry in this: Death initially came by a man, and resurrection from death came by a man. Everybody dies in Adam; everybody comes alive in Christ. But we have to wait our turn: Christ is first, then those with him at his Coming, the grand consummation when, after crushing the opposition, he hands over his kingdom to God the Father. He won't let up until the last enemy is down—and the very last enemy is death!

1 Corinthians 15:19–26 MSG

According to the Bible, death is not the end of life, but it is an earthly doorway to a different kind of life. Death is merely the separation of the invisible from the visible, the immaterial aspect of a person from the material. Upon death, the physical body ceases to function and immediately begins to decay; the material world reclaims our molecules. Meanwhile, the inner, invisible qualities that define our personalities—our spirits and/or souls—continue to exist.

Destiny. For those who die before the return of Jesus, their physical bodies are destined for the grave. Nevertheless, death and eternal destiny are two distinct matters. Whereas bodies perish, souls live on. Once someone has passed through the doorway of death, one of two destinies awaits him or her.

Those who die without having placed their trust in Christ, those who either refuse God's offer of a restored relationship or try to make their own way, will not cease to exist. Death for them is still a doorway to a different kind of existence; however, their destiny is very different from those who die "in Christ." They do not go on to enjoy God's presence forever. They will go to a literal place where they will be eternally separated from God.

Jesus described this other destiny as "unquenchable fire" and "outer darkness, in that place where there will be weeping and gnashing of teeth" and "eternal punishment." As heaven is unimaginably good, hell is unspeakably horrific—beyond our comprehension. It is not temporary.

There is no "purgatory," in which a person suffers for a time to become purified of "smaller sins" before entering heaven, and no one can pray to have another removed from there. The choice between these two destinies must be made before passing through the door of death. Upon crossing that threshold, eternity is sealed permanently.

Fortunately, no one has to go there. Everyone has a choice. Jesus Christ died for the sins of the entire world and now offers another destiny as a free gift. To be "in Christ" is to place one's trust in Him for salvation from sin. To be "in Christ" is to trust His goodness, not our own; to trust that His sacrificial death on the cross paid the complete debt of death we owe for our sin; to trust that His resurrection gives us eternal life instead of relying upon our own ability to please God. To be "in Christ" is to claim, by faith, the free gift of salvation. To be "in Christ" is to enjoy a completely restored relationship with our Father in heaven by virtue of His Son's righteous standing.

Paul stated earlier in his letter to the Corinthians, "We [in Christ] are always full of courage, and we know that as long as we are alive here on earth we are absent from the Lord—for we live by faith, not by sight. Thus we are full of courage and would prefer to be away from the body and at home with the Lord" (2 Corinthians 5:6–8 NET). In other words, life "in Christ" is a win-win proposition. To be alive on earth is to anticipate a grander future. And to be separated from our bodies is to be enjoying eternal life in heaven with our Maker!

Paul said those "in Christ" will be made alive; not merely restored to the same kind of life—like Lazarus, who was raised and later died of injury or illness—but eternally, abundantly alive, never to suffer or die again. The resurrection Jesus promised and about which Paul taught is a profoundly different concept than anyone understood before.

The Christians in Corinth—some of them skeptics—were asking, "How are the dead raised? And with what kind of body do they come?" Paul described the resurrection using a marvel of nature we commonly take for granted. He noted that a seed must die and go into the ground before it can realize its destiny. A germ of wheat grows to become a stalk. An acorn becomes a giant oak tree. And, when the seed dies, it doesn't become something different; it becomes a much greater expression of what it was before.

> What you sow is not the body that is to be, but a bare seed—perhaps of wheat or something else. But God gives it a body just as he planned, and to each of the seeds a body of its own. All flesh is not the same: People have one flesh, animals have another, birds and fish another. And there are heavenly bodies and earthly bodies. The glory of the heavenly body is one sort and the earthly another.
>
> 1 Corinthians 15:37–40 NET

Resurrection. At this point, the believers undoubtedly wondered, Well, then what if Jesus comes back before I die? How will I experience this new resurrection life if I haven't died? Paul then set forth another *musterion.*

> Now this is what I am saying, brothers and sisters: Flesh and blood cannot inherit the kingdom of God, nor does the perishable inherit the imperishable. Listen, I will tell you a mystery: We will not all sleep, but we will all be changed—in a moment, in the blinking of an eye, at the last trumpet. For the trumpet will sound, and the dead will be raised imperishable, and we will be changed. For this perishable body must put on the imperishable, and this mortal body must put on immortality. Now when this perishable puts on the imperishable, and this mortal puts on immortality, then the saying that is written will happen,
> "Death has been swallowed up in victory."
> "Where, O death, is your victory?
> Where, O death, is your sting?"
>
> 1 Corinthians 15:50–55 NET

This old bag of bones—this aging, ailing, antiquated body—isn't equipped to last throughout eternity. We're fortunate to get seventy years out of it. Some make it to eighty or even ninety. I read of Mary Thompson, who died in Florida at the age of one hundred twenty years! According to relatives, she lived that long because she ate well, never smoked, continued to work in her yard until she was one hundred five years old, and always carried a .22 pistol in her bra! Even if we follow every proven recipe for longevity, our bodies will ultimately wear out. They must be changed in order to live forever. Relatively speaking, those who have already died, though their bodies have decayed, are not in any worse condition than those who are alive. Neither is fit for eternity. Mortal bodies must be made immortal. When Jesus returns to take His people to be with Him, a radical physical change must—and will—take place.[2]

Christ's return. Paul revealed that when the trumpet blasts and Jesus appears in the sky, the people who are "in Christ" and have not yet died will "all be changed, in a moment, in the twinkling of an eye" (1 Corinthians 15:52). The Greek word translated "moment" is *atmos*, from which we derive our word *atom*. It's an indivisible moment in time, not the batting of an eye, but the time it takes for light to flash across the eye. Those who are alive when Jesus returns will instantly receive a body fitted for eternity just like those in graves who were raised from decay.

Theologians call this new physical existence a "glorified body," because it is immune to the destructive, toxic effects of a world that has been poisoned with sin. This new "imperishable" body will never contract a disease, never suffer injury, never sin, never experience sorrow, never wear down or die. Death will have been "swallowed up in victory" (v. 54).

THE BEGINNING OF THE NEW BEGINNING

Jesus warned His disciples about the days to come, of false prophets and false messiahs, of rumors and false sightings. Despite the Lord's assurance that no one knows when He will return, people have worked tireless hours to calculate the day and have published their predictions with astounding confidence. In 1833, William Miller began to proclaim from the pulpit, through pamphlets, and in books that the Lord would return in 1843. (He didn't.) Then some of Miller's followers published the corrected date as 1844 . . . October 22, to be exact. When that date passed without any sign of Christ's return, still others adjusted the date to April 1878. Nonsense!

Jesus said false teachers would proclaim, "Look, He's in the wilderness!" or "Look, He's come secretly!" But He assured His followers, "Just like the lightning comes from the east and flashes to the west, so the coming of the Son of Man will be" (Matthew 24:27 NET). His return will be sudden and it will be plainly visible to everyone.

Nevertheless, some of the early Christians worried that they might have missed Jesus' return. They also wondered if the people who had died would not experience the joy of the new kingdom. To reassure them, Paul provided additional teaching.

> But we do not want you to be uninformed, brethren, about those who are asleep, so that you will not grieve as do the rest who have no hope. For if we believe that Jesus died and rose again, even so God will bring with Him those who have fallen asleep in Jesus.
>
> 1 Thessalonians 4:13–14

Imagine how much you would grieve over someone if you didn't believe in this future resurrection. How much more tragic is death if no hope exists beyond the grave? But the certainty of eternal life gives death an entirely different meaning for the believer. Paul used the term "asleep" not merely as a euphemism, but to communicate an important truth. Christians grieve at the loss of a loved one because it's painful. But they grieve with the certainty that their believing friend is alive and that they will be together again. Though death has separated them, it is only temporary.

Having settled the issue of the resurrection, Paul then turned to the matter of Jesus' return and how the dead will be affected at that time.

> For this we say to you by the word of the Lord, that we who are alive and remain until the coming of the Lord, will not precede those who have fallen asleep. For the Lord Himself will descend from heaven with a shout, with the voice of the archangel and with the trumpet of God, and the dead in Christ will rise first. Then we who are alive and remain will be caught up together with them in

the clouds to meet the Lord in the air, and so we shall always be with the Lord.

1 Thessalonians 4:15–17

When Jesus met His followers on a mountain in Galilee and commissioned them to become His witnesses throughout the world, He then rose into the sky and disappeared into the clouds. Then, an angel said, "Why do you stand looking into the sky? This Jesus, who has been taken up from you into heaven, will come in just the same way as you have watched Him go into heaven" (Acts 1:11).

Jesus will not be reincarnated. He will not return as another person. He will not return as merely a spiritual presence. He will not arrive secretly and begin a subtle, underground takeover of the world's governments or religions. Jesus will return, physically and literally, through the clouds, and the event will be unmistakable. A shout, an angel's voice, a trumpet blast, the dead will appear, and then believers will be transformed. No one will fail to recognize the return of Jesus Christ when it occurs.

Once the dead have been raised and the believers transformed, all the followers of Jesus will meet Him in the air. And they will forever be with Him, never to be separated from their God again. This would become a great comfort to Christians soon after receiving Paul's letter. With Nero ruling the world as emperor, they would need to reassure one another often.

KING JESUS

"In the beginning, God created the heavens and the earth" (Genesis 1:1), filled the universe with truth, gave it order, and called it "good." Then the first man and woman disobeyed this simple command of God:

> "From any tree of the garden you may eat freely; but from the tree of the knowledge of good and evil you shall not eat, for in the day that you eat from it you will surely die."

Genesis 2:16–17

Adam and Eve's willful disobedience changed *everything*, for in that moment sin began its cascading corruption of the world, transforming it from the "good" God had created into a menacing perversion of it. The earth now produces crops hampered by weeds and thorns. Work has become grinding toil, full of stress and struggles. The joy of childbirth comes at the expense of enormous pain and anguish. Even our nature as people—created to bear the very image of God—has been twisted by sin so that even the good we do is laced with selfishness. Evil now corrupts every good as if to insult the Creator. And sin brought with it the ultimate affront to God: death, the termination and decay of everything He created to be good.

This is the world as I described it in chapter 3. This is the world Jesus invaded for the purpose of eventual transformation. At present, the world still operates according to the rules of the fall. Evil continues. Relationships fracture. Wars erupt. Disease afflicts. Loved ones die. Hearts break. But when Jesus returns, all of that will change. When Jesus returns to this planet, He will come in power and with judgment. The Messiah the religious leaders originally desired, the warrior king who takes the throne of Israel, defeats its enemies, and establishes a worldwide kingdom, will accomplish everything the prophets had predicted, but on a global scale, profoundly larger than anyone could have imagined.

In the final chapter of the earth's history, even creation will be transformed. All evil will be consumed in the fire of God's glory, leaving only those things He made "imperishable."

BELIEF IN THE IMPOSSIBLE

I fully acknowledge that this final chapter has taken a surreal turn. I can appreciate how outlandish some of this must seem for someone who does not know very much about Jesus or the Bible. Biographies of even the most extraordinary lives don't end with the subject rising from the dead and then ascending to the clouds, promising to return someday. But, as I stated in the beginning, this is no mere chronicle of a great historical figure, because Jesus was no mere man. Nor is His story merely the account of one life. His birth, growth, death, and resurrection comprise the story of all humanity—at least as God desires it. Apart from Christ, our story concludes with a chapter on our demise; an epilogue ties up the loose ends and we go into the ground to return to dust. But "in Christ," our story ends like His, with a final, outrageous, contrary-to-nature triumph over death—an ending that introduces an unimaginable beginning in a entirely new realm of existence.

I also acknowledge that what God asks us to believe is humanly impossible. These truths rest beyond the reach of science, which can only observe and quantify the material aspect of the universe. But let me point out that while supernatural, spiritual truths defy our experience, they do not defy logic. Faith does not demand that we shut off our brains and blindly leap. We have been given evidence that the impossible exists outside this realm of the material. A supernatural Someone condescended to tell us of a much greater realm, and He did impossible things to validate His claims.

Jesus doesn't ask us blindly to believe; He invites us to believe Him. The ineffable, transcendent God became a material, flesh-and-blood human to give us all the evidence we need. And to claim that abundance, all we must do is trust Jesus—trust His words and trust the authenticity of His gift.

Allow me to make this much more personal.

You are a sinner. I know this to be true because the Bible says every man, woman, and child who has ever lived has done what is wrong. And more than once . . . in fact, many times. Furthermore, the Bible says that the penalty for committing those sins is eternal death—unending torment in a place that Jesus described as unspeakably horrible. But the free gift of God, through His Son, is eternal life. This is grace. Unmerited favor. Mercy you had not earned, did not deserve, had no right to demand, and could only receive. Grace is free. Completely free.

God became a man in the person of Jesus Christ. As a man, He suffered the penalty of sin on your behalf. He bore all the punishment you deserve, leaving you none to pay, none to work off. Not even a little. In this supreme act of grace, the Judge voluntarily took off His robe and took the place of the convicted. But He will not push you aside. He will not take back the gift He gave Adam and Eve, the honor of making your own decisions and the privilege of living with the consequences. However, God could not have made His gift of salvation any easier.

All you need to do is exercise the use of your first gift, choice, to receive another, eternal life.

Will you accept it? If so, take a few moments to offer this simple prayer:

Dear God,

I know that my sin has put a barrier between You and me. Thank You for sending Your Son, Jesus, to die in my place. I trust in Jesus alone to forgive my sins, and I accept His gift of eternal life. I come to Christ alone, by faith alone. I ask Jesus to be my personal Savior. I trust Him completely to forgive my sins. Thank You.

In Jesus' name, amen.

If you are able to say this to God and mean every word, then you have received the gift of inestimable value. You have received eternal life beyond death. Furthermore, abundant life is yours to claim on this side of the grave. Because you believe in Jesus Christ, His life is now yours, and your life is now His. You have entered into the greatest life of all.

Notes

INTRODUCTION

1. Robert Bowman and J. Ed Komoszewski . *Putting Jesus in His Place* (Grand Rapids: Kregel, 2007), 17. Used by permission of the publishers. All rights reserved.

CHAPTER ONE
THE IDENTITY OF DEITY

1. *Mere Christianity* by C.S. Lewis copyright © C.S. Lewis Pte. Ltd. 1942, 1943, 1944, 1952. Extract reprinted by permission.
2. Bill Counts, *Once a Carpenter* (Irvine, CA: Harvest House, 1975), 28.
3. Lewis, *Mere Christianity*, 40–41.
4. Gerhard Kittel and Gerhard Friedrich, eds., *Theological Dictionary of the New Testament: Abridged in One Volume*, trans. Geoffrey W. Bromiley (Grand Rapids: Eerdmans, 1985), 506.
5. D. R. W. Wood, ed., *New Bible Dictionary*, 3rd ed. (Downers Grove, IL: InterVarsity, 1996), 693.
6. Elaine Stedman, *Adventuring through the Bible: A Comprehensive Guide to the Entire Bible* (Grand Rapids: Discovery House, 1997), 528. Used by permission of Discovery House Publishers, Box 3566, Grand Rapids, MI 49501. All rights reserved.

CHAPTER TWO
A RELATIONSHIP, A COURTSHIP . . . A MIRACLE

1. Macrobius, *The Saturnalia*, trans. Percival Vaughan Davies (New York: Columbia University Press, 1969), 171.
2. Leland Ryken, James C. Wilhoit, Tremper Longman, III, et al., *Dictionary of Biblical Imagery* (Downers Grove, IL: InterVarsity, 1998), 75.
3. Geoffrey W. Bromiley, ed., *Theological Dictionary of the New Testament*, vol. 5 (Grand Rapids: Eerdmans, 1967), 828.
4. Excerpted from Charles R. Swindoll, *A Bethlehem Christmas: Celebrating the Joyful Season* (Nashville: Thomas Nelson, 2007), 117–19. Reprinted by permission. All rights reserved.
5. M. G. Easton, *Easton's Bible Dictionary*, 1897, public domain; accessed through Libronix (Oak Harbor, WA: Logos Research Systems, 1996), s.v. "incarnation."

CHAPTER THREE
DEITY IN DIAPERS

1. Charles Colson, *Kingdoms in Conflict* (Grand Rapids: Zondervan, 1987), 81.
2. *Encyclopaedia Britannica*, www.brittanica.com, s.v. "censor." © 2006 Encyclopædia Britannica, Inc. or its licensors. All rights reserved. Encyclopædia Britannica is copyrighted 1994-2006 by Encyclopædia Britannica, Inc.
3. Thomas Mott Osbourne, *Within Prison Walls* (New York: D. Appleton, 1921), 24.
4. The Persians issued no fewer than four decrees granting permission to restore various parts of Jerusalem, starting with the temple: Cyrus (538 BC), Darius I (520 BC), Artaxerxes Longimanus (457 BC), and Artaxerxes Longimanus again (444 BC). Four hundred eighty-three Jewish lunar years (consisting of 360 days each) equals 173,880 days. Converting this to the Gregorian solar calendar involves adjusting for 116 leap years (centennial years are not leap years except those occurring each 400th year).
5. Phillip Keller, *Rabboni . . . Which Is to Say Master* (Old Tappan, N. J.: Fleming H. Revell, 1977), 56–57.
6. Gerhard Kittel and Gerhard Friedrich, eds., *Theological Dictionary of the New Testament: Abridged in One Volume*, trans. Geoffrey W. Bromiley (Grand Rapids: Eerdmans, 1985), 316.

CHAPTER FOUR
RESPONDING TO THE REDEEMER

1. Josephus, *The Antiquities of the Jews*, 17.6.5.
2. Gerhard Kittel and Gerhard Friedrich, eds., *Theological Dictionary of the New Testament: Abridged in One Volume*, trans. Geoffrey W. Bromiley (Grand Rapids: Eerdmans, 1985), 219.
3. Os Guinness, *The Call: Finding and Fulfilling the Central Purpose of Your Life* (Nashville: W Publishing Group, 1998), 4. Reprinted by permission. All rights reserved.
4. Ibid, 162.

CHAPTER FIVE
LIFE . . . AS GOD INTENDED IT

1. Johannes P. Louw and Eugene Albert Nida, *Greek-English Lexicon of the New Testament: Based on Semantic Domains*, vol. 1 (New York: United Bible Societies, 1989), 331.
2. Warren W. Wiersbe, *Wiersbe's Expository Outlines on the New Testament* (Wheaton, IL: Victor, 1992), 21.
3. Merrill Tenney, *Expositor's Bible Commentary*, vol. 9 (Grand Rapids: Zondervan, 1981), 47.
4. Ibid.
5. Gerhard Kittel, Gerhard Friedrich and Geoffrey William Bromiley, *Theological Dictionary of the New Testament* (Grand Rapids: Eerdmans, 1995), 828.

CHAPTER SIX
RESTING IN CHRIST

1. Brennan Manning, *Abba's Child: The Cry of the Heart for Intimate Belonging* (Colorado Springs: NavPress, 2002), 79–80.
2. John F. Walvoord, Roy B. Zuck, and Dallas Theological Seminary, *The Bible Knowledge Commentary: An Exposition of the Scriptures*, vol. 2 (Wheaton, IL.: Victor, 1983), 45.
3. *Theological Dictionary of the New Testament*, vol. 6 (Grand Rapids: William B. Eerdmans, 1976), 647.
4. Ibid.
5. Gerhard Kittel, ed., *Theological Dictionary of the New Testament*, vol. 3, ed. and trans. Geoffrey W. Bromiley (Grand Rapids: Eerdmans, 1967), 827.

6. Marvin Richardson Vincent, *Word Studies in the New Testament*, vol. 1 (Grand Rapids: Eerdmans Co., 1946), iii.
7. William Barclay, *The Gospel of Matthew*, vol. 2 (Philadelphia: The Westminster Press, 1958), 18–19.
8. William Hendriksen, *New Testament Commentary: Exposition of the Gospel According to Matthew* (Grand Rapids: Baker, 1982), 504.
9. Kittel, *Theological Dictionary of the New Testament*, 483.
10. Paul J. Achtemeier, *Harper's Bible Dictionary* (San Francisco: Harper & Row, 1985), 357.
11. Manning, *Abba's Child*, 80.

CHAPTER SEVEN

IT IS BEST TO REST

1. Robert L. Wise, *Your Churning Place: Your Emotions—Turning Stress into Strength* (Glendale, CA: Regal, 1977), 9–10.
2. See, for example, Deuteronomy 3:19–20; 12:8–9; 25:19; Joshua 11:23; 21:44; 22:4; 23:1–2.
3. Johannes P. Louw and Eugene Albert Nida, *Greek-English Lexicon of the New Testament: Based on Semantic Domains*, vol. 1 (New York: United Bible Societies, 1989), 260.
4. Mark Twain, *Following the Equator, Pudd'nhead Wilson's Calendar for 1894* (New York: Century, 1893).

CHAPTER EIGHT

THE ASTONISHING POWER OF JESUS

1. Flavius Josephus, *The Works of Josephus: Complete and Unabridged*, William Whiston, trans. (Peabody: Hendrickson, 1987), Wars 2.164–66.
2. Flavius Josephus, *The Works of Josephus*, Antiquities 18.16.
3. A. B. du Toit, *The New Testament Milieu* (Halfway House: Orion, 1998), 659.
4. Gerald L. Borchert, *John 1–11*, The New American Commentary, vol. 25A (Nashville: Broadman & Holman, 1996), 258.

CHAPTER NINE
THE ULTIMATE HEALER

1. William Barclay, *The Letters to the Corinthians*, rev. ed. (Philadelphia: The Westminster Press, 1977), 258–59.
2. Tony Snow, "Cancer's Unexpected Blessings," *Christianity Today* vol. 51, no. 7 (July 20, 2007): 30–32.
3. Ibid.

CHAPTER TEN
ABIDING IN CHRIST

1. Andrew Murray, *Abide in Christ: Thoughts on the Blessed Life of Fellowship with the Son of God* (London: James Nisbet & Co. Limited, 1864), 1.
2. Lewis Sperry Chafer, no source available, based on the recollection of Charles R. Swindoll and John Walvoord.
3. Reprinted from *God's Pursuit of Man* (Previously titled *The Divine Conquest* and *The Pursuit of Man*) by A. W. Tozer, copyright © 1950, renewed 1978 by Lowell Tozer. Used by permission of WingSpread Publishers, a division of Zur Ltd., 800-884-4571.
4. Gerhard Kittel, ed., *Theological Dictionary of the New Testament*, vol. 1, ed. and trans. Geoffrey W. Bromiley (Grand Rapids: Eerdmans, 1972), 185.
5. Ibid.
6. Warren W. Wiersbe, *The Bible Exposition Commentary*, vol. 1 (Wheaton, IL: Victor, 1994), 356.

CHAPTER ELEVEN
THE GATHERING STORM

1. Alfred Edersheim, *The Life and Times of Jesus the Messiah*, vol. 2 (Grand Rapids: Eerdmans, 1962), 11.
2. James Russell Lowell, "The Present Crisis" in *Poems by James Russell Lowell*, vol. 2 (Boston: Ticknor, Reed, and Fields, 1849), 57.
3. Ibid.

CHAPTER TWELVE
BETRAYED AND ARRESTED

1. William P. Barker, *Twelve Who Were Chosen: The Disciples of Jesus* (New York: Fleming H. Revell, 1957), 121.
2. Frederick Godet, *A Commentary on the Gospel of St. Luke*, vol. 2, M. D. Cusin, trans. (Edinburgh: T. & T. Clark, 1881), 280.
3. A. T. Robertson, *Word Pictures in the New Testament*, vol. II (New York: Harper & Brothers, 1930), 265.
4. John Calvin, *A Harmony of the Gospels: Matthew, Mark and Luke*, vol. III, A. W. Morrison, trans. (Grand Rapids: Eerdmans, 1972), 125.
5. Darrell L. Bock, *Luke* (Downers Grove: InterVarsity, 1994), 346.
6. C. J. Wright, *Jesus, the Revelation of God: His Mission and Message According to St. John* (London: Hodder and Stoughton, 1750), 164.

CHAPTER THIRTEEN
ANALYSIS OF A COURTROOM FIASCO

1. See Laurna L. Berg, "The Illegalities of Jesus' Religious and Civil Trials," *Bibliotheca Sacra*, Vol. 161, No. 643 (July–September, 2004), 330–42, and Darrell L. Bock, "Jesus v. Sanhedrin: Why Jesus 'Lost' His Trial," *Christianity Today* 42, no. 4 (6 April 1998): 49.
2. *International Standard Bible Encyclopedia*, Vol. 1 (Grand Rapids: Eerdmans, 1979), 128.
3. George Matheson, *Thoughts for Life's Journey* (New York: Hodder & Stoughton, 1908), 266–67.

CHAPTER FOURTEEN
THE LAST TRIALS AND TORTURE OF JESUS

1. Philo of Alexandria, *The Works of Philo: Complete and Unabridged*, Charles Duke Yonge, trans. (Peabody: Hendrickson, 1993), 784.
2. Flavius Josephus, William Whiston, trans., *The Works of Josephus: Complete and Unabridged* (Peabody: Hendrickson, 1987), 392.
3. W. D. Edwards, MD, W. J. Gabel, MDiv, and F. E. Hosmer, MS, "On the Physical Death of Jesus Christ," *The Journal of the American Medical Association* 255, no. 11 (21 March 1986): 1457.

4. Frederick T. Zugibe, MD, PhD, *The Crucifixion of Jesus: A Forensic Inquiry* (New York: Evans, 2005), 22.

CHAPTER FIFTEEN
DELIVERED UP TO BE CRUCIFIED

1. Cicero, *The Verrine Orations*, vol. II, L. H. G. Greenwood, trans. (Cambridge: Harvard University Press, 1976), 655.
2. Ibid., 655–57.
3. Gerhard Kittel, ed., and Geoffrey William Bromiley, trans. and ed., *Theological Dictionary of the New Testament*, vol. 7 (Grand Rapids: Eerdmans, 1978), 573.
4. Frederick T. Zugibe, MD, PhD, *The Crucifixion of Jesus: A Forensic Inquiry* (New York: Evans, 2005), 53.
5. W. D. Edwards, MD, W. J. Gabel, MDiv, and F. E. Hosmer, MS, "On the Physical Death of Jesus Christ," *The Journal of the American Medical Association* 255, no. 11 (21 March 1986): 1459.
6. Zugibe, MD, PhD, *The Crucifixion of Jesus*, 92.
7. Jim Bishop, *The Day Christ Was Born and the Day Christ Died* (New York: Galahad, 1993), 491–92.
8. Edwards, Gabel, and Hosmer, "On the Physical Death of Jesus Christ," 1461.
9. Kittel, *Theological Dictionary of the New Testament*, 288.

CHAPTER SIXTEEN
NOT TO WORRY . . . HE IS RISEN!

1. Frederick T. Zugibe, MD, PhD, *The Crucifixion of Jesus: A Forensic Inquiry* (New York: Evans, 2005), 106.
2. Merrill C. Tenney, *The Reality of the Resurrection* (New York: Harper & Row, 1963), 119.
3. Ibid.
4. Peter Marshall, *The First Easter* (New York: McGraw-Hill, 1967), 137.

CHAPTER SEVENTEEN
ENCOUNTERING JESUS ALONG LIFE'S ROAD

1. Author unknown, quoted in Jerry Bridges, *Growing Your Faith: How to Mature in Christ* (Colorado Springs: NavPress, 2004), 181.

CHAPTER NINETEEN
CHALLENGED BY JESUS ON THE MOUNTAIN

1. Joseph C. Aldrich, *Lifestyle Evangelism: Crossing Traditional Boundaries to Reach the Unbelieving World* (Portland, OR: Multnomah, 1982), 15–16.
2. Henry Gariepy, *Daily Meditations on Golden Texts of the Bible* (Grand Rapids: Eerdmans, 2004), 180.
3. Charles R. Swindoll, *Growing Strong in the Seasons of Life* (Grand Rapids: Zondervan, 1994), 110–11.

CHAPTER TWENTY
WATCHING FOR JESUS IN THE AIR

1. Flavius Josephus and William Whiston trans., *The Works of Josephus: Complete and Unabridged* (Peabody: Hendrickson, 1987), 613.
2. The Bible clearly teaches that two events will take place at some definite, yet unknown, future time. Jesus will appear in the air and summon His followers to join Him, at which time the dead will rise and the living will be transformed, leaving all unbelievers behind. Theologians call this event "the rapture." Jesus will also set foot on earth to conquer those who oppose Him and establish a literal, functioning monarchy, by which He will rule over the world. Whereas some theologians believe these two events will occur concurrently, I am convinced from my study of Scripture that the Lord will rapture His followers, "a great tribulation" (Matthew 24:21) will fall upon earth for seven years, and then He will return to establish His government. For more information, see Three Views on the Rapture (Grand Rapids: Zondervan, 1996)."

Ordinary People, Great Lives

ISBN 978-0-8499-1382-2   ISBN 978-0-8499-1386-0

ISBN 978-0-8499-1383-9   ISBN 978-0-8499-1342-6

The *Great Lives* series explores ordinary men and women whose lives were empowered by God when they surrendered to Him. Learn from the great lives of our faith and how their stories can help us become who we were created to be.

Available Now

CPSIA information can be obtained at www.ICGtesting.com
Printed in the USA
LVOW062353020212

266855LV00001B/5/P